Principled Policy

(A Conversation about America)

By Victor Bolles

For Charlie

PART 1

GETTING OUR BEARINGS

PART 2

CHARTING OUR COURSE

PART 3

TACKING TO OUR NEW COURSE

Preface

This is a slim book but it covers a lot of important topics. Many of the topics certainly deserve greater study and analysis but, because we are rapidly approaching an inflection point concerning the future of our country, I felt that publication should not be held up for deeper analysis. In writing on these topics I have often felt that I had an inadequate understanding and thus I have spent much time doing further research. At times, it just seemed impossible to put down the thoughts swirling in my brain in an understandable way. But I felt a sense of urgency and have plowed on as best I could.

I am reminded of another slim book by a then unknown writer with an unremarkable background. Thomas Paine wrote *Common Sense* on the eve of the American Revolution. He wrote, not to the intellectual elite, but to the common people. You may think it a bit egotistic of me to arrogate this book to the heights of such a classic transformative document. But America needs such a transformative document at this point in its history; your humble author can only attempt to do his best.

We will be talking about what is the proper role of government in a modern society: more specifically, a modern democratic, free-market society. We will be talking about what is the appropriate balance between liberty and security; what is the difference between a right and a so-called entitlement. We will be talking about the duties of citizens and the role that taxes should play in a modern free-market economy.

Most importantly, we will be talking about the American Social Contract: what it is and how it binds us together as a people and nation. We will be talking about making changes in the direction of our society to reinvigorate and strengthen the American Social Contract. There has been much talk about the fact that America is on an unsustainable path but there has been little rational discussion on what a sustainable path would look like. I hope that this slim book can be one of the stepping-stones leading to that new path.

Victor Bolles, July 4, 2015

Prelude

Have you ever sat on the porch on a hot summer night watching the heat lightning in the distance, feeling the oppressive calm before the coming storm, dreading the tempest to come but at the same time having an itch of anticipation for the fresh new morning? Although your logical mind says that the storm will damage the corn on the back forty and even knock down some of the old oaks, your heart longs for the cathartic blasts of wind, bolts of lightning staggering across the sky, the sudden coolness blowing away the heat, the sheets of rain crawling across the hills.

In 2008, the atmosphere throughout the world was pregnant with the storm clouds of oncoming change. There was a visceral feeling that history was at an inflection point and that the future was going to be very different from the past. Every indicator pointed toward doom or salvation. Oil and commodity prices spiked, financial markets collapsed, a black man was nominated by the Democratic Party to run for President – everything seemed on the verge of transcendent change – either for good or bad. The whole world seemed to be clamoring for change – NOW! You feared the coming changes, but at the same time felt a tingling; things were going to be different!

By the time of the election in 2012, the storm clouds had dissipated yielding little life giving rain and leaving a stunned feeling of incompleteness; where was the change we had feared/longed for? True, a black man had been elected President of the United States; however, commodity prices had regressed to normal levels and financial markets had muddled through (albeit with ample assistance from the US Treasury and the Fed). Many now think that some of the change that did occur (massive deficits, mandatory health care, etc.) wasn't actually the change that they had sought. Instead of catharsis we reaped...incompleteness.

The run up to the elections in 2012 seemed different - ugly and nasty. The Republicans and Democrats were locked in a titanic struggle over the future course of America, a course that neither side could clearly express. Divided government became a gridlock of repeated crises that were never actually resolved; only postponed. Barack Obama won the presidency and the Democrats won the Senate while the Republicans held on to the House of

Representatives. So what was the result of an election that cost in excess of a billion dollars? The status quo – and another looming crisis, the fiscal cliff.

Throughout history, few people have recognized the massive changes going on around them. They are too close to events and lack perspective. Most people see events from their own individual point of view (how things affect them) and not in historical terms. The Luddites in 18th Century England attacked the machines of the industrial revolution because they had lost their jobs to new automated looms. They thought that by venting their rage against the looms that made their jobs obsolete they could regain their employment, not realizing that the nature of their work had changed and that they had to change in order to adapt to their new reality.

I believe that we are still in the midst of a transformational change; that the storm clouds we saw in 2008 were only the outer bands of a much larger tempest coming our way. Further, I believe that the outcome of this transformational change has not yet been determined and (even more importantly) that individual men and women can have an impact on the type of change that will come about.

As the greatest power in the world, much of this coming change will affect and, in turn, be affected by the actions of the United States and, by implication, by the actions of its individual citizens and their leaders. Not all of the possible future outcomes are propitious for the US or its citizens. Americans have a vested interest in making sure that the US plays a prominent role in determining the outcome of the changes that will roil the 21st century.

Together we must think about the events that have affected our world, analyze their impact on us and the rest of the world and then determine what actions need to be taken in order to assure a favorable outcome. We need to continue to believe in American exceptionalism, that changes that favor America will be beneficial to the entire world. Conversely, we must reject moral relativism that states that America is no better than any other nation; that we are hopelessly flawed sinners that have no right to assume the mantle of leadership.

It is true – sadly – that America does not have an unblemished historical record. The institution of slavery, enshrined in our most sacred political document – the Constitution – is a stain on the bright new world envisioned by the Founders. The treatment of the indigenous people of the North American continent (mistakenly called Indians by the early settlers) is shameful, although in fairness, more died from poorly understood disease than from outright war or violence.

The reason we feel shame for these and many other events is that we aspire to be better. We know that America was founded on noble concepts and that our government and leaders (as well as we ourselves) often fail to live up to these concepts. This causes us to feel deep shame as a people and a country. Well, look around folks! Nobody else feels this type of collective guilt. No other country goes around apologizing for not living up to the ethical standards espoused by their founders and enshrined in their constitution.

All the contending parties in the US claim that their actions are motivated by American values. Everyone is talking past each other and not with each other. Let's go back to the beginning and try to determine what are the American values that created the freest most prosperous country on earth, assess the continued validity of those values for today's world (or change them as necessary) and see what we need to do to continue to live up to those values.

Principled Policy

Part 1

Getting Our Bearings

The American Social Contract

The founders were well aware of the concept of the social contract; a concept developed originally by the enlightenment philosophers of the seventeenth and eighteenth century. The social contract is one of the key underlying tenets of the Declaration of Independence and the Constitution of the United States. The Declaration of Independence states "When in the course of human events, it becomes necessary for one people to dissolve the political bands which have connected them with another...". The referenced political bands were the social contract between the people of the colonies and the people of Great Britain. The Revolutionary War was essentially a war between social contracts.

The colonists, being emigrants from Great Britain (to a large extent), believed that they belonged to a grand social contract of English people. When Parliament imposed taxes, tariffs and unequal terms of trade on them, they felt incensed because this was a violation of the social contract as they understood it. If you recall, they were not opposed to taxes, they were opposed to "taxation without representation". The injustice was not the taxation, but the unequal taxation between Britons living in England and the colonists on the other side of the Atlantic. For their part, the Britons living in England felt that the unwritten social contract was between themselves and that the colonists were subjects to the British Empire. The British government treated the American colonists as they would any native people in a subject colony. It was this different view of the social contract that led to the Revolutionary War.

The social contract is what binds a people together. It is essential that the largely unwritten social contract (the Constitution of the United States makes up only a part of the American social contract) be well understood by the people of the contract. Different perceptions of the social contract will lead to discord and conflict.

The Nature of the Social Contract

In the view of enlightenment philosophers, prior to entering into a social contract, human beings lived in a state of nature where they retained all rights but had no protections against others who also had all rights without restriction. There was no mechanism to resolve the differences between people arising from this situation. Hobbs, in *The Leviathan*, felt that without a social contract, life would be "nasty, brutish and short". Under Hobbes' conceptualization, any authority, even an absolute authority or sovereign (the "Leviathan"), was preferable to the state of nature and that humans should rejoice even to be a part of brutal autocratic regime, however imposed. Rousseau, Locke and others felt, no, the type of regime did matter. They believed that humans voluntarily joined together in society for mutual protection and benefit. They believed that humans voluntarily ceded a portion of their natural rights to a central authority so that this authority would have the necessary powers to be able to provide the benefits of a civilized society. Under this view, the ceded natural rights went to a central authority or state, not to other individuals, as would be the case under Hobbes. In the American Declaration of Independence, the Founders clearly stated that "when any government becomes destructive of these ends, it is the right of the people to alter or to abolish it". The government provides the framework for the social contract that allows people to live together in harmony and it is the duty of the government to preserve that framework for the benefit of the people.

Although Benjamin Franklin's statement that "those who can give up essential liberty to obtain a little temporary safety deserve neither liberty nor safety" makes for a good bumper sticker; the nature of the social contract is exactly that. Some liberties must be ceded to the government so that it has the power to maintain the framework. The key word in Franklin's phrase is "essential". What are the essential rights and liberties that we cannot give up and still remain free? The U.S. Constitution elucidates what rights are ceded to government and by subtraction, what rights are retained by the people. But the interpretation of what the Constitution means has evolved over time. In some areas new rights are created or derived from previously existing rights (such as abortion and homosexual marriage) while other rights are constrained (such as the right to bear arms). As the circumstances of the nation change what we view as essential rights also changes.

The Coercive Power of the State

In order for the social contract to function, the citizens collectively must grant coercive power to the central authority. There are two principal aspects of this coercive power; 1) the power to be able to provide the anticipated benefits, and 2) the power to preserve the functionality of the state.

If the State does not have the power to preserve its ability to function it will not have the ability to provide the anticipated benefits of the social contract. To Hobbes, this meant the cession of virtually all rights to the sovereign authority in order to obtain the ability to live together in peace. Most people, however, would not agree with Hobbes. The difficulty is to find the appropriate balance between state power and liberty of the people.

The exercise of state power is not static even if there is a written constitution delineating the powers of the state. It is a dynamic function where the state, like an all-consuming black hole, tends to accrete more and more power to itself. This is the nature of all governments. To the extent that the state has power to achieve a common goal, a little more power would help the state to achieve the goal more quickly or easily.

For example, if the state has the power to regulate commercial activity, then more regulatory authority would facilitate the job of regulating the industry. If the increased regulatory power reduced or constrained commercial activity, this would not directly affect the state since a reduced or constrained industry would actually be easier to regulate.

The ability to tax gives the state great power. Taxation not only funds the government, it also molds how people live their lives. The power to tax can determine which industries are successful and which fail, which activities are to be curtailed or promoted. It is the power to tax that also gives the state the ability to assure its continued functioning. But it is a power that must be strictly controlled so that the government does not encroach on essential liberties.

The Founders' Fear of State Power

The colonists were very familiar with social contracts. From the Mayflower Compact in 1620 and the Fundamental Orders of Connecticut in 1639, Americans had been developing social contracts and democratic governmental organizations from the very start of colonization. Being far from England they were largely self-governing, a habit that became entrenched over the course of a century and a half. When England tried to assert more state power over the colonies, they resisted.

At the time of the Revolution, most of the Founders viewed the colonies as thirteen independent countries that shared a common language and ancestry but otherwise were very different. It took many days to travel from one state to the next. They banded together because they shared common grievances and also because no one colony could hope to defeat Great Britain on its own. The Founders feared remotely exercised power. What did a king on his throne in England know about the American colonies and their needs?

After winning independence the first attempt to create a political entity (not quite yet a nation) was the Articles of Confederation, which gave the central authority very little power. It lacked sufficient authority to tax and was dependent upon the States. The confederation therefore flunked one of the key requirements of a central authority in a social contract, the ability to preserve itself. This lack of power in the central authority as represented by the Confederation was a direct result of the Founders' fear of the coercive power of the state.

The second attempt to create a central authority to exert state power under the social contract has been more successful. The US Constitution is a seminal document that has not only preserved essential liberty for the people of the United States but has been a beacon to oppressed people around the world.

Concentration of Power in the State

In order for the state to function it needs a certain level of coercive power. As noted above, the Articles of Confederation gave the central authority too little power for it to function. Without central government power the state will fall resulting in anarchy and discord. The question is, of course, how much power is necessary and how do we, the people, control government once we have given it so much power?

The Dynamic Nature of State Power

State power is not fixed, but ebbs and flows. We now live in an era where State power is growing quickly. Government needs power to fulfill its function but a little more power can always help it fulfill its function better or more easily (or it finds new functions to perform that require more budget and more power). The world today is complex and internationalized, requiring a strong central government to regulate powerful corporate interests as well as to protect citizens from ever more sophisticated threats from abroad. Regulations are written to ease government's ability to function, and with each new regulation a little bit of freedom erodes away. The NSA listens in on our telephone conversations to catch spies and saboteurs among us, but it is our enemies that gain as our freedoms are eroded bit by bit.

The power of the state has five aspects: administrative or bureaucratic power, political power, economic power and, ultimately, police and military power.

Administrative Power

The bureaucracy of the state is necessary for the day-to-day running of government but the bureaucracy serves the government, not the people. Bureaucrats are not elected and, lacking additional motivation such as the allure of profit in the private sector, there is little reason to provide superior customer service. Instead, they become self-serving, quasi-autonomous, driven by the ability to justify their annual budget. Complaints about bureaucracy abound throughout recorded history so the particular bureaucratic idiosyncrasies of any government are not unique. Regulations are written and forms developed to meet the regulatory requirements of the bureaucracy and to ease *their* workload. As you write your social security numbers into a series of forms for the third or fourth time you wonder why they are making such redundant information requests. Then you realize that one bureaucrat will look at one part of the form and a different one will look at another section and they can't be bothered to search other areas of the form to find the information.

Political Power

Government, acting through the legislature by means of law, or by the executive through executive action or decree, has the power to make policy that affects your daily lives. New laws and decrees are disseminated on an almost daily basis. However, old laws are rarely eliminated such that the mass of laws governing our lives becomes larger and larger. Politicians feel they must be seen as doing something and what they do is pass laws and enact decrees. The bulk of these laws creates an ever-growing burden of law with which citizens must comply. As a former government employee, I had to take periodic ethics training. The regulatory structure covering the ethics of government employees is so complex, contradictory and redundant that the ethics trainer stated, "don't try and understand the laws. Just come to us whenever there is any question regarding ethics." Citizens are often at the mercy of complex and overlapping laws (not to mention jurisdictions) that make compliance difficult.

Economic Power

Government decisions affect us daily in how we live our lives. Between withholding taxes on income and added value taxes (like sales tax) on our purchases the government is omnipresent in our economic lives, affecting our decisions and often guiding us to the Government's preferred outcomes. We depend on our own economic power to manage our daily lives. The ability of government to enhance or deplete our economic power affects us greatly. The government regulates our companies and financial institutions, mandates the fuel efficiency of our cars, where and how we build our homes. The point here is not to debate whether or not these policies are beneficial but only to show the tremendous extent of state power in our lives.

Police Power

We also give the government police power, which is the ability to arrest, detain and punish people for things they do (or don't do). Hopefully these are things that the community agrees people shouldn't do, like rob or kill other people. But the state also has the power to detain people for its own state reasons, like not paying your taxes. Government can also detain and incarcerate people for other reasons of policy. Dictatorial governments use police power to arrest people who criticize state power as exercised by the dictator. Examples abound; I need only mention President Putin's arrest of the young girls in the band Pussy Riot for their annoying but essentially harmless performances. The

Founders were careful to limit the police powers of the state. However, due to the dynamic nature of state power, the people must constantly be on guard against encroachment of police power on their freedom. Americans are right now only just becoming aware of the enormous intrusion of the National Security Agency (NSA) into our daily lives in the name of national security. This is a conversion of military power, which is employed outside US borders, into police power, which is employed within our borders.

Military Power

The government also has military power, which is necessary to protect the nation from outside forces. The goal is to defend the nation but the same power that can be used against our enemies can also be tuned against us. The history of Latin America is rife with military coupes d'état where military power was used to overthrow civilian government. The US military is without equal in the world. But in the wind-down of the wars in Iraq and Afghanistan, returning military equipment is being made available to local municipalities and other law enforcement agencies for domestic use, again commingling the military and police powers of the state.

State Power under Socialism

Freidrich Hayek noted in his book, the Road to Serfdom, that it is the nature of socialism to ever increase its power and control over the economy and the people in it. Having economic decisions made by a central economic planning authority is fraught with problems. Adam Smith in his seminal work the Wealth of Nations gave the example of the thousands and thousands of economic inputs that went into the making of a simple pin including the clothes on the worker and the feed for the horses bringing ore from the mine. A Central Economic Planning Board cannot hope to make all the millions of economic decisions that make up an economy. Therefore, they simplify by eliminating "unnecessary" economic decisions. Socialist man (or woman) doesn't need shirts of different colors and the color chosen will be the one most easy for state enterprise (Mao jackets were fashionable in the US but were all that was available in China). When the State Planning Board decides, it eliminates the possibility of you deciding.

Even in so-called mixed economies, where government allows the private sector a secondary role in the economy, independent economic decisions will always be circumscribed because the state cannot allow independent decisions to frustrate government plans. When the private sector undermines the State's plans, the private sector must be subjected to increased state control. Price controls in Venezuela cannot stop roaring inflation which, in turn, requires the government to intervene in privately operated companies, confiscating their goods or the entire business (even though the inflation is caused by government policies). This reality requires the government to encroach step-by-step on the private sector's (and your) freedom of action either by increased regulation or through confiscation of private property. The socialist march towards greater and greater control seems inevitable.

This raises the question: is economic freedom equivalent to personal freedom? Can you give up some or all of your economic freedom and still be free? Later in this book we will try and delve more deeply into this when we discuss economics.

Remedies for the inexorable growth of State Power

The Founders justly feared state power and wrote protections against the rise of state power in the Constitution and in the first ten amendments to the Constitution, known as the Bill of Rights. The tenth amendment states that "powers not delegated to the United States by the Constitution .... are reserved for the States, respectively, or the people" (although I would have preferred the people to come first). Many States refused to ratify the Constitution without the additional protections from the Bill of Rights. Since that time, the federal government has clearly and steadily encroached on the rights of the States and also the people, often through tortured interpretations of the Constitution. The principal political discussion that is going on right now in our country is precisely this: how to preserve our freedom in the face of encroaching government power. There are those that label folks trying to roll back encroaching government power as radical. But my dictionary defines radical as "departing markedly from the usual or customary". If greatly increasing the size and power of the federal government is not a radical departure from the form of government envisioned by the founders, then I am afraid I don't know what radical is.

Constitution as a Constraint to the growth of the Coercive Power of the State

The Constitution was designed to define the limits of the power of the government, which is probably why progressives now see it as an antiquated and dysfunctional document, a mere nuisance and obstruction of the efficient implementation of government policy. What remedies do we have to stop encroaching government?

Elections

The Election process, as flawed as it might be, must be considered the expression of the will of the people. The ability to throw people out of office is one of the most powerful restraints on governmental power. However, it has been less and less effective in recent years as the power of the incumbency has grown as a result of the fundraising power of political parties, gerrymandering of electoral districts, and influence of special interest groups. Many states as well as the presidency have term limits in order to constrain this power; however, such a remedy has not yet been applied to Congress. We will discuss the limits on the right to vote later in this book.

Checks and Balances

The government of the United States is, as we all know, divided into three branches that act to check the abuse of power by the other branches and to balance the formulation of government policy. This is all very inefficient. State power is all about increasing the terrible efficiency of the State. One of the polemical arguments convulsing Washington in 2014 was the President's assertion of executive power to rule by decree because of his inability to get his policies approved by a recalcitrant Congress. His statement was paraphrased by the Washington Post as "I won; you lost. Deal with it." But the Republicans in the House also won, so he is the one who also has to deal with it. The Constitution and the American Social Contract do not permit rule by decree (something Venezuela's Hugo Chavez and his successor, Nicholas Maduro, loved to do). If you want to push policies through then get a bigger mandate by winning both houses of Congress rather than a presidential election by a few percentage points.

State's Rights

Throughout the history of the United States, states' rights have been tainted by the curse of slavery. But that does not mean that the concept of states' rights is totally invalid. At the time of the Founding, communication and transportation severely limited the central government's ability to exercise power. The colonies, now states, were used to running things pretty much on their own. Over the centuries, the federal government has taken on much of the power once exercised by the states. Another method of expanding central authority has been the use of federal mandates to enact the will of the central government on the states. Likewise, the federal government makes states beholden to it by means of federal grants and transfers. Still many states still choose a different path as to tax policies, labor policies, etc.

Balancing Power – The State, the Private Sector and civil society

The time of the Founding was also a period that could boast a vibrant civil society. In a period when the powers and abilities of government were limited, citizens filled the gap with a plethora of civil institutions: library societies, Masonic organizations, hospital associations, workhouses, rescue missions, etc. Benjamin Franklin was a chronic joiner as well as founder of some of these civic societies. These civil institutions were a counterbalance, not only to the power of the central government, but also to the growing power of corporate institutions that were forming in America. As the power of government to perform these functions grew it not only took over or supplanted these civic institutions, but it also eliminated the melting pot of ideas bubbling up from the citizenry.

Technology and the Social Contract

The social contract is a larger concept than the Constitution. The Constitution defines the relationship of the federal government, the state governments and the people. The social contract defines the relationship of the people amongst ourselves, of which the Constitution of government represents only a part. The Constitution was elaborated by the social contract accepted at the time it was written. It was therefore limited by the technology that existed in the late eighteenth century. The form of our government is a representative republic because direct democracy was impossible in that era except for very small communities of people where they could meet in public assembly (as is still done in some communities in Vermont and elsewhere). It would have been logistically impossible for the entire people to gather to discuss and vote on a national issue. Many of these technological impediments have now been overcome as we have the ability to access the public debate at any time (for example: the President's State of the Union speech which can be seen by virtually every citizen that wishes to participate). Many of these technological advancements have affected the social contract among the people. Other potential innovations (such as on-line voting) could also have a major impact. Is it timely and appropriate to consider revising the Constitution to reflect these changes? We also need to keep in mind that the pace of technological change is accelerating and think how we can preserve lasting institutions that can withstand the onslaught of change and still be relevant.

Is the Constitution Antiquated and Out of Step?

A research paper by David S. Law and Mila Versteeg (Declining Influence of the United State Constitution) described the U.S. Constitution with other constitutions around the world. I would not use this argument as a justification to modify the U.S. Constitution. Many of the other constitutions around the world are overly complex and unenforceable. A friend of mine, who is a legal expert, noted while we were working on a project that the constitution of the country we were in had 226 articles while the U.S. Constitution has six. There is something to be said for simplicity; at least it's understandable. Having worked all over the world I have been confronted by convoluted, confusing and unenforceable constitutions that provide little but grandiloquent and appropriately progressive words that are principally apparent by their absence in application. Are the citizens of Russia and Venezuela well served and protected by their constitutions? No! I think we need to look to America – our history, our philosophy, our view of the rights of all humans – and not to other countries where their constitutions have only been effective under the umbrella of the American post-war institutions.

A Modern Social Contract

The U.S. Constitution is clear on what the anticipated benefits the government will provide from the liberties ceded to it by the people: "establish justice, insure domestic tranquility, provide for the common defense, promote the general welfare, and secure the blessings of liberty". The government's obligations under the Constitution are to be the guarantor and enforcer of the social contract. We will discuss later two key elements of the social contract entrusted to the government: the rule of law and equality of opportunity (the level playing field).

Has the Constitution been able to keep up and adapt to the changes as the modern American social contract has developed over more than two centuries? Many people will assert that the government has overstepped its constitutional authority or sidestepped its constitutional obligations. Many of these issues are now in the hands of the Supreme Court. Do we need to modify or re-write the U.S. Constitution to assure the benefits of the twenty-first century version of the social contract? In this book we will discuss some of the philosophical and practical reasons why we may want to adjust some of our long standing institutions, including perhaps the Constitution, to better meet the needs of a modern society.

The Free Market Economic System is the Most Moral

There I have said it. The free market economic system is the most moral and ethical of all economic systems. This may seem incredible to you, what with the Pope railing against greed and poverty and the Occupy movement excoriating the one-percenters. Let me explain.

What Constitutes a Moral Economic System?

The Pope has been excoriating the so-called capitalist system[1] practiced by western democratic nations as evil, however the history of evil and corruption in the Catholic Church give the Pope little standing to criticize others. The history of the Catholic Church is rife with Crusades, political manipulation, the Inquisition and the covering up of rampant pedophilia. The truth is: all human economic/political systems and their institutions, including churches, charities and other supposedly noble institutions, are subject to our human frailties in addition to our better human attributes. Good kings are followed by their less noble offspring. Wise administrators are replaced by bored bureaucrats. Over time the vibrancy of institutions becomes sclerotic. Transparent processes become opaque.

The Fallibility of Institutions

The American economic and political system is not immune to these weaknesses and, indeed, it is the objective of this book to change the course of an America that is drifting toward the fate of so many institutions and nations that came before us. The hope for the American social contract lies not in its invincibility to such problems, but rather in its ability to reform and renew itself. Democratic institutions must be transparent in order to function properly. Economic processes must undergo constant renewal in order to remain competitive. A system of checks and balances is constantly at work to reform

---

[1] You will note that I do not refer to our economic system as capitalism. Capitalism is an antiquated notion based on Marxian and Keynesian thought. Later on I will explain why capitalism is an insufficient and misleading descriptor of our economic system.

outdated practices or uncover activities some wish to keep from view (recent probes of the IRS by congress are a case in point).

Other economic systems are, by their inherent nature, less transparent, less able to reform internally. Decision making in command and control economies such as socialism and communism is by nature restricted to the few cognoscenti or apparatchiks in charge of policy formulation. Neither the processes of governance nor the bureaucrats in charge of the processes are subject to any checks or balances – except the commissars charged with maintaining party discipline. Their goal is the maintenance of state power and control. Change, any kind of change, threatens that control.

The social welfare states lie in a netherworld between free economic systems and command and control economies: aspiring to control but hesitant to wield the necessary power. The European models for this system range from German success to Greek distress. But the German success is based on their ability to limit and cut back on the excesses of the social welfare system while the Greeks have succumbed to the lure of false promises. How long can the Germans resist the siren call of ever-greater social welfare benefits? Teutonic stoicism can only get you so far.

The essence of the American social contract lies in its transparency to its citizens. We have the First Amendment, the Freedom of Information Act and a long tradition of investigative journalism. This transparency exposes corruption and promotes reform and renewal. Of course, our transparency isn't perfect, and reforms are often overdue, improperly applied or incomplete. But other systems, cloaked in ritual and privilege, lack even this basic transparency, and therefore have greater difficulty in reforming their practices.

The Role of Profits

There is a wide range of issues cited by critics of the free market economy to illustrate its moral depravity including (but not limited to): income inequality, low wages, periodic recessions or depressions, unemployment, unfair prices and pollution. I am sure there are others that you may wish to raise as well. But if you think about it, all the proposed solutions to these problems revolve around one thing: they seek to limit or eliminate profits. I could go into a long discussion of each of these criticisms and other perceived problems with the free market system but in the end the proposed solutions would all boil down to constraining profits in the name of some supposedly greater good.

However, profits or surplus are an essential element of economic progress. Without surplus we are all just subsistence farmers trying to eke a meager crop out a small plot next to the encroaching jungle. Profits or surplus are essential elements of all economic systems that have any hope of providing a decent living for its citizens. Primitive farming communities need surplus seed for the next harvest. More advanced communities produce excess grain not only for the next harvest but also to trade for other products not produced by the farmer such as tools to make the farming easier or food not produced locally to supplement his simple fare.

Let us also keep in mind that taxes are profits that are appropriated by the state through the exercise of its coercive power. All the benefits supplied by government come from appropriated surplus. It must .be surplus or the producer will starve or go bankrupt from the onerous tax burden (not that this hasn't happened time and again). In earlier societies the emperor, king or chief (and sustainers, courtiers and concubines) was the primary beneficiary of these extractions of profit.

Under communism or socialism extracted profits or surplus (at least the surplus not siphoned off by party cadres and apparatchiks) are appropriated by the state. Logic would suggest that the elimination of profits would mean lower prices or greater benefits for everyone. In the real world this is rarely the case. Government control of the means of production is monopoly and the goal of monopolies is self-preservation. Without competition there is no impetus to provide high quality products or services. Consumers orient their consumption to what is available even if it is not exactly what they want. A diversity of products and services just makes the job of central planning more difficult.

The surplus is used to maintain the state's hold on power. Once in power, the state resists change as any change might weaken its grip. There is no role for innovation in a socialist state unless it helps the state to tighten its hold over the people. Competition only comes from the outside. The Soviet Union could be very innovative in war. It beat the United States into space during the cold war. But internally it was rotting away. Lacking innovation and creative destruction, socialist economies are doomed to very little growth, leaving the workers' paradise an unending purgatory of unfilled dreams.

In theory the modern welfare state extracts profits from the one-percenters and redistributes these excessive (as defined by the state) profits to the rest of the people. In reality, surplus is taken from everyone in value added taxes, reduced services or shoddy infrastructure. Since the extraction of surplus is often fiercely opposed by the producers of surplus, many welfare states (including the United States) fund redistribution programs through debt without realizing that these debts must be repaid by future surpluses (in other words, repaying current expenditures from surpluses that haven't been made yet — keep in mind that these surpluses are to be extracted from our children and grandchildren).

Many people do not understand the role that profits play in the modern economy. Most people assume that profits go into the excessive consumption of the superrich who flaunt their wealth in the face of the struggling people on Main Street. It is true that some profit is consumed stupidly by arrogant boors, but a substantial portion goes to reinvestment. This reinvestment supports innovation and innovation creates economic growth, as we shall see in more detail in the next chapter. But investment in new companies and products is risky and investors need to get a return on their investment. So how do you define excessive?

So profit is what drives the free market economic system and the economic growth and technological advancement it produced has given us the quality of life we currently enjoy. But profit is what progressives want to put in chains for the supposed benefit of society. What the question boils down to is: is economic growth incompatible with a moral economic system? The progressives will deny it. They will say that without profit there will be more for everyone else. But the lack of surplus will slow economic growth and central planning will limit innovation. Such societies would be lucky to be able to maintain the status quo. Citizens would be condemned to the unending drabness of the socialist state. But this goes against one of the most basic aspirations of a human being to provide a better future for his or her kids. It is no wonder that soviet citizens suffered from depression and alcoholism.

Some people will say that some profit is good but the too much profit is harmful. That excessive profit is extracted from exploited workers, shoddy products, special tax benefits, corporate welfare and high prices. But these symptoms are evidence of abuse of the free market system arising from our human fallibility. The free market system is based on the social contract not laissez-faire as many believe. Each economic system is abused by elites, aristocracies, oligarchies and apparatchiks. The American Social Contract is under constant attack from those who would pervert it to their own uses. It is the principal function of a democratic government to prevent this from occurring. Only the democratic free market system has the ability to reform itself peacefully, to reestablish the social contract and make sure it works for all citizens. All the other systems require revolution to reconfigure the social contract and the elites in control will employ all the coercive power of the state to prevent reform.

The Exercise of State Power to Achieve Ideological Goals

All economic systems use the coercive power of the state to extract surplus from the producers of the surplus to be used as the state deems fit. In democratic states, there must be some consensus on the amount of surplus to be expropriated by the state. This is true even in the case where a large amount of the expropriation comes from a small segment of the population (presumably the wealthy). Under socialist and communist systems, the ideological goals outweigh the need for consensus so the state uses its coercive power to extract larger amounts of surplus than would otherwise be possible. The necessity of vast state power limits the freedom of the individual and the need to fulfill the ideological objectives of the state make democracy impossible.

The social welfare state attempts to navigate a middle ground between absolute state power and the condition of personal liberty where the people limit the power of government. It attempts to provide services that a majority of the population desires such as public transportation, free healthcare, income redistribution, etc. Of course, some personal liberty must be sacrificed in order to provide the service although it might be a relatively small portion of the total population. The workers in these areas must now work for the state. And entrepreneurs who would have provided such services are denied the opportunity. Many would say that this is a small price to pay in return for the benefits, but the services that the state could supply are unlimited. If healthcare and transportation are considered essential services that must be supplied by the state, what about food, clothing and shelter? At what point does the social welfare state become a socialist state. The logic is the same, profit is bad and the state can deliver more benefits by eliminating the profit motive. However, as the state dominates more and more of the economy, personal liberty must also be increasingly restricted. In America, a prime example of state coercion is the Affordable Care Act, which requires everyone not already insured to enroll in one of the government's insurance exchanges or be subject to fines.

Are there societies or economic systems that can overcome the lure of profit and provide benefit to mankind? Monasteries and nunneries would probably qualify as institutions where profit plays no role. In these types of societies, religious objectives are paramount, much like the ideological objectives are paramount in socialist states. But not everyone wants to live in a monastery or nunnery. Monks and nuns must give up their personal liberty when they put on the habit, which they do willingly. If force were required to make everyone adopt the monastic lifestyle, these institutions would become as evil and corrupt as the Soviet Union. I respect monks and nuns but I don't want to be one. How about you?

The Essence of an Ethical Economic System

So we have looked at the essence of an ethical economic system from three perspectives: the fallibility of institutions, the role of surplus, and the use of state power to manage the economy. What we have found is that economic systems and the institutions of which they are made are all fallible and subject to ossification, opaqueness and collapse. In these situations, the systems' ability to adapt, reform and evolve is vital. We have investigated the role of surplus in economic systems and see that it also play a vital role for economic growth and progress. Finally we have seen the use of state power to achieve ideological goals can only result in a limitation of the freedom of the individual.

The Social Contract Governs Ethical Conduct in a Free Market Economy

Some people (especially leftists and progressives) believe that because their motives are pure, their actions, whatever they may be, are justified. Great evil has been done in the name of lofty goals. And progressive goals cannot justify trampling on the personal liberties of citizens. The essence of the free market economic system is an emphasis of the processes of economic activity and it's governance over achievement of particular goals. It is the presumption of the free market system that if the processes are good the end result will also be good. Unfortunately, in the United States we have allowed these processes (which are the inner workings of the American Social Contract) to be abused, fall into disuse or be overwhelmed by ideology or special interests.

The Economic System is Part of the Social Contract

The social contract is not limited to the Constitution. It includes how we interact with each other. We interact with each other constantly and much of this interaction is economic. For a democratic economic system to work there should be a broad consensus that it functions well for most of the population. I can hear the chorus saying "but the current free market system isn't functioning well for most of the population". And I agree. But the current economic system in the United States is not a free market system. It is, rather, a corruption of the free market system, an economy where a portion has been taken over by rent seekers, monopolists and fraudsters abetted by government leaders that are supposed to keep this from happening. At the same time, another portion of the system is being directed away from free markets toward by leftwing ideologues. The challenge we face is how to get the free market economic system to work the way it is supposed to work.

Trust is essential to the Free Market Economic System

I say the free market system is moral because it is based on trust. If you buy a product you expect it to be well made and safe to use. If you enter into a contract you expect the other person to honor it. In the small Scottish village of Kirkcaldy where Adam Smith lived and wrote The Wealth of Nations, this is what you would expect to happen. If a local merchant offered shoddy goods, he would soon be out of business. If a local person had the reputation of a schemer or serial defaulter no one would enter into a contract with him.

In a large, complex, modern society this is not so easy to do. If you are buying meat that was trucked across the country, how do you know that it is safe to eat? You don't know who the producer is, let alone if he has a reputation for good quality products. You don't know the shipper or if his trucks are refrigerated. One of the principal functions of modern government is to provide that assurance through inspections of the meat plant, grading of the quality of meat and inspections of the truckers' equipment.

We rely on a system of trust and entrust the government with the responsibility to assure that trust. This is one of the most important functions of government, a function that it is currently failing to adequately provide as resources for these functions are redirected to social welfare payments.

Rule of Law

The participants in the social contract (called citizens) create the Rule of Law between themselves and entrust a governing body with its enforcement. In the case of the United States, the representatives of the people, the Congress, are empowered to write the laws that make up the Rule of Law, and the Executive has been empowered to enforce those rules. When conflicts arise in the interpretation of the Rule of Law, the judiciary is charged with deciding the merits of the case.

Many people feel that the Rule of Law is not working correctly in America and I tend to agree with them. But it is incorrect to merely state that the problems with the implementation of the Rule of Law invalidate the free market system. We need to fix the problems but many of the proposed fixes are mere Band-Aids that don't address the real problems in implementing the Rule of Law. But in order to address the true underlying problems we must first try and define what the Rule of Law is and then come up with the solutions to resolve the problem.

Equality of Opportunity/The Level Playing Field

In a democracy, the Rule of Law should guarantee a level playing field for all citizens. What does this mean? It means that the law must apply equally to everyone. I don't know the details of the US tax code; how could anyone? It's 77,000 pages long. But I can tell you that at least 76,000 of those pages are giving some special interest an advantage over the rest of us. The US tax code is the antithesis of the Rule of Law and the legislators that wrote the tax laws and the bureaucrats who wrote the regulations should be ashamed of themselves. There are many examples of the un-levelness of the legal framework in the US -- too many to list in a small book like this.

Inequality of Outcomes does not prove there is an Un-Level Playing Field

But it is important that we not use the lack of equality of outcomes as proof of an un-level playing field. If equality of outcomes was the proof that the rules of the game were unbiased, nobody would ever go to a football or soccer game again. People are different and even with a level playing field; different people will have different outcomes.

It is, of course, important that the outcome not be caused by an uneven playing field. But proving that an unequal outcome was caused by an un-level playing field can be difficult. Many factors affect our hypothetical football game on the hypothetical level playing field such as: the size and strength of the players, the coaches' strategies, the weather conditions, the health and well-being of the quarterback. This list goes on and on (which is why I do not bet on sports).

Correlation (such as the relationship between gender and pay) does not does not prove causality. Special interest causes often use correlation as proof of the inequity of their situation. But correlation does not give you any clues as to how to resolve a problem: for that you need to understand the causality of the problem. A good example is the gender pay gap. There is a very strong correlation between one's gender and one's level of pay. Women generally earn less than men. If the sole reason for this pay gap was a person's gender it would be an easy problem to solve. The problem, however, is more complex. There are many factors that affect the pay women receive, although some are clearly gender linked. The factors include, the type of jobs women choose, their aggressiveness in seeking promotion, etc. One of the most significant factors is the time women spend on child rearing. In most age cohorts, women generally tend to have less work experience than their male counterparts (in the age cohorts 16-24 and 25-34, where the experience difference is less, the pay gap is much reduced). Simply mandating increased pay on the basis of gender would increase the pay of less experienced women to the cost of the more experienced men. People in the feminist special interest group might rejoice, but this "solution" only replaces one unequal outcome with another. A true solution of the gender pay gap would have to resolve the child-rearing problem among other factors causing the gap. Trying to resolve correlations by fiat without changing the underlying causation will only result in further inequity that damages the social contract among citizens.

In America the Rule of Law must provide equality of opportunity in order to live up to the promises of our founding documents. The Rule of Law must also assure that citizens of the American community strive to achieve their goals within the level playing field and by abiding by the rules of the game. In this way trust is engendered among the citizenry, which not only prevents abuse of the system but also unlocks the potential of all people to attempt to realize their dreams in confidence. When there is an inequality of opportunity (as noted by Dr. Mohamed El-Erian) the social contract cannot fulfill its proper function.

Trust Among Citizens

One of the principal reasons for banding together in a community is to assure personal safety and security. The nature of the social contract provides security from outside dangers but also provides for security within the community. It is not just security of our persons but also in our interactions with other citizens. Having lived in countries with a weak or twisted Rule of Law, I have seen how people act when they cannot trust their fellow citizens. It results in a virtual paralysis of free personal and economic interactions. If you don't trust your elected representatives then you will not vote or not care how you vote – rendering the vote meaningless. If you don't trust the police then you don't report crimes. If you don't rely on the police to keep you safe, you hire bodyguards or carry weapons or join a gang for mutual protection.

Trust among citizens is essential for democracy to work. This does not imply agreement or unanimity. We need to be different for the democratic experiment to work. But we also need to trust each other. That means we need to respect other people in order to expect their respect of us. Of course, not everyone is trustworthy or respectful. The role of the Rule of Law is to define the limits of appropriate behavior in order to restrain the uncivil behavior that may not come naturally to some and to punish those that go beyond the limits of the law. The role of punishment within the Rule of Law is not to try and extract some biblical form of vengeance. Rather, like the referees in a football game, it is to prevent the occurrence of the infractions so that those playing the game (and us citizens) can rely on the behavior of others to conform to the rules. Without this trust, it would be very difficult to live together.

Trust in Economic Dealings

Trust is also essential in economic transactions within a free market economic system. Because economic decisions in a free market economic system are voluntary (unlike other economic systems), trust is needed by all the parties to the transaction. This is especially important in modern societies where we don't always know the other party. When we buy a hot dog we don't know the manufacturer except for the name on the package. While some people rely on rabbis, most of us rely on government meat inspectors to assure us that the hot dog meets minimal standards.

Government not only formulates the laws making up the Rule of Law, it is also in charge of enforcement of the rules. Many people rail against regulation as a restraint to economic activity but a certain level of regulation is needed in order to promote economic activity. What happened to beef consumption when people first heard about mad cow disease and didn't know if the beef in the grocery store was safe? Sales plummeted. In financial transactions the government assures the safety of the deposits of ordinary citizens through deposit insurance that allows depositors to feel secure in their financial transactions with their bank. It is this trust that allows for the free flow of goods and ideas that makes the American free market economy such a potent economic system.

Later we will discuss in greater detail why trust in economic transactions is another reason why socialist economic systems don't work. In the free market system, the private sector produces the product and the government assures its safety through regulation. In a socialist system, the government is the producer of the product and the regulator that assures its safety, a clear conflict of interest. When a defective product is produced in a socialist system the government's instinct is to protect itself by covering up the facts, not in eliminating the problem and punishing the offenders.

Confidence in Outcomes

I have lived in countries where the Rule of Law is very weak or virtually nonexistent. It's not that there aren't rules; there's usually a plethora of rules and laws. It's just that the rules only apply to the powerless (that's you and me) and not to the powerful. Corrupt politicians are never prosecuted, even by their political enemies (who know that some day the tables might be turned on them). Toxic effluents from manufacturing plants and strip mines run through villages with impunity. Criminals operate openly in the barrios and the police do nothing. Contempt for the law is so pervasive in such societies that people, all people, have no compunction about violating the law. On one trip to work in Central America I saw three cars and two buses run red lights. This was not uncommon. I saw people run red lights almost every day.

Not only must we have rules. They must be enforced. People were running red lights because they know the laws are not enforced. In some countries, politicians are corrupt because they know they are unlikely to get caught and, even if they are caught, they are unlikely to be punished.

On Main Street, people are outraged that the people on Wall Street that caused the economic crisis in 2008/9 were never punished. As bad as Bernie Madoff was, he was not one of the causes of the crisis (although he may have been emblematic of the greed). The reason that no one on Wall Street went to jail for the crisis is that they broke no laws. In violation of the Rule of Law, the framework of financial laws had been jiggered to allow the types of behaviors that led to the crisis. The ability to do these shenanigans was embedded in the tax code and other regulations and their attorneys and auditors duly approved their implementation. The crisis could not have happened without the collusion of Wall Street and the Halls of Congress (with a little help from K Street). This is the trust that was broken.

Without faith in the Rule of Law, democracy cannot function. As Rudy Giuliani noted in his broken windows theory, once there is no respect for the rule of law, civil society starts to break down. Faith in the Rule of Law is what holds the fabric of society together. Without that faith the people are despondent or angry; they fall under the spell of narcissistic populists or revolutionaries. Right now in the United States we feel that we are heading in the wrong direction, down the wrong path. Many may have the sense that something is wrong but are unable to identify the cause. The cause is the breakdown of the social contract that has held us together for over two hundred years.

Factors Impeding the Implementation of the Rule of Law

When talking about restoring the Rule of Law there are several factors that must be included in the process. We will be returning to these concepts as we discuss the remedies for the current economic and social malaise afflicting our country.

On Fairness

Fairness is a concept that is over-used and under-analyzed. People always strive for fairness but never achieve it. That is because fairness is not a philosophical concept but an emotional reaction. When do humans first become aware of the concept of fairness? When they are about three year's old. Little Bobby says, "Mommy, Mommy! Jimmy won't share his toys with me. That's not fair." The justice of the matter (in that the toys are, in fact, Jimmy's) is lost on little Bobby.

Fairness is a concept rooted in emotion and, as we will discuss in the next chapter, in our instinctual brain. It is not a concept that can be used for policy making. What is fair for one person may not seem fair to another. There is no way to resolve these differences because they are not made based on rational thought. When talking about the rule of Law we must defenestrate (my favorite word) fairness.

Fairness as an Instinct for Survival

Some may argue that the concept of fairness is deeply ingrained in our human nature and that we have an innate sense of right and wrong. They have a point. In times of hardship, getting your fair share can be the difference between life and death. Those in the pack that don't get their "fair" share of the kill don't survive. Our "innate" sense of fairness was probably honed in the hard times of the Ice Age. Most of the time that modern humans have been on earth (about 200,000 years) has been during ice ages (the recent rise of civilization due, at least in part, to global warming). It is no wonder that that much of what we call humanness was forged from those tough times. But this only reinforces the argument against using fairness for the development of policy. Fairness resides in our instinctual brain, but our instinctual brain was designed to help us survive the Ice Age. Now that we are "civilized" we need to develop different standards.

Unfairness as a Policy Standard

The reason that fairness doesn't work as a policy standard is that it is very subjective and personalized. While the concept of fairness is innate to all of us, the specifics of fairness vary from person to person based on our personal circumstances. Any government policy will have its proponents and opponents but it will never achieve unanimity on its fairness. Something that is totally fair to one person or group will be unfair to many others. There are no qualifiers to fairness, there is no "sort of" fair or "pretty" fair: there is only fair. Any qualified fairness has elements of unfairness in it.

Based on the concept that the definition of a good deal is when both sides are unhappy, I propose to use unfairness as the basic standard for government policy. There are many levels and qualifiers to unfairness. If there is a policy that is unfair to me (say taxation) but I can see that it benefits many other people I can consider whether the unfairness I am subjected to is tolerable given the general benefit it provides. In other words, the policy is not too unfair. This process takes rational (not instinctual) thought to evaluate the costs and benefits and can be used as a tool for policy making.

On Complexity

The social contract must be understandable by the citizens of the community. Complexity confounds the ability of citizens to understand the world they live in and how the social contract is supposed to function. A 77,000-page tax code is beyond the comprehension of all but a very few cognoscenti (who probably only know the certain bits that interest them and their clients). There is no transparency intended in such a series of documents. An excess of data is as bad as no data. So why are documents (and our lives as a result) so complex? Because it suits the interest of certain parties. Special interests can benefit if the understanding of others is frustrated by complexity.

Complexity is part of modern life. An iPhone is a complex device. I have no idea how to replicate one. Modern government must also be complex in order to function in a complex world. But there is a world of difference between technological complexity designed to make our lives easier, and bureaucratic complexity designed to make our lives more difficult (while making the life of bureaucrats easier). If it is virtually impossible for a regular citizen to understand the tax code, how is that citizens are supposed to understand additional complex laws such as the Affordable Care Act? We cannot eliminate complexity but we can reduce it. It won't be easy. We can't reduce it to an episode of Sesame Street or a 12 minute segment on 60 Minutes. But we can demand more responsive government and a good faith effort from public servants to inform the public and to write reasonable legislation. We will be discussing some mechanisms to reduce complexity later in this book.

Asymmetries of Power and Knowledge

The different parties to economic transactions are subject to asymmetries of knowledge and power. The seller of a product knows both the benefits and flaws of the product he is selling but is likely only to communicate the benefits to prospective buyers. Legally required disclosure (such as nutrition labels, SEC filings and prescription drug warnings) can help remedy this asymmetry but there are many areas of our lives where these disclosures are not required or not enforced. Also, many unscrupulous counterparties rely on complexity to obfuscate full disclosure (have you ever actually read disclosure statements on the web before clicking "agree"?).

A similar asymmetry is that of power. When dealing with large corporations or other large institutions, regular folks like you and me either assume the entities know what they are talking about or are unwilling to take on a fight that we will probably lose. Of course, the greatest asymmetry of power is that between you (or me) against the government. When some people talk about limited government they mean small (and cheap). When I talk about limited government I mean limiting government to the functions of maintaining the rule of law as allowed by the Constitution.

The free market economic system is the democratic expression of economic activity just as democracy is the free market of political activity. The two notions are not just linked they are, literally, the same. Of course, unbridled laissez-faire economics and unrestrained personal liberty are not only practically unfeasible; they are ethically and morally repugnant. People cannot live together as a community under such conditions. The social contract is the mechanism to manage the civil and economic activities among citizens. It is government that is charged with managing these competing interests and it is the democratic will of the people that controls the power granted to government.

The march toward a social welfare state upsets this balance. In order to meet the requirements of the welfare state, the government must take over more and more of the free market and exercise greater power over not only economic transactions but also the people implementing them. People beholden to government cannot effectively control it and therefore the democratic power of the citizenry is diminished. This diminished freedom may be relatively benign as is apparently the case in Europe (time will tell) but the ability of the citizens to control the coercive power of government has become circumscribed by their dependency. Should this power granted to government become malignant, the people may be powerless to stop it. Many people initially supported the Nazis and democratically elected Hitler as Vice Chancellor. Putin currently maintains his popularity in Russia. However, if the mood changes it will be very difficult to change leadership peacefully.

Redefining the Free Market Economic System

Much of modern economic thought is burdened by the chains of Marxian and Keynesian theory and does not provide an adequate explanation of what drives economic activity nor can it provide solutions to current economic problems. They defined capitalism as the interplay between two forces, labor and capital. Marx felt that the elites that controlled capital exploited workers in order to produce the manufactured goods of a modern society. His solution was to take the capital from the elites and give it to the government thereby creating a "classless" society. Keynes had a more nuanced approach but believed that government should play a significant role in "managing" the economy. He felt that the government could, through management of fiscal policy, control aggregate demand and how it affects wages (the cost of labor) and interest rates (the return on capital).

Although Marx and Keynes came to different conclusions, they both used the same materials to construct their theories. Both Marx and Keynes assumed, as did most economists at the time, that people were rational and made rational decisions. In order for their formulas and prescriptions to work, they had to maintain this assumption that, in turn, required many additional assumptions. A second problem was that they assumed the economy was basically static. Production could go up and down (booms and busts) and price could go up and down (inflation or deflation) and these both affected interest rates. But what they ignored was economic progress and technological advancement – in a word: innovation. They ignored innovation because they couldn't fit it into their formulas. No one can predict innovation or the impact it might have on the economy. In 1990 almost no one had heard of the Internet or the World Wide Web. That's only 25 years ago (a literal blink of the eye in historical terms). But the Internet has profoundly changed how we do business, how we do our daily shopping, how we communicate with friends and family, and even how we wage war. There are two things we should take from this example: 1) anyone in 1990 attempting to predict economic activity 25 years in the future would have been completely wrong, and 2) the numbers and statistics used by economists cannot describe the profound changes that have occurred.

What Drives Economic Growth

Today most economists (and the politicians they advise) are focused on fostering economic growth in order to provide more jobs in the economy. But what drives economic growth? Most people today say they are Keynesians without knowing what that means: thinking that government spending and deficits can drive economic growth and provide employment for the masses. But I think we all need to take a step back and think a little about what really drives economic growth (assuming of course that economic growth is a good thing – not everybody agrees with that).

As far back as ten thousand years ago, economic activity consisted primarily in hunting and gathering to meet the needs of daily life. These needs or demands arose primarily from hunger but also for the need of shelter from the cold (remember this was during the Ice Age) and protection. The physical needs of the body demand action. Our primitive ancestors took action by hunting meat on the bleak tundra and in gathering the berries and grains on the wide savannah in order to fill their stomachs. In other words, they worked to meet their demands.

For the previous 190,000 thousand years (or so) that modern humans had walked the earth, there had been little economic progress as we currently define it. They continued hunting and gathering, making stone tools and hiding in caves or other protected areas at night. Progress was slow. One day was much like the day before, the years rolling by unnoted and unrecorded. Our ancestors labored mightily to survive. Falling asleep exhausted with a partially full stomach was considered a successful day. In philosophical terms they lived a Hobbesian life. The social unit was probably familial tribes similar to those of chimpanzees and gorillas today.

But they did make progress, slow painful progress. Fire was tamed, stone tools became more sophisticated, the power of speech was developed, art and religion were practiced, and dogs joined the human family as fellow hunters and companions around the fire. There was probably a little trade between these family groupings but not much in what we would call economic activity. The subsistence level existence of these primitive tribes did not provide much surplus that could be traded. The search for food and shelter absorbed almost all of their time and they consumed most of what they found or killed. There was likely very little specialization in these little tribes: perhaps a shaman for religious rituals and healing, the old and infirm watched the little children while the hunters and gatherers searched for provisions. One person might be better at making stone tools but making the tools was everybody's job.

This began to change at the end of the last ice age about ten thousand years ago with the invention of farming. The principal reason that change had been so slow in coming was the lack of surplus. The wandering nomads had to carry everything on their backs (they would have to wait many thousands of years more for domesticated pack animals) limiting the supplies they could carry. There was little surplus, little innovation, little change. Farming changed all that.

Farming is not possible without surplus. You must save the seeds from the current harvest for the next planting season. You must save your best animals for future breeding. And with surplus comes innovation, the thought process of what to do with the surplus and how to best utilize it. The innovative use of surplus is what we call economic growth and progress.

Surplus also allows for specialization. For hunters and gatherers, every able-bodied member of the tribe must be dedicated to the hunt for food. Specialization would be at the periphery, occurring when special circumstances allowed. But with farming, fewer people had to be dedicated to producing food. This allowed some people to specialize in providing products and services to the population. People could work fulltime as potters or weavers.

With surplus and specialization, trade could flourish; within the community and with other communities. Surplus allowed for larger populations. Hunting and gathering is a very dispersed occupation. Surplus allowed for a greater concentration of people and that allowed even greater specialization. Familial tribes grew into towns, towns grew into cities, cities grew into kingdoms. On the down side, the specializations included kings and priests because greater concentrations of people required government to manage the interrelationships of people and their economic interactions.

Without surplus, innovation is difficult if not impossible: a surplus of time to think of innovative ways of doing things and a surplus of resources to implement the innovative thoughts. All of our economic advances have had to do innovation arising from surplus. But our economic well-being isn't the only things that surplus delivers. Our culture, all art, music and literature, is possible only from surplus.

Traditionally, economists have ignored innovation and creativity. It doesn't fit well into their formulas. Labor and capital are much easier to quantify. Supply and demand are easily converted to numbers. But supply and demand, labor and capital, don't explain economic development very well. An RCA 21-inch color television cost $495 in 1960. In 2015, an LG 55-inch LED flat panel HDTV costs $499 (available at your local grocery store, of all places). The TVs cost about the same in dollar terms but the modern HDTV is infinitely superior to the clunky old RCA model. And keep in mind that $495 in 1960 would be the equivalent of around $3890 today.

Gross Domestic Product (GDP) is the standard measure of economic activity, but GDP has problems with innovation. Moore's Law states that computing power doubles approximately every two years which has resulted in a substantial reduction in the cost of computing. An improved product at a lower price would have a negative impact on GDP, which only looks at the numbers.

Working without the creation of surplus to be used in innovative ways is mere drudgery (equivalent to our ancestor's exhausted sleep in a cave). Innovation is the mechanism to meet demand more effectively or in new ways (or in Steve Jobs' case, to create demand). The real drivers of economic growth are demand, surplus and innovation. Trying to generate economic growth by ginning up demand alone through deficit spending with no thought to surplus or innovation is not sustainable.

Surplus has a cumulative compounding effect. We can build on surplus – not on consumption. Our primitive ancestors were great consumers, they consumed everything they could find or produce. That is the reason progress was so slow. But with surplus you can build houses and barns that will last many seasons. These assets help produce future surpluses and reduce the amount of human labor needed to produce a crop or product (that's productivity), freeing our simple producer to think of new innovative ways to improve his or her products. Animals have only instinct and direct experience to help them survive but humans, thanks to language, can communicate to others the dangers and opportunities in the environment. Oral tradition helped our primitive ancestors, but the innovation of writing meant that the knowledge gained from these innovations would never be lost. Our civilization is built on surplus.

The Keynesian Thought Process

Marx considered surplus a form of exploitation in that it accrued to the supplier of capital rather than the supplier of labor (which is where he thought it belonged). Everything produced was the product of labor and capital and the goal of the economy was to provide employment for the workers. Keynes felt that the government had a role in stimulating aggregate demand, which would drive the economy toward its full potential and would maximize employment. Politicians of all stripes have adopted Keynes' theory as it defines government action as key to national economic growth. (Since politicians will take the blame for unemployment, it makes sense for them to use government stimulus in the form of deficit spending to take the credit for employment).

But Marx and Keynes did not include innovation in their thought processes. Without innovation there is no economic growth except for increasing population and longer work hours. How many Trabants (clunky old cars produced in Communist East Germany - https://en.wikipedia.org/wiki/Trabant) do you want? They hardly changed in the 30 years they were in production so there was no need to get a new one unless it broke down (which they did fairly regularly as quality control and customer service are also not part of the Marxian economic production paradigm).

Behavioral Economics

Economists love numbers and statistics. They are a very precise way to describe economic activity: much more precise than trying to describe human activity. Humans are very unpredictable. A new kind of economics described by Daniel Kahneman, Amos Tversky and others combines psychology and economics (Kahneman won the Noble Prize for Economics although he is a professor of psychology). Behavioral Economics tries to study the economic activity in human terms. The penchant of traditional economists for using numbers and statistics requires people to make rational economic decisions and most economic texts discuss how this rationality works. In the real world people often do irrational things, like buying a red convertible instead of a family sedan. The people in the marketing department know this! They don't give you a bunch of performance statistic on the convertible; they show you a sexy blonde with her (or his) hair blowing in the wind. They don't appeal to your rational brain, they appeal to your emotional heart (or lower).

In order to make the numbers and statistics work economists are forced to make innumerable simplifying assumptions. We will discuss later how economic theories and simplifying assumptions have affected policies in the real world. The point here is to show that traditional economic theories do not do a very good job of describing the free market system. Policies designed to generate aggregate demand based on Keynesian theory address the underlying causes of economic activity only tangentially. Deficit spending can only change aggregate demand if it changes the mindset of the population. Deficit spending to stimulate the economy after the Great Recession in 2008 was ineffective because the mood of the people was unchanged (instead of spending they saved, called by Keynes the Paradox of Thrift).

It is not so much that traditional economic is wrong. You need to know about the theories and mechanics of the economy. But they are just the beginning. The real world is just too complex to fit within their assumptions. We don't live in a ceteris paribus world.

The Free Market System and the Social Contract

If the government's economic and fiscal policies are based on erroneous theories using meaningless or misinterpreted statistics, then its no wonder our economy is in a mess. But it is even more than that. The government has become more focused on manipulating the economy than is in preserving the American Social Contract. This is the obligation laid on the government by the Constitution. All this market manipulation by the government may have been based on good intentions but they have been focused on outcomes rather than processes. And it is true that focusing on the underlying causes does not have the dramatic impact that politicians crave. But good governance is notable only in its absence.

The primary purpose of a democratic government is the preservation of a social contract based on a set of national principles agreed to by the citizenry. Allowing the erosion of the social contract not only creates difficult societal problems that are hard to resolve but also causes the people to begin to doubt the very principles on which the country is based. The only way to truly resolve these societal problems is to fully understand the principles on which the country is based and apply those principles in restoring the American Social Contract.

Arguments Against the Free Market System

Many of the thoughts and ideas in this book are based on the notion that economic growth, technological advancement and personal liberty are beneficial for the well-being of the human race. These beliefs, however, are not universally shared. Uneven economic growth has been cited as the cause of much unhappiness in the world. Technological advancement has been opposed since the beginning of the Industrial Revolution. Numerous cultures value individual liberty less than communal well-being or cohesiveness.

Uneven Economic Growth

The boom and bust cycles of the free market system are the bane of economists and politicians but uneven economic growth is inherent to the free market economic system. It is not just an unfortunate side effect of the economic system but is an essential element of how the free market system works.

Economic cycles

The free market economic system is made up of hundreds of millions of individual economic decision makers. Classical economic thinking assumes that each of these millions of decision makers is making rational choices that maximize the utility to each individual. Each of our economic decision makers, however, is not totally rational in making economic choices (later we will discuss how little rationality is actually involved in these choices). Further, this absence of rationality can affect large groups of decision makers who can be hopelessly optimistic or wildly pessimistic based on small amounts of data (or even the total lack thereof). The effect of these irrational economic decisions on the overall economy results in the booms and busts of the economic cycle. Irrational optimism (excessive exuberance as defined by former Fed Chairman Alan Greenspan) can result in build-ups of inventory, over-production or asset bubbles. Pessimism can result in bank runs, wholesale layoffs and recessions. The severity of these adjustments can be exacerbated by the efforts to prevent them.

Politicians and economists (Keynesians all) dedicate themselves to reducing or eliminating these economic fluctuations, primarily because of their impact on employment (keeping in mind that it is not the economic hardships felt by the unemployed that is their primary motivation but rather the voting preferences affected by unemployment). But they focus on the effects of the business cycle rather than on the causes of the business cycle. The business cycle treats the causes but can have some painful side effects. While the causes of a recession may be a build-up of inventories, the ultimate cause of expansions and contractions is the perception of the future held by market participants, whether rational or irrational.

The long boom times of the 1990's convinced many policy makers that they had overcome the impact of economic cycles. Such thinking led economic decision makers to become unreasonably euphoric about the future of the economy and their ability to control it. This thinking led them to repeal long-standing controls (such as repealing Glass-Steagall and loosening the underwriting criteria of Fannie Mae and Freddie Mac) and to adopt reckless stimulus measures, which led to a surge in the prices of real assets that eventually collapsed in 2008. The destruction caused by the Great Recession was inevitable given the level of unreasonable expectations. Unfortunately for the Keynesians, the lingering depression of the populace in the wake of the Great Recession blunted all the stimulus efforts of the government resulting in one of the slowest and most painful of recoveries in recent memory. It was only the slow healing of the psyches of the economic decision makers that eventually led us out of the recession, not the hundreds of billions of stimulus dollars.

Creative Destruction

So economic cycles are not only inevitable, they are also necessary. During boom times many companies can get by with inefficient operations and outmoded products due to the general euphoria. But in hard times, these companies begin to fail causing economic disruption and unemployment. The instinct of the politicians is to prop up the failing companies even though their outmoded processes and products are not what is demanded in the market. (Left to politicians the government would still be subsidizing buggy whip makers to the tune of billions of dollars in order to appease the members of the Buggy Whippers International Union –an affiliate of SEIU.)

Booms and busts facilitate the process of creative destruction (as first described by Joseph Schumpeter), which is an essential element of economic growth. Creative destruction weeds out inefficient operations and outmoded products, sometimes with ruthless efficiency. There are negative side effects such as unemployment but the cleansing effect of creative destruction clears the way for new and expanded economic growth. This has been the case since at least the start of the Industrial Revolution when more efficient factory workers replaced home workers in cottage industries. The cottage workers were not happy and perhaps you, too, might even long for the good old days of simpler times. But in order to go back to those times would require you to give up many (if not most) of the things you are accustomed to (especially at affordable prices).

The Distribution of Wealth

The free market system assumes that people who work smarter, harder or longer than others will achieve greater economic success. It is the ultimate meritocratic system − in theory. In practice, because human systems are inherently flawed, the meritocratic adjudication of success in the free market system is often skewed to the advantage of certain elite groups. But elite groups exist in every economic system and all economic systems are flawed for the same reasons that the free market system is flawed. Let us take a look at the underlying nature of the problems with unequal wealth distribution and then apply this understanding to the current environment.

Poverty
I think we need to further define what poverty is; there is absolute poverty and there is relative poverty. During prehistoric times, the base case scenario for early humans was a life of poverty. Scientists speculate that the human population may have been reduced to as few as 10,000 individuals about 70,000 years ago and that the global population 10,000 years ago was only around 5 million. In the intervening 60,000 years humans lived a precarious existence often in a state of dire absolute poverty. They lived a largely nomadic existence, following the herds of animals they hunted and the seasonally changing crops they scavenged for food. The concept of poverty probably had no meaning to them; they just had a hard life. Money did not exist and the economy consisted of barter trade between wandering tribes.

The slow growth of the human population from near extinction to around 5 million individuals 10,000 years ago can only be attributed to technological advancement that fostered a form of pre-economic growth (pre-economic growth would be an improvement in quality of life in the form of better diet, longer life, etc.). Humans slowly introduced better tools and ways to adapt to changing climatic conditions. Still, they lived in very harsh conditions that would be equivalent to dire poverty by modern standards.

Yet even in this early stage, economic growth benefitted some people more than others. Some tribes may have had an exceptionally good location that provided them a better life than others who dwelt in deserts or the arctic tundra. Within the tribes there probably was also a hierarchy among the individuals of the tribe. Some individuals would have been the warriors that exploited the labor of others (this is speculation but has been observed in other primitive societies).

The poor have always been with us. In biblical times religious leaders urged compassion for the poor, much as Pope Francis is currently advocating. However he errs in his economic analysis.

r>g

Thomas Piketty in his book, Capital in the 21st Century, asserts that capitalism is inherently flawed because the return on capital (r) is always greater than the growth on the economy (g), hence the nifty formula. Based on this assertion he deduces that the wealthy (being owners of capital) will always continue to get wealthier resulting in an evitable impoverishment of the vast majority of common folks (the ninety-nine percenters). This might be true if the world were the simplistic two-dimensional construct he envisions. There are many flaws in his basic thesis, as many other economists have been pointing out. Let me put in my two cents worth.

The Keynesian liberals (to draw a distinction between them and classical liberals) jumped all over this assertion as proof of the need for a greater role for government in the economy in order to counteract the growing income inequality that will destroy us all. I don't dispute that income inequality exists. In fact, to a certain extent, I am all in favor of income inequality. It is one of the principal motivators of the free market system. Some economists will say that Piketty's numbers are flawed because he did not calculate taxes correctly, or did not count all the subsidies and government services received by the poor. But this book attempts to go the basic roots of economic growth and democracy and these quibbling critiques barely scratch the surface.

Piketty's book makes no mention of innovation (neither does Marx or Keynes in their tomes). But as we will see later in this book, innovation is at the root of economic growth. Piketty uses GDP as his standard for measuring economic activity and changes in GDP as a standard for growth (this is very common among economists) but GDP doesn't capture many aspects of economic growth. An old rotary dial phone probably had an economic impact (in GDP terms) similar to that of an iPhone or Samsung Galaxy (i.e.; adjusted for inflation the cost of an iPhone is in the same ball park as an old rotary dial phone). But the additional functionality of a smart phone has had an enormous and transcendental impact on how we live our lives. Further, Piketty asserts that economic growth (barring exogenous events such as world wars) creeps along at a pace of 1 to 1.5 per cent per year. One and a half percent growth over a century would result in a GDP almost four and a half times larger. But looking back one hundred years the changes we see far outstrip a factor of four. The world has been transformed (or at least the parts of the world that have free market economies have).

An underlying presumption in Piketty's writing is that the wealthy do not deserve their wealth; they are merely rentiers living off the labor of others. He further asserts that entrepreneurs such as Bill Gates and Steve Jobs, although providing some miniscule service to society, become rentiers as their wealth increases. Piketty is stuck on the concept that labor intrinsically has value and that capital does not. Later on I will show that labor actually has no value — no value that is unless needed to meet some demand. If there is no demand for labor then it has no value. Presumably, governments could supply this demand for labor but governments are poor at delivery of goods and services and they absolutely suck at innovation (unless there is a war which changes the equation). It is the innovator that improves products and creates new products that drive demand. And demand drives the economy.

Piketty's solution to this situation is an intentionally confiscatory taxation of the wealthy to give the disadvantaged the money hoarded (and by definition not being used for socially beneficial purposes) by the wealthy. One of the (many) problems with this solution is that under this scenario more and more of the productive base is confiscated for redistribution (ingeniously renamed as entitlements) the overall economy becomes progressively less productive and less innovative resulting in slower growth (which requires even greater confiscation of wealth). Ultimately, Piketty's solutions to unequal outcomes (income inequality) have the fatal flaw of not addressing the causes of the problem and therefore are doomed to failure.

There is, however, an important point within Piketty's arguments. The perception that income inequality is due to an unfair economic system stacked against the little guy tears at the fabric of the social contract. One of the contentions of this book is that this is, indeed, the case. The system is stacked against the poor, minorities and middle class working stiffs. However, the confiscation and redistribution of wealth, only treats the symptom of the problem without addressing the problem itself. What needs to be done is to reform the social contract in order to level the playing field. Now you will say that this will be incredibly difficult to do, and I agree. But real solutions are worth the effort, especially when facile simplistic solutions are proven to be ineffective. The path that offers real solutions to intractable problems is usually difficult but is immensely more desirable than an easy course that only offers false hopes.

Socialism is not the Answer

Many have advocated socialism (or communism) as the answer to the uneven apportionment of wealth. This concept is flawed on two basic levels: 1) elites still exist in such societies, and 2) socialistic economies are slow growth systems such that impoverishment becomes more generalized.

Being flawed human systems, socialist economic systems (which cannot exist without a socialist political system) suffer from many of the same failures as a free market system. Greedy and ambitious individuals try to use the system for their own benefit. As usual, these individuals gravitate toward the centers of wealth and power, which in socialist systems is the central government. They form the apparatchik that operates the socialist system and take advantage of the perquisites available to those in power: luxury apartments, cars with drivers, dachas on the Black Sea. The key problem is that in socialist systems there are reduced (and in many cases no) checks and balances to stem the abuse of the system, allowing the apparatchiks to consolidate power and resist reform.

Perhaps the thefts by the entrenched socialist apparatchiks could be condoned, if the magnitude of their abuses did not lower the incomes of the rest of the population too much (i.e.; their appropriation of income was less than the one-percenters). However, there is another element of the socialist system that must be taken into account. Because central authority governs the economy, innovation and technological advancement is greatly reduced because so few people are making economic decisions. As noted earlier, the lack of innovation reduces economic growth such that socialist systems are slow-growth or no-growth economic systems. This means the pie to be shared is much smaller. In the old Soviet Union an apparatchik's three bedroom apartment in Moscow generated as much anger and envy as the one-percenter's mansion in Palm Beach.

Education
Although America spends more per student on education than almost any other nation on Earth, the return on this massive investment has been less than impressive. This problem is most acute in poor communities whether white or minority. Charles Murray notes in his book Coming Apart, the problems facing white youth in America: poor education, broken families, joblessness, estrangement from society -- the same problems facing many in minority communities. Murray sees a growing division in America between married, educated middle and upper class families (who pass on these benefits to their children) and rootless, poorly educated and unmarried (but not childless) lower class families (who are condemning their children to the same fate). The only solution to this problem is education.

Throwing money at the problems of our education system doesn't seem to have worked (no matter what the teachers' unions say). Nevertheless, the political solution to this problem is always more money. We need to rethink, not just how schools function, but why schools function. Alexis de Tocqueville, in his book Democracy in America, marveled at the literacy of Americans in an age when most people in Europe were illiterate. Literacy is essential to democracy and the proper function of schools is to prepare students for citizenship. This is the only logical rationale for the government to pay for education (or, in reality, to force taxpayers to pay for the education of other people's children). It is not to make children feel good about themselves (although this will come if they are properly educated). It is not for them to be respected but to be respectful (respect is earned which they will gain over time with hard work). It is not to get them off the streets and out of their parents' hair but to teach how to learn for the rest of their lives (because in order to survive in modern times they will have to reinvent themselves over and over).

Gangs

Gangs are the scourge of poorer communities and the schools within such gang-infested communities are fraught with peril for innocent students. Getting rid of drugs and extortion will not rid these neighborhoods of gangs. Gangs arise to counteract the hopelessness perceived by the youth in these neighborhoods. It is their perceived inability to control their own lives that drive youths into gang affiliation as a means of feeling powerful. Their hopelessness is so acute that even the realization that they are unlikely to survive their twenties is not a sufficient deterrent to gang membership. This hopelessness is derived from their belief that the deck is stacked against them and that any effort to live within the rules is foolish. They are not wrong. It is very difficult for poor children to escape a fate of joblessness, poverty and dislocation from society. This is where the playing field is most skewed.

A proper education is another (and better) form of empowerment. Only education will allow them to escape the downward spiral they are trapped in. It is essential that schools be the beacon that transforms their lives, not the institutions that condemn them. This is a function that the current educational system has utterly failed to do. We will talk about this later.

Dislocation from Technological Advancement

Another criticism of the free market economic system is the dislocation of employment arising from technological advancement. Our cottage workers and buggy whip makers were made unemployed by technological advances of the Industrial Revolution. This caused a great deal of individual hardship and I am sure that there were a lot of anecdotal narratives that would break your heart. But many more people were well served by these advances. We must take care not to let anecdotal narratives drive our decision-making processes (despite the efforts of politicians of all stripes to the contrary).

The process of technological advancement is accelerating. Technological advancement was extremely slow in pre-history (although the discovery of fire and the invention of language were two biggies). Without the written word, development was chained to oral traditions, handed down from father to son (or mother to daughter) over the millennia. Ancient poems and stories had to be memorized verbatim and repeated. Such limitations made it very difficult to build up a cumulative knowledge base. The invention of writing meant that these oral histories could be stored in books and scrolls, liberating the mind to take on other challenges. Our civilization sits atop an ever-growing base of knowledge from almost all previous learning (some unfortunately has been lost over time). This ever-increasing mountain of knowledge allows us to not be forced to reinvent the wheel every generation, thus permitting not just technological advancement, but an accelerating momentum of advancement. Barring a new dark age, this process appears to be able to advance indefinitely.

Although this process of change is being generated by many millions of people (engineers, scientists, artists, etc.) many millions more are only able to react to the changes occurring around them. How they react to change will determine whether they benefit from the changes occurring around them or whether they become the victims of change. There are many forces in society that will resist change in order to protect their place in the existing order. However, the existing order no longer exists - it has already changed. Resistance can, at best, only slow the transition, often making the eventual readjustment more difficult.

This process of change is facilitated by the free market economy. Other economic systems might be able to slow the pace of change but only to the disadvantage of their citizens and at the cost of their place in the world as other nations pass them by. Slowing change can only be done on a global basis and would require the suppression of economic freedom (which can only be done with a corresponding suppression of political freedom) to achieve this dubious goal.

Personal Liberty versus Community solidarity

There are a number of cultures and philosophies that do not value personal liberty as highly as does American democracy. Socialism and communism value communal interests (as represented by the state) above those of individuals, the rights of the community as a whole over the rights of the individual. Asian cultures, Islam and many traditional societies do not elevate the individual over the community. In fact, western culture is pretty unique in its high valuation of the individual and personal liberty (and none higher than America).

The emphasis on the community over the individual, however, does not imply that these traditional cultures are necessarily democratic. In fact, most are not. Many of these cultures denigrate individual rights in order to better control the populace. Centrally planned economies cannot abide individuals making their own economic (or political) decisions. Traditionally communal societies also have a leadership structure, hereditary families or religious orders that control the community.

Communal societies not only devalue the individual, they also discourage innovation and technological advancement. Because the individual does not benefit directly from his efforts, there is little motivation to innovate, invent or improve. This is often called the tragedy of the commons where the communal orientation suppresses growth and development. Marx railed against the expropriation of communal lands in England but without this expropriation English agriculture would have remained inefficient and beset by low productivity that was holding back the economic advancement of the entire country.

Culture and Genetic Determination

Nicholas Wade in his book A Troubled Inheritance makes the case that 1) genetic evolution can occur in relatively short time periods, and 2) culture (including geographic separation from other cultures) determines the path of genetic selection such that people are genetically preprogrammed for the culture in which they live. If true, the implications to how we, as Americans, view the world and how we conduct our foreign policy are enormous.

Since the end of the Second World War, America has tried to establish a world order based on personal liberty, democracy and free market economics on the assumption that all people are basically the same and that all people aspire to the same ideals as we do. We have spent billions in foreign aid to foster the growth of U.S. style institutions in developing countries around the world. Daron Acemoglu and James Robinson, in their book Why Nations Fail, assert that lack of advancement in many developing countries is due to their inability to adopt and maintain western style institutions.

If Wade is correct, many people may not have the genetic programming to foster these institutions or thrive in them. In Wade's analysis it took many centuries (a brief moment in evolutionary terms) for Europeans to reprogram their genes to reduce the grip of tribal cultures and institutions so that the modern national state could be developed. If it will take generations for Iraq and Afghanistan to break the hold of tribal institutions, how should we modify our foreign policy to accommodate this fact? We were able to impose western democratic institutions on Germany and Japan after WWII. Why can't we do the same in the Middle East? But Germany was already a western European country and Japan had already been turning to the west for at least a century. Add to this the fact that after seventy years the U.S. still has military bases in Germany and Japan, while troops have been withdrawn from Iraq and are programmed to be withdrawn from Afghanistan after little more than a decade. To our mind, Middle Eastern leaders are stubborn and corrupt in their resistance to adopting western standards and institutions. If however, they are genetically predisposed to tribal behaviors and institutions, how can we expect them to act otherwise?

Americans are reluctant to dominate the world in a manner that would be necessary to foster the type of change that would make other societies more democratic and able to adopt free market economic ideas. It would be a virtually impossible task in any case. However, until such time as there is greater certitude regarding the concepts raised by Wade, Americans need to stand their ground regarding the moral rectitude and economic efficiency of our system. Even if we are preprogrammed toward personal liberty and economic freedom, we can back up our beliefs with more than tradition as will be shown later in this book. We will need to think more profoundly about the implications to foreign policy (as well as immigration policy).

The Level Playing Field - Equality of Opportunity

The foundation of the social contract in America is the concept of the level playing field. The social contract assumes that all citizens start out on the same footing with equal access to education, employment opportunities and financial resources. Differences in outcomes are supposed to be derived from differences in our intelligence, talent and drive and not because of the color of our skin or our gender.

The goal of a perfectly level playing field is, as is true of all human endeavors, impossible to achieve. Some people will have advantages due to genetic predisposition: good health, high intelligence or athletic ability. These differences are impossible to avoid except in the realm of science fiction (although much of science fiction is becoming science fact).

Other distortions of the playing field arise from inheritance and family businesses. It is a natural human motivation to want to create a family business or farm to leave to your offspring. There is nothing inherently wrong with this motivation. It is perfectly natural. However it does result in such offspring having an advantage over their peers. Family wealth can allow access to better schools, assured employment in the family business or opportunities through business and political connections. These types of distortions are hard to avoid. Even people of modest means strive to leave something for their kids whether it is a family home or money for a college education.

Other distortions arise from a deliberate and willful attempt to gain advantage over others though unethical and/or illegal means. A 77,000-page tax code may be legal (as it has been approved by our elected legislators) but it is an abomination of the level playing field and the rule of law. As mentioned earlier, I can guarantee you that at least 76,000 of those pages are designed to give advantage to some special interest (whether corporate or otherwise). Many of the distortions in the level playing field arise from a collusion of private and public interests (which we will discuss later in greater detail).

In order for democracy to function correctly, there is a necessity for not just the perception but also the reality of a level playing field. Keeping in mind that an absolutely flat playing field is an impossibility we must focus on the process of nurturing and maintaining as level a playing field as possible. A democracy must constantly be restoring and correcting the distortions arising over time.

Education

A good education, as noted above, is probably the single best determinant of your ability to thrive in a democratic, free market environment. Today we require more than just basic literacy. To survive and thrive in modern America you need a very good education, which should include some form of advanced training or specialization. It is impossible to create anything approaching a level playing field if a large portion of our population is hampered by poor educational skills. Poor kids, without many of the advantages accruing to middle and upper class kids, must have a good education to have any hope of social mobility. Advancing technology makes this requirement even more critical. It appears that schools now are training kids to be complacent about their situation: high self esteem in the face of poor results, awards for all competitors (if you can call them that) no matter in what position they finished, etc. Poor kids today are being trained to be able to do little more than cash their welfare checks (excuse me, entitlement checks) but not feel bad about it.

This must stop. The entire concept of public education needs to be rethought and made relevant. Unless we do this, we will not just lose the future potential of large segments of our population, we will lose America itself.

The Justice System

The justice system, both civil and criminal, is one of the greatest responsibilities of government and it is the duty of government to assure that there is equal justice for all, that we are all equal before the law. It is, however, irrelevant that justice actually be equal for all. Today in America, there is a wide spread perception that justice is not equal for all. This perception, whether justified or not, undermines the social contract between citizens.

Race/Ethnicity and Justice

In 2015, protests exploded across the country in reaction to a series of killings of unarmed black men and boys by policemen. Protesters demanded that the police be punished for the killings. When grand juries from New York to Ferguson, Missouri decided to not indict the police officers involved protesters believed this to be a prime example of unequal justice. Were they justified in their belief?

Blacks and Hispanics disproportionately populate our nation's prisons. Is this because of prejudice against minorities or are minorities more likely to commit crimes: or is some other factor(s) involved? Crime is also highly correlated to socio-economic status and blacks and Hispanics tend to be poorer and less educated than whites or Asians.

There are many theories as to the causes of criminality but an in-depth investigation of the causes of criminality go far beyond the scope of this book. As noted previously, correlation does not prove causation: however, correlation can affect perception. In the United States there is a perception of inequity in the justice system as it relates to race and ethnicity.

Money and Justice
People feel that there is a different justice system for rich people and corporations than for the rest of us. It is true that money can buy good lawyers and expensive trial preparation. But does that mean that money buy justice? It matters little that the US justice system is far less corrupt than many of others around the world.

Politicization of the Courts
Ideologues from the left and right attempt to use the legal system to advance their particular ideologies. These battles for court appointments is most fierce when the ideological faction can't make their case to the public at large and rely on the courts to make changes that can't find majority support in state or federal legislatures.

Reform of the legal system must try and address these perceptions whether they are justified or not.

Affirmative Action
Affirmative action has been put forth as a remedy for the un-level playing field faced by disadvantaged minorities in college admissions and hiring.

But affirmative action isn't a solution; it is only a Band-Aid to ameliorate the symptoms of the underlying problem. But what is the underlying problem? Is it animus against blacks and other minorities or are there other reasons that have hampered these minorities from getting the opportunities available to others? I believe that this animus and racial hatred has diminished greatly in my lifetime but am also sure that many blacks and Hispanics will also assert that it continues to exist although perhaps in more subtle forms.

The point here is not to discuss whether racial discrimination exists. Further, the point is not to find ways to alleviate the problems arising from the unlevel playing field that cause certain groups to have fewer opportunities for advancement; but rather it is to find ways to level the playing field that are the cause unequal opportunities.

While racial discrimination may be the root cause of some of the unequal opportunities that exist, it does not explain the entire problem. Many poor whites also suffer from the same lack of opportunity that afflicts blacks and Hispanics, as noted by Charles Murray in his 2012 book, Coming Apart. Affirmative action programs often assist middle class blacks that do not need assistance while underserving poor blacks and ignoring poor whites that might need assistance.

Justification of Affirmative Action as a Temporary Measure

Affirmative Action is, by definition a distortion of the concept of the level playing. It is a conscious decision to provide advantages to certain selected groups at the expense of others based, not on merit, but rather race, gender or other determinant. This is clearly not in line with the goals of the social contract. Such a distortion can only be justified if there is a legitimate grievance that is in need of redress. A strong case could have been made (and indeed was made) fifty or so years ago, that blacks were discriminated against solely on the basis of their race. The epitome of this discrimination was the concept of "separate but equal" where the races went to separate schools but where the schools were supposed to be of equal quality. The schools were clearly not of equal quality and this was reflected by the inability of blacks to get into the better colleges and universities in the country. Even when these institutions did not discriminate on the basis of race, blacks were at a disadvantage because the poor quality of their schools that left them poorly prepared to meet the entry standards in the form of SAT tests or other tests. Some of the actions during the Civil rights Movement were meant to change this situation. School desegregation and busing programs were intended to eliminate the problems of the separate but equal concept. These programs, however, would take a long time to have the intended impact. Affirmative action was plausibly necessary during the transition period. So why, more than fifty years later do we still have affirmative action?

One reason is that blacks often still go to substandard schools and thus still have problems meeting the entry standards of elite institutions. But why? One reason is that poorer neighborhoods have poorer schools and many blacks tend to live in poorer neighborhoods (although this is changing). But if poor schools are the problem, then wouldn't other minorities as well as whites that also live in these neighborhoods have many of the same problems getting into higher education as to blacks? This is exactly the case Charles Murray asserts in his book, <u>Falling Apart</u>. Poor white kids (as well as Hispanics) suffer many of the same problems as the blacks in the 'hood.

In a way, this is good news. The un-level education system affects blacks, whites and Hispanics in much the same way. This would tend to indicate that current affirmative action programs are geared to solve a fifty-year-old problem and not today's problem. Whatever the cause, poor kids in the 'hood suffer from the un-level playing field. And not just them, the whole country suffers from this underutilization of human potential.

<u>Tax Code</u>
A 77,000-page tax code is an abomination. The only possible explanation of such a gargantuan code is that special interests, working with lawmakers, have concocted a tax code that has been modified to meet the specific requirements of the rich and powerful. This problem is more than that of mere perception and represents a severe distortion of the level playing field that needs to be corrected. Later in this book I will analyze this problem in more detail and make recommendations to level this very slanted section of the playing field.

The Role of Government

It is not only an appropriate but an essential function of government to assure equality of opportunity as part of the American Social Contract. However, most of the problems identified above are under the management and administration of the government. Education and the court system are direct responsibilities of government. Even segregation used to be official policy.

It is true that government has been trying to resolve these problems for example by establishing a policy of affirmative action. But affirmative action is only a Band-Aid that does nothing to fix the underlying problem of the crappy, dangerous schools that minority kids go to. Band-Aids are for symptoms not causes. Not that Band-Aids aren't good and useful. But if your only treatment is Band-Aids then you will have to be constantly applying Band-Aids and other temporary fixes instead of curing the problem. Affirmative action is Band-Aid that violates the principle of equality of opportunity and can only be of value if it is a temporary treatment while the underlying cause is resolved.

Government needs to refocus its efforts to restoring the American Social Contract so that temporary fixes become a thing of the past.

The Problem with Democracy – Us

So, if democracy is the most ethical and rational political system, and if the free market is the most rational and ethical economic system, why are we in such a mess? Well, Brother, look in the mirror. It's us! Us humans, with all our foibles and frailties. We all know that humans are imperfect and all these imperfections are reflected in the institutions that we create. The question to be answered is as follows: is democracy and the free market system the best mechanism to deliver the most benefits to the most people or is there a better mechanism? In order to address this question let's analyze the factors that may affect our decision making.

True Evil

We know that there are truly evil people in the world and that they do truly evil things. Historically, evil people have been able to gain power through lies, deception and violence. Adolf Hitler was democratically elected as vice chancellor of Germany. He then used lies, deception and violence to advance his ambition to become dictator (Fuhrer). More recently, Daniel Ortega bootstrapped a 28% plurality in a fair election into presidency-for-life through the use of deception and coercion. These are people who use democracy but don't believe in democracy. The 21st century is replete with these villains who use sham elections, phony ballot counts, media controls and whatever other deceptive tools are handy to rig their permanent re-election. The ALBA countries (Venezuela, Ecuador, Bolivia, Nicaragua and (above all) Cuba) have not seen a democratic change of government since they came to power. Only infirmity (Fidel Castro) or death (Hugo Chavez) has been able to cause a change of leadership. Putin has made a mockery of the Russian constitution to remain in power for 15 years and is unlikely to leave any time soon. Robert Mugabe in Zimbabwe has been reelected president for the last 27 years with mobs of supporters murdering, intimidating or forcing into exile most of his opponents. Hell, even Kim Jong Un in North Korea goes through the motion of elections (he gets 100% of the vote by the way).

These shenanigans fool very few, although some methods of election rigging are more obscure than others. Is this truly an indictment of democracy or of people who believe in democratically elected governments? It would be easy to say no, that these are exceptions, which don't disprove the benefits of a true democracy (whatever that is). However the truth is a bit different and disturbing. Demagogues and populists (often in combination) have the ability to manipulate the emotions of the populace in order to stay in power. Many of the petty dictators in the world today would be popularly elected in free elections because the opposition is hampered by the ability of the party in power to control the media (the licenses of opposition TV stations in Venezuela were not renewed), to direct resources to vulnerable populations using state funds in anticipation of elections (a woman in Honduras said she would vote for Mel Zelaya because he gave her a club sandwich), and to mobilize supporters to intimidate the opposition (the *colectivo* motorcyclists in Venezuela beat up and shoot people with impunity).

A brow beaten and oppressed population (often poorly educated) will vote for whom they are told to vote. This is the coercive power of the state used for evil. There are no checks and balances in these countries. Is democracy inherently fated to degenerate into demagoguery and populism? Is the Welfare State just a stepping on this path to dictatorship? A case can be made that the unsustainable spending on welfare payments binds a dependent population more closely to the party in power justifying (in the minds of party leaders) continuation and expansion of benefits in order to remain in power. A further complication of the welfare state is that you can have an evil outcome without evil intent. Many people believe that the welfare state is a benefit to mankind; that a wealthy nations needs to provide for all of its people. We will analyze the welfare state in greater detail later in this book. Suffice it to say at this point that the welfare state can be used as a mechanism to perpetuate a party in power and that this can lead to an evil result.

Self-Interest

Self-interest and greed are often blamed as the root causes of the problems with the free market system. Opponents of the free market system often use these two terms as synonyms. The truth is actually far different: the terms convey very different concepts of human activity.

Self-interest is one of the most basic of human instincts and is derived from the survival instinct that seeks to preserve the life of the individual and the species. Self-interest is hard-wired into our brains and humans are one of the few animals that can overcome the demands of the survival instinct. We admire this kind of sacrifice when we see it displayed by heroic men and women, however many of us fail to live up to that standard. Most of us do what is best for ourselves and our families (preservation of the species). But self-interest is not necessarily shortsighted. By entering into a social contract with other human beings, individuals forego self-interest for the benefit of the community. This not only benefits the community but also the individual who gains more (by being part of the community) than the rights or other goods given up. This is a win/win situation. It has to be or otherwise humans would not be banded together in large social groups, a process which has made the advancement of civilization possible.

Greed is very different. One of the seven deadly sins, it has been around for a very long time. The seven deadly sins are sins of excess. Lust (sinful) is an excess of desire (a good thing). Sloth is an excess of recuperations and relaxation (a good thing necessary for the revitalization of body and spirit). Likewise, greed is an excess of self-interest, an aberration of normal human behavior. Greed is a Christian sin because greed for money and possessions leaves no room for God. Greed is also an economic sin because greedy behavior disrupts the rational behavior of markets in an attempt to gain outsized profits from monopolistic practices or other distorting manipulations of free markets (insider trading, bribery of officials, etc.).

Adam Smith posited that enlightened self-interest was the invisible hand that moved markets. Many people now aver, continuing the illogical equating of greed and self-interest, that greed is the driving force of the free market economic system. Nothing could be farther from the truth. Not only is self-interest separate and distinct from greed, Mr. Smith further modified the term by requiring the self-interest to be enlightened (another way of saying rational). Enlightened self-interest posits an economic system where market participants understand that actions that benefit the market will, ultimately, benefit them as well. Thus actions that provide short term profits such as the use of shoddy materials, substandard or unhealthful working conditions, and monopolistic practices undermine the smooth functioning of the market and ultimately, the profits of everyone. Markets work best when based on trust. Practices that violate that trust are like sand in well-oiled gears; it slows things down and can in the end bring everything to a halt. Rationally functioning markets guided by enlightened self-interest operate for the benefit of everyone.

Socialist Man

The Communist solution to self-interest is Socialist Man. Self-interest is incompatible with the communal focus necessary for the socialist or communist state. It is this latent self-interest that necessitates the dictatorship of the proletariat to protect the incipient communist state, not only from the vestigial class struggle, but also from the latent self-interest of the working class themselves. Everyone has self-interest, even the working class. In modern democracies unions are intended to meet the needs of self-interested workers. This is the reason that one of the first actions of socialist and communist regimes is to replace workers' unions with state unions. The goal of the state unions is to serve the needs of the state, and not the workers. The purpose of the dictatorship of the proletariat is to root out remaining class divisions and to re-educate (i.e.; brain-wash) the masses. The problem is that people need self-interest to motivate them. The benefits to an amorphous community are lost on the individual worker. Absent self-interest there is no art, no culture – only the state. Life becomes drudgery in service to the amorphous community. Innovation dwindles, individual cheating becomes rampant, and productivity stalls. The principal reason for the collapse of the Soviet Union was the failure to create socialist men (and women) who would be willing (no, eager) to sacrifice their labor to the needs of a state that faced mounting challenges from a resurgent America under Ronald Reagan.

The Instinctual Brain

Nobel Prize winner Dr. Daniel Kahneman, in his book <u>Thinking Fast and Slow</u>, asserted that the brain has two systems. He called these systems System One and System Two, probably to keep people from making snap judgments about the two systems as a result of giving them names (an attribute of System Two). The brain is more complex than that (we also know that the different sides of our brains perform different functions and that there are gender differences as well), but we will use this theory for now because it has great explanatory power. I call the two systems the rational brain and the instinctual brain (because I am not concerned about your snap judgments).

Enlightenment philosophy is based on the assumption that people make rational decisions regarding politics and the economy. In politics, it is assumed that we evaluate the character, the experience and the platforms of the candidates and make a rational decision about which candidate to elect. Likewise in the economy, theory assumes that we do the appropriate research and rationally determine which products meet our needs the best. The problem is that this is not how we make decisions – either in politics or in economics.

Dr. Kahneman asserts that our rational brain is lazy and is usually quite happy in letting the instinctual brain run our mental operating system. The instinctual brain is very different from the rational brain. It is running all the time like one of those annoying computer programs that runs continually in the background (at times using up a lot of memory) while you are trying to do something else using another program that you opened for that specific purpose (i.e., a rational decision).

Like self-interest, the instinctual brain is designed to help us survive. Of course, it is designed to help us survive on the African savannah or the pre-historic tundra as we wander around hunting and gathering. The instinctual brain is not so well adapted to helping us survive in the urban jungles we currently inhabit.

Because quick decisions can be the difference between life and death on either the savannah or the tundra, the instinctual brain makes snap judgments based on what may be incomplete facts, filling in the gaps of data from past experience. This can, of course, lead to bad decisions. If you mistake your cousin for a lion lurking in the tall grass, you merely appear foolish. However, it would be a very different outcome if the data were reversed.

Prejudice
Because things that appear different from what we are accustomed to can have a bad result, we tend to view things that are new, strange or different with suspicion. We know the members of our family and our tribe, but strangers are treated with suspicion and are not easily trusted. When confronted with

something new or different, the instinctual brain immediately tries to classify it as something safe or dangerous, with a bias toward dangerous because of the asymmetry of the potential outcomes.

Because the human brain is limited in its ability to process data, we need to simplify and categorize the data in order to comprehend it. If we have two trees in our yard, we can come to know them individually and in great detail; this tree is Bob and this other one is Dave. But if we are confronted with an entire forest, we cannot get to know each tree as intimately as we do Bob and Dave. So we simplify and categorize. Bob and Dave have certain general characteristics like heavy bark and small pointed leaves (e.g. both are oak trees) and so if the trees in the forest are similar enough to Bob and Dave as to bark and leaves we quickly classify them as oak trees also.

Similarly, we can know intimately everyone in our family and, to a slightly lesser extent, our tribe. But when we are confronted with a large city, we must begin to categorize and stereotype the other people we encounter. And because we have a bias toward suspicion, we are very wary about strangers that are different from us. We, lacking evidence to the contrary, assume that people of the same ethnic or linguistic background share other similar traits with us. Our assumptions are likely to be very wrong since ethnicity and language are only two of the many factors that determine who we are. It takes time to go beyond easily determined factors to understand the complexity of the individual. But in a country of over 300 million people, we don't have time to get everybody's full story before having to take action for any reason.

There are people who insist that they are not prejudiced, but to me that is like saying they don't have an instinctual brain. Nonsense! Everyone has an instinctual brain and everyone has the momentary twinge of reaction when encountering stranger on a darkened street, categorizing them and putting them in a nice, safe compartment somewhere in the storage closet we call our brain. We need to deploy the rational brain in order to overcome prejudice.

John H. Miller made an interesting discovery when running Monte Carlo simulations on complex adaptive systems, which he discussed in his book, A Crude Look at the Whole. In running the simulations it took only a mild predisposition to produce a very segregated result. Dr. Miller was, of course, using colored balls, not people using their instinctual brain. But you get the idea. You don't have to be extremely prejudiced to end up in a highly segregated community.)

Manipulation

It's called nudging if done by benevolent left-wing progressive governments and manipulation if done by hard-hearted right-wing conservative regimes, but it all comes down to the same thing. People are easily swayed. Professor Kahneman and the references he quotes (particularly Thaler and Sunstein who wrote the book, Nudge) show that test subjects can be influenced by subtle changes in how information is presented (such as changing the order of presentation). Recently, Facebook experimented on its customers by seeing how their moods were affected by the way information was presented. Grocery stores influence you by locating items they prefer we purchase at eye level (compared to the items you want which are usually at your feet or on the top shelf).

Manipulation is part of everyday life. We do it all the time, often unaware that we are trying to influence someone else. But the (easy) ability to manipulate people has enormous repercussions on democracy. Studies have shown that people who look more honest (as defined by symmetrical features or certain ethnicities) have significant advantages over less attractive opponents, no matter their qualifications. More sinisterly, politicians use attack ads primarily because they work. Attack ads do not appeal to our higher cognitive abilities but to our baser (more intuitive) emotions.

The Nazis were known for their propaganda machine but they didn't invent the concept. Propaganda has been around for centuries. When dictators take power, one of their very first actions is to eliminate the free press. This includes all forms of media including newspapers and magazines, radio and television and censoring the Internet. There are so many examples of countries trying to control information and manipulate their populations that I literally don't know where to begin.

The sad (and most troubling) thing is that people often do not know when they are being manipulated. People in North Korea may be aware that they are not being told the truth, but they have no idea what the truth is. They have nothing to compare with so they think that the entire world is starving just as they are. Some people in China are aware that their government controls what they see on the Internet, but they don't know what they are not seeing. They don't have to believe all the lies of their government. Just a few believable lies can change attitudes and how people react.

Manipulation of Polls and Surveys

Ever been confused by all the polls that support the position of whoever is doing the polls? How can different polls support opposing positions? There are many ways to manipulate polls: how to phrase the question, limiting the options, targeting the group to be polled (everyone/registered voters/likely voters) etc. There is no need to discuss all the variety of techniques that can be used to manipulate polling results. The important issue to raise is that the reason they manipulate polls is to manipulate you. If manipulating polls didn't potentially affect the outcome of an election there would be no reason to publish the poll.

How can democracy exist in the face of these subtle manipulations and our vulnerability to them? The American answer has been a vibrant (and protected) free press. It is not that the press does not try and manipulate us as well (this has been happening at least since the time of Jefferson who published surreptitiously all sorts of lies about John Adams). It is that we have a large and pluralistic free press so that we can pick and choose from many sources of information (although we could be accused of manipulating ourselves through these choices).

The Fairness Problem

If you talk to progressives their conversation on economics and politics will be laced with references to fairness (or more likely unfairness). I have a problem with that. I have tried to write this book without reference to fairness at all, except that I have to deal with other peoples' perceptions of fairness. Why?

Where does the concept of fairness arise? Not from Socrates, or Aristotle. Nor from any of the great philosophers. It comes from toddlers. "Mommy, Timmy's piece of cake is bigger than mine. That's not fair." Fairness is one of the earliest concepts of children and, some could say, among the most base and mean. Fairness isn't a search for justice but an attempt to get what others have. It is rooted in envy.

The basic problem with fairness is that it is based on emotions, not logic; which is why issues of fairness are so potent. But each person's concept of fairness is different. It is based on their personality and background. Fairness is hard to define but you know it when you see it. Only someone else who sees the same things may have a different opinion about what is fair.

Take, for example, the flat tax; a tax on income that is the same percentage for everybody. Many people believe that to be a very "fair" tax. Many other people, however, disagree – strenuously. Most likely, people who believe the flat tax is "fair" would have their taxes lowered under such a scheme. Those who strenuously oppose a flat tax are most likely to have their taxes increased. That's not logic; that's self-interest.

Fairness and Complexity

It would be a stretch to state that the attempt to achieve fairness is a principal cause of complexity in our society. However, it is clearly a contributing factor. Complexity is an unavoidable characteristic of modern society. Smart phones and LED flat-panel TVs are incredibly complex and are based on the accumulated wisdom of centuries of scientific study and technological advancement. But this type of complexity is easy to use and actually makes our lives simpler and more productive.

The other type of complexity is the kind you encounter when you want to improve your property and need the approval of your homeowners' association. You are told that what you want to do is "complicated". Things get complicated when what you want to do in your own interest (improve property) potentially conflicts with the interests of others. Improving your own property can be deemed "fair" as it is your property. However, the HOA may object if your idea of improving your property includes painting your house purple.

Fairness and self-interest are inextricably linked. Living in large societies involves a plethora of self-interests, many of which are in conflict. Resolving these conflicts on the basis of fairness is impossible. This is why I avoid the use of the concept of "fairness" as a standard for conduct within the social contract. We have to seek a better way.

Love, Compassion and Artistic Expression

The model of the human brain as described by Kahneman, Thaler and other economic behaviorists is a very limited approximation of a very complex organ. They have restricted their analysis to explain human behavior in economic situations and similar activities. I have attempted to expand the scope of activities to include politics and policy (you can judge how successfully). Clearly we are much more complex creatures than this simple analogy of a two-system brain. How do attributes such as love, compassion and artistic expression fit into this two-system brain? These expressions of our humanness are not based on rational thought but in our emotions. They are an inseparable part of who we are and, as such, would appear to part of our instinctual brain derived from our more primitive ancestors.

Like fairness, these basic elements of humanity are difficult to incorporate into policy. While the modern welfare state can be considered more compassionate than a laissez-faire capitalist system, this compassion comes at the cost of the core American principle of personal liberty: making the recipients of compassion dependent on the state. They receive material benefits at the cost of their souls.

Our American principles include love and compassion because we are a good people. But compassion alone is insufficient for developing policy. There must be limits to compassion. Just as love can become an obsession, too much compassion smothers the human spirit.

So how do we objectively set standards for community actions or government programs (or just about anything) if we have recourse to only the flawed concept of "fairness"? The standard I propose is not the "fairness" of the ideas. Rather, I propose the "not too unfair" standard. If you try to hold a government program or tax system to a standard of fairness, everyone will be trying to mold the program to their understanding of fairness. This is an impossible standard that results in horribly complex laws and programs as they are jury-rigged to conform to many different standards of "fairness". The sponsor of every one of the special clauses and treatments in the tax code probably believes that the special clause relating to their situation is "fair". The result is a 77,000-page mess that is not only "unfair" but also horribly expensive and unworkable. A greatly simplified tax code would benefit everyone in the nation even though it would be less "fair' to certain special interest groups in certain situations. However, such a simplified tax code would work as long as the majority of citizens felt that it was not "too unfair".

The basis for the "not too unfair" standard is a rational ethical system. By "fairness" I refer to the emotional appeal of a proposition, while I use the term "ethics" in the sense of that which is rational. Underlying the social contract is a shared ethical system. It is impossible to assert that a flat tax system is "unfair" but it is clearly possible to state that it is unethical when it violates our shared ethical system. Under a flat tax system, poor people would have to divert expenditures from purchase of food or shelter for their family in order to pay taxes that the rich would pay from their cash reserves. Such tax payments by the poor would exacerbate their poverty. This is unethical and not in keeping with the ethical standards we have incorporated into the concept of America.

Genetic Determination

As noted previously, Nicholas Wade, in his book, <u>A Troublesome Inheritance</u>, posits that human genetics can evolve fairly quickly and that evolutionary changes can occur in a few thousand years and, perhaps in even less time. He also asserts that, because we are social animals, the way we interact socially is genetically hard-wired into our DNA. This assertion, if true, would have enormous consequences for our democracy and the policies that we need to implement. Wade further posits that people from Europe, over several thousand years, developed the social systems of what we now call Western Civilization and that these western social systems have been genetically encoded in our bodies. We have discussed before about the problems black people have faced in adjusting to life in an America. Humans first migrated out of Africa about 70,000 and the populations remained separated until recent times. In addition, since being brought to America as slaves about five hundred years ago, blacks and whites continued to live separately until very recently. Wade's theory would appear to explain at least one of the factors affecting blacks ability to fully integrate into American society. However, genetic differences in no way affect the rights of black people but only offer a possible explanation of one the difficulties we face in American democracy. There are many people who disagree with Wade but we must make sure that this disagreement is based on scientific grounds and not ideology.

Dealing with Human Frailty

It would appear that humans are ill suited for democracy. We are intellectually lazy, prejudiced, self-absorbed and easily manipulated. Further, there are actual bad people out there that try to twist the forms of democracy and the free market system to their own purposes. Added to that there are a number of folks that (many through no fault of their own) just can't cope with modern society. Rather than contribute they must be taken care of by the rest of society. Given all these hurdles that compound the problems of democratic and free market society we have discussed, how can we expect the democratic system to function in a way that benefits society?

First, I never said it would be easy. The 200,000 or so years since modern humans evolved, life has been a constant struggle. As hunting and gathering nomads and as primitive subsistence farmers, humans created only a meager and tenuous life for themselves. For much of our existence we were an endangered species until we were able to develop the tools (such as language and writing) to overcome precarious existence by becoming "civilized". This harsh life nonetheless is genetically encoded in our DNA and we struggle to adapt to a modern society with accelerating technological advancements. Our struggles with democracy and the free market system reflect our slow adaptation to accelerating changes in circumstances. If there are problems with democratic and free market institutions the fault lies with us.

A Statement of Principles

(and their Limitations)

We hold these truths to be self-evident, that all men are created equal, that they are endowed by their Creator with certain unalienable rights, that among these are Life, Liberty and the Pursuit of Happiness, That to secure these rights, Governments are instituted among Men, deriving their just powers from the consent of the governed, That whenever any Form of Government becomes destructive of these ends, it is the Right of the People to alter or abolish it, and to institute new Government,
      - The Declaration of Independence

The government of the United States is based on these principles. Unlike other nations that are based on geographic proximity, ethnicity or religion, the United States is based on principles. Without principles the United States would cease to exist. Let's enumerate the principles we have been discussing: the powers of government are derived from the consent of the governed, the people have the right to equality of opportunity, the rule of law guarantees the social contract among citizens, all citizens are equal before the law, the people have the right to acquire, possess and protect property, the people are free to engage in commerce with one another, and (very important) powers not granted to the government by the Constitution are retained by the states or the people.

But the absolutes defined by these principles cannot be fully achieved because; 1) their implementation is limited by our humanity, and 2) these principles, at the extreme, can be in conflict with one another.

As noted above, humans are flawed and the institutions we create are inevitably flawed as well. We create these institutions (the Executive Branch, the Courts, the Legislature, etc.) to fulfill the goals delineated by our principles but being human institutions they are destined to fall short. Does the fact that we cannot hope to live up to our principles mean that we should completely abandon them and seek other lesser principles?

I cannot imagine what other principles could replace those outlined above. Other ideological belief systems such as socialism or communism (and we can include a lot of other "isms" as well) are inherently flawed and the attempt by humans to implement such systems will only compound the essentially flawed nature of these concepts. The result of such implementation of flawed principles, even if attempted by good people with the best of intentions, will be, at best, failure and, more likely, very evil.

Thus, even though our attempt to be faithful to the underlying principles of America will fall short, we are obligated to make the attempt as the best prospect for creating a just society.

Conflict between Principles

While it is clearly apparent that we cannot fully live up to these stated principles, it is less apparent that it is actually impossible to do so due to inherent conflicts between these principles.

For example, the right of people to have equality of opportunity must be limited by the right of citizens to try and provide the best for their children. Even if we assume that public schools provide an excellent education, our principles state that we cannot infringe on a parent's right to further educate their child by hiring a tutor, home schooling or some other mechanism to provide his or her child with some form of advantage over other children not receiving this additional education.

Likewise, the right of citizens to be equal before the law can be in opposition to the right of another citizen to provide the best defense possible. If a person has the money to hire the best lawyer in his defense, by what right could we prevent him from that effort?

Living within the confines of a social contract obviously requires concessions of personal liberty no matter what Benjamin Franklin said.[2] It is the function of the government to enforce the social contract in a way that benefits

---

[2] Those who would give up essential liberty to purchase a little temporary safety deserve neither liberty nor safety. Benjamin Franklin

society as a whole without an undue limitation of personal liberty. The government can define parameters of acceptable behavior and attempt to limit abuses. It can permit a wealthy citizen to send his child to an excellent private school but not allow that wealthy citizen to deny a good education to other children by refusing to fund high quality public schools. The result of this compromise of basic principles may be sub-optimal (a good education for one child and a superior education for the other) but it is better than the result of not adhering to our basic principles at all (a poor education and a superior education).

If our guiding principles are not absolutes, then we must rely on sound institutions, reasoned processes and good judgment to navigate these dilemmas. This can be difficult as everyone has a different opinion of how to weight the various options in order to obtain a balance acceptable to a large majority of the populace (this is where "fairness" becomes problematic).

Not Too Unfair

The standard I try to employ is the "not too unfair" standard. As noted above, fairness is not a reasonable standard as everyone interprets fairness differently and these interpretations are based on instincts, not reason. The concept of fairness dwells in the instinctual brain and is based solely on the perspective of the individual. A person knows what is "fair" but is unable to define exactly why it is fair. It is based on perception and people's perceptions differ. These perceptions are not rational and are subject to various emotions of the individual. Many people can share common perceptions of fairness even though they can't necessarily define why they agree. Fairness is a lot like pornography, you can't define it but you know it when you see it.

I prefer the "not too unfair" standard. Many people can agree to accept things that do not seem to be fair as long as they are deemed to be not too unfair. In order to reach this stage of acceptance, the person must leave his instinctual brain and engage his rational brain. The "not too unfair" determination must take into account the feelings and perceptions of other people, it must weigh facts and make determinations. Professor Kahneman asserts that the rational brain is lazy and it lets the instinctual brain run things most of the time. The rational brain only works when it has to. The "not too unfair" standard forces the rational brain into action.

The smooth functioning of the social contract of a democracy depends on a certain degree of rationality. This rationality can break down when people come under the influence of populists and demagogues who appeal to emotion and not rationality. Fairness is the fodder of demagoguery. The "not too unfair" standard engages rationality and this can promote the smooth functioning of the social contract and of the government charged with maintaining it.

The Costs of Principle Based Policy Making

Adhering to our principles does not come without cost.

Corrupt Practices

There is a cost to maintaining our principles in a venal and corrupt world. American ethical practices extend to our business activities overseas. American businesses are subject to the Foreign Corrupt Practices Act under which American companies and businessmen can be subject to penalties such as fines or even jail time. This American law is unique to my knowledge, as countries not established upon a set of principles have no problem with allowing its citizens to commit crimes in foreign countries as long as they do not commit crimes in their home country. At the urging of the US (our principles require us to try and convince others of the public good provided by adherence to a set of guiding principles) many countries have signed conventions prohibiting corrupt practices but enforcement is spotty.

In many countries, business practices are opaque and the wheels of government (for permits, licenses, procurement, etc.) move slowly. The slower and more complicated to government procedures, the more likely people are to try and cut the red tape through strategic payments to the right individuals.

In my international experience I have seen many deals lost to foreign competitors because we in the U.S. do not allow our businesses to expedite matters through these types of payments.

"Enhanced Interrogation"

There has been a lot of discussion regarding the use of enhanced interrogation (labeled torture by many) to extract information from terrorists.

Progressive pundits assert that enhanced interrogations provided no actionable information to our security forces, while pundits on the right assert that the use of enhanced interrogations is essential to our security and that it has saved American lives and led to the killing of Osama bin Laden. They are both wrong.

Unless our security forces are lying (in which case we have even bigger problems), the use of enhanced interrogation or torture clearly provided information that saved lives. But that's not the point. The use of torture is not in keeping with our American principles. Our principles prevent us from the use of torture or enhanced interrogations. What makes America exceptional is our principles, and the use of torture makes us no better than the terrorists we are fighting (they have no qualms about the use of torture).

What progressives who favor banning the use of torture won't tell you is that banning torture of terrorists will cost American lives. What the rightists won't tell you is that there is a cost to standing by our principles and that cost is American lives. We are accustomed to sacrificing American military lives when our armed forces fight our enemies, but balk at losing American civilian lives. It is an evil world we live in that forces us to make this choice.

There is no front line in the war on terror. Afghan civilians (many of them relatives of the terrorists) have been killed and have been given the euphemism of "collateral damage". They die because they stick to their principles of placing family or tribe above acts of evil. Our civilians will be at risk because of the ban on torture. But that's what we do, what we must do. We are Americans.

The point here is not to highlight specific instances of the application of our principles around the world, but rather to show that there is a cost to maintaining our ethical position. Sometimes the cost is relatively minor, lost business opportunities or reduced profits, but sometimes the cost is dear.

The Benefits of Principle

Although it is true that there is a cost to sticking to your principles, there can also be many benefits. Much of the post-WWII world is structured around American principles. Former enemies and brutal dictatorships are now models of peaceful democracies. After the war, America tried to be inclusive and to bring many countries into a world system of governance and trade; creating the United Nations, The International Monetary Fund, the World Bank, the World Trade Organization, the World Court. While there were many wars and revolutions, death and destruction in the second half of the Twentieth Century was much less than the first half. The Cold War ended with the collapse of the Soviet Union in the face of American global economic dominance rather than in a catastrophic nuclear conflagration. World poverty has been greatly reduced, cut in half between 1981 and 2008 according to the World Bank. Much of this is attributable to Chinese economic growth; however, this growth resulted from the abandonment of communist economic principles in favor a market based system. By almost every measure, the world has greatly benefited from America sticking to its principles.

Where America has not done well on the world stage has been in cases where it did not stick to its principles. When we propped up dictatorial regimes to fight communist insurgencies we reaped anger and resentment from local populations. When we abandoned allies, people came to distrust us. The examples are legion; we have often not lived up to our ideals and principles.

In the twenty-first century many of the post-WWII American world institutions are in danger of losing their relevance. What worked in 1950 may not work so well in 2015. Even the concept of democracy is coming into question. But revamping institutions is a very different proposition from abandoning our principles. The necessity of creative destruction applies to democratic institutions as well as businesses. The economic balance of the world has changed in the intervening years and this needs to be reflected in how voting rights are weighted in some institutions. But the importance of American principles in these institutions cannot waver. Certain groups of countries in opposition to American dominance are trying to create alternative institutions. But these institutions lack core moral and ethical values; they are merely political creatures designed to meet the political goals of their creators. Without a principled ethical framework, these institutions will appeal primarily to non-democratic countries, to strongmen and dictators who shun a moral compass and abhor anything that limits their absolute power.

The Role of Religion in Defining American Principles

Some people define America as a Christian nation. It is true that many of the people arriving on America's shore during the sixteenth until the nineteenth century were from largely Christian Europe and that many came expressly for the purpose of religious freedom.

But the founders took a more expansive view of the role of religion in developing the moral and ethical principles to guide a new country. The Age of Enlightenment was an outgrowth of the Renaissance where scholars rediscovered the ancient philosophical texts of the Greeks and Romans. Although partially derived from Christianity and including many Christian sentiments, the Enlightenment philosophies were secular in nature and based on reason and tolerance. Our founding documents are religiously neutral. The Declaration of Independence refers to Nature's God and the Creator but makes no reference to Jesus or any specific religion. The Constitution is even more secular, noting only that there will be no religious tests as a requirement for public office (this was not the case in Europe at this time). The Bill of Rights prohibits the creation of a state religion (also not the case in many European countries at the time) or the creation of any law to limit the free exercise of any religion.

Much of the religiosity found in American government (such as "In God we trust" or "one nation, under God,") came much later. The words "under God" were added to the Pledge of Allegiance in 1954. In God we trust was adopted as our motto in 1956. Such sentiments may work for some, but the genesis of these attempts to insert religion into government arose more from politics than from the fear of God.

It is essential to our notion of liberty that our principles be based on reason and not solely on religion. We are a nation of many faiths and religions. Murder isn't against the law just because it is one of the Ten Commandments. It is against the law because one of the primary duties of the government within the social contract is to maintain public security and to protect the lives of its citizens. When religion or ancient texts become the basis for law, trumping reason or science, we are in danger of becoming a dictatorship of the clergy. The founders feared this type of dictatorship and strove to protect minority rights.

Because our citizens come from many different religions and also because there is a growing number of secularists and atheists in our country, our laws and principles cannot be based on any particular religion but must be derived from universal principles. These principles have much in common with Christian beliefs but will also have much in common with other religions. Much of the resistance to homosexual marriage is based on passages from the Bible. There can be no reconcilement between opposing groups if public policy is based on religious belief (which is based on faith, not reason). Take religion out of the public discourse on this topic and you will have a very different discussion.

Application of Principle in the Development of Policy

Principle is theoretical and straightforward while policy is practical and can be complex. Therefore the application of principle in developing policies can be difficult.

Moral Aspirations versus Jobs
From her beacon-hand
Glows world-wide welcome; her mild eyes command
The air-bridged harbor that twin cities frame.
"Keep, ancient lands, your storied pomp!" cries she
With silent lips. "Give me your tired, your poor,
Your huddled masses yearning to breathe free,
The wretched refuse of your teeming shore.
Send these, the homeless, tempest-tost to me,
I lift my lamp beside the golden door!"
New Colossus, Emma Lazarus

The aspirational policies as represented by the Statue of Liberty are difficult to apply in real life. Real immigration impacts the real jobs of real people. When vast stretches of the North American continent were undeveloped (as opposed to uninhabited) it was relatively easy (and a practical necessity) to accommodate waves of immigrants to fill the land and make it productive. In the early twenty-first century, with land almost fully occupied and very expensive, and dealing with the aftermath of the Great Recession of 2007/08, it is more difficult to accommodate new immigrants.

However, a principled nation has the moral obligation to live up to its principles (or at least try to). Many of our ancestors arrived on these shores penniless with no job or visa. It would be a sacrilege of our civic responsibility to turn away immigrants desiring to become Americans. It is true, however, that unfettered immigration causes disruption to our society and can negatively affect our citizens. We must, therefor, develop an immigration policy that honors the government's obligation to its citizens under the social contract, while at the same time living up to the principles that guide this nation. Not an easy task.

Developing principle-based policy is not easy. There will be conflicts between principle and the legitimate needs of the people (as well as the less legitimate needs of those who live without the burden of principles). The second part of this book reviews the current situation facing our nation and makes some suggestions for principle-based policies that will benefit the people of the United States.

Principled Policy

Part 2

Charting Our Course

Winds of Change

The principal struggles of the 20th Century were ideological:; against fascism in the first half of the century, and against Communism in the second half. Americans were convinced of the superiority of the democratic system and the freedom it provided us.

From our perspective in the 21st Century, the appeal of fascism would seem incomprehensible. However, we must look to the Great Depression to get an inkling of the insecurity and fear for the future felt by the people of the that time. Economic insecurity combined with weak regimes and the devastation of the First World War made day-to-day life almost unbearable; causing people to look for something – someone – who could ease their fears; someone strong, someone who told them their problems were not their fault, who offered facile solutions. Hitler was elected (Vice Chancellor) by a frightened populace and then manipulated his way to total power. Once in power, Hitler was able to use the enormous power of the state to, not only create a powerful war machine, but also to mobilize an entire population to commit the most horrific acts including world war and genocide. We face similar times now and can bear witness to the return of the strong man in leaders such as Vladimir Putin and the late Hugo Chavez. Latin America has been especially hard hit by elected leaders that manipulate the institutions of democracy in order to stay in power indefinitely.

America was also hard hit by the Great Depression. Was it the strength of our democracy or just dumb luck that we didn't fall into authoritarianism? It is true that we had a longer tradition of democracy than the countries of Europe. Although he was freely elected, it was only his death that ended the presidency of Franklin Roosevelt. America was able to survive world war and depression with our democracy intact. In a country with less independent people and fewer civil institutions, the result could have been different.

The Soviet Union was created when Lenin was able to use the chaos of World War One to topple the czar and install an all-controlling state regime unparalleled in history. The ideological struggle between the two opposing powers (U.S. and USSR) was never so clearly drawn up. The two behemoths of the Soviet Union and the United States bestrode the entire world and their surrogates fought nasty little wars in steamy jungles from Viet Nam to Angola to Nicaragua. The two super powers appeared evenly matched with only the mutually assured destruction (MAD) of their nuclear arsenals keeping the giants from direct confrontation. Only the internal rot of the Communist economic system (about which I will have more to say later) and a land war in Asia (Afghanistan) were able to ultimately cause the collapse of the Soviet Union. Although the policies of Ronald Reagan pushed them to the limit and probably hastened their demise, the collapse was already written in the stars.

America emerged from the struggle with the Soviet Union at the pinnacle of its power,; the sole super power of the entire world,; causing some to declare the End of History. The Washington Consensus advised other countries to emulate us if they wanted to live in peace and prosperity. So why, after only a few short years, does America seem debilitated, confronted by rising authoritarianism (Russia and China), socialism of the 21st century in our own hemisphere (Venezuela, Cuba and Bolivia) and mired in the longest war in it's history against a group of rag-tag Islamic terrorists that can project their power from the mountains of Afghanistan to the center of our democratic system. The very fabric of our economic system seems to be coming apart at the seams as we stagger between financial crisis and acute recession while being swamped by a mountain of debt. Hitler and Stalin pointed to real or fabricated enemies to retain power. We can't point to them, because "them" are us.

The Attack on the Free Market Economic System

Critics have pointed to the "Great Recession" of 2008/2009 as highlighting the weaknesses of free market capitalism and pointing out the need for greater state intervention in the economy. It was also a great factor in convincing many people of the need for "change now" (but be careful what you ask for). The Great Recession was precipitated by two bubbles; a housing bubble, primarily in the United States, where house prices reached unsustainable levels, and a commodities bubble generated by rising demand due to the rapid growth of developing countries (primarily China) competing for limited resources, exacerbated by speculators bidding up commodity prices. The reaction of governments around the world has been to slap on greater controls on banks and tighter regulation of the financial system motivated more by a desire to go after and punish "evil" capitalists, investment bankers and speculators than in substantial reform.

Five years into the reforms following the crisis, the global financial system remains as unstable as before the crisis, banking is even more concentrated in a few too-big-to-fail banks, the amount of global debt has increased, and a new bubble has been created in the equities markets. All of these instabilities have been created or exacerbated by government: banking concentration was caused by the bailouts, rising debt has been the result of sovereign borrowing and the equities bubbles by the accommodative policies of central banks.

But before analyzing the causes of and the cures for the Great Recession, let's think a bit about what a free market economic system is and also what it isn't. For this we have to go back, way back. The primogenitors of today's capitalism have been around since the dawn of time, scampering around like minuscule mammals amongst the dinosaurs. The earliest human tribes often traded amongst themselves exchanging seashells and mollusks for beads and deer antlers. Entrepreneurial merchants ran the spice trade across the deserts of Asia. Free markets further developed as the mercantilist captains of renaissance Italy expanded the range of their trade. The economic systems under which they lived might not yet have been free markets as we understand it. But look at the traits these early entrepreneurs exhibited: risk taking, innovation and investment of capital – sounds a lot like the free market system, doesn't it.

Free markets work because they are well adapted to people, to their psyches. It is a form of economy that has existed (sometimes underground, sometimes on the periphery of society) despite the efforts of potentates, princes and priests. Powerful leaders want to control the economy because it is the most effective way to control people – more effective than police or armies. The people opposed to free markets tend toward autocracy and dictatorial powers. They fear the power of people and allowing them to make their own economic decisions (which may lead to a desire to make their own decisions on other matters – like who their leaders are). Whether from benevolent paternalism or the lust for power, they want to take away from you the power to decide what is in your best economic interests. They want to grab that Big

Mac and Coke out of your hands and make you eat a veggie wrap and drink green tea.

But the fact that free markets are well adapted to people's desires means that free markets are subject to the vagaries of human psychology: the fears, the excessive exuberance, the wretched depression. Bubbles, such as those that wracked the world financial system in 2008-2009, are nothing new. The first recorded bubble was the Tulipmania in 1636-37 where florists and merchants bid up the prices of tulip bulbs using futures contracts. This bubble burst when the Dutch government stepped in to curb the rampant speculation. Although dramatic and also emblematic of the frenzy that can accompany some market activity, the actual economic impact was limited. The South Sea Bubble in 1720 had a greater impact in Britain causing bankruptcies and implicating numerous government officials. Bubbles have continued to occur on a periodic but irregular basis.

Bubbles occur because people forget that prices go up *and* down. They think that prices can only go up (very common for a limited resource such as real estate) and they speculate that even if they buy at a high price that they will still make a handsome profit when they sell at an even higher price (i.e. they think there is always a bigger fool out there than themselves). But bubbles are not just limited to a few speculative investors: entire markets have a tendency to go boom and bust. It's part of the built-in adjustment system characteristic of free markets. Rising prices motivate more production which then cools down prices. In theory these small adjustments between prices and production should be almost unnoticeable. But people appear to be oblivious to theories and prices often get far ahead of production (and vice versa).

A classic recession would result from an overheated economy that motivated businesses to build up inventory to meet anticipated demand that does not materialize resulting in a cut back in production to help pare inventories. The production cutback would result in lost jobs that further dampen demand exacerbating the downturn. The decline in production and job loss would feed on itself in a vicious cycle until inventories were so depleted that production had to be restarted. These cycles have a profound impact on individuals (if you lose your job it's a recession, if I lose my job it's a depression).

But these same cycles of boom and bust also purge inefficient operations, clear out stale inventory and prepare the economy for a new wave of expansion. Just like the seasons prepare the land for new growth, economic cycles renovate the economy. The measures often employed by governments to eliminate downturns (which can be onerous) can also cripple the return to economic growth by preserving inefficient companies or saving jobs in outmoded industries. The operation of the free market system is an organic process that is more easily observed than predicted. It can only be described like a botanist observing the propagation of plant species. It cannot be intellectualized by theoretical conceptualizations and formulas (although that doesn't mean that people don't try- just ask all those PhD's at Long Term Capital Management who thought they had it all figured out — before they went bust).

This makes economic activity very difficult to predict. There are too many variables to put into any formula. The law of unintended consequences trumps almost any theory. I am reminded of Adam Smith's description of the complexity of economic activity back in 1776. He took one of the simplest products imaginable, a simple straight pin, and thought about all the people (and economic decisions) that were involved in producing that simple pin. The straight pin was produced by a factory worker at a stamping or extruding machine: one guy, one machine and a simple product. But that pin was made of steel, produced by a steel plant with hundreds of workers, made from iron at a foundry, smelted from iron ore transported from the north of England, dug from the earth by miners, and so involved hundreds of people in the production of that simple straight pin. But we have not yet even considered the farm workers needed to provide food for all those workers, or the innkeepers putting up the teamsters transporting the ore, or, or, or ... the list goes on and on. Many thousands (if not millions) of people were involved in the production of that simple pin. No computer existed in 1776 that could manage all the calculations needed to accomplish that task, but yet the task was done. Not just for straight pins but for everything consumed by all the people in England at that time.

One could think of that little pin as having the economic DNA of all those inputs. A similar product, let's say a staple, would have much the same economic DNA: the same miners, the same teamsters, etc. but yet be a distinct product (much the same as Chimpanzees have DNA closely approximating humans DNA but are still very different).

The free market system is similar in many ways to biological systems we observe in nature. Species find their ecological niche, thrive, adapt, mutate, and then in the face of changing circumstances die out or adapt to the new environment. Economic concepts (usually in the form of companies) are similar to these species as they adapt to the changing economic environment. This is the essence of the free market system. It strikes me as very strange that people opposed to the free market system (I will discuss them in greater detail later) and all the diversity of economic choices it brings want to replace the free market system with a single command driven economic system (such as communism) while at the very same time protesting against forces that are (supposedly) reducing or eliminating biodiversity in the organic world. This form of illogic (which will be demonstrated repeatedly in the forthcoming analyses) arises from the lack of a philosophical basis from which you can organize your thoughts and decision-making.

The boom and bust cycle is inherent in the free market system because the excessive optimism of market participants (that results in inventory build-up or bubbling price increases) and, likewise, their excessive fear (that results in cutbacks, mass layoffs and crashing prices). It reflects the ups and downs of human nature; free markets allow the greatest scope of expression to our inherent human nature. Command and control systems (such as communism or socialism) start by trying to subordinate human nature to economic theory (and eventually discover than human nature prevails in the end).

Primitive economic systems are limited by lack of resources or technology such that people must adapt to their limitations rather than explore possibilities. Change is slow in such societies. Traditions become ingrained and people are locked into a subsistence level existence subject to the vagaries of wind and rain. People are chained to these tribal structures because there is no surplus that can support a more complex society. They must adapt their society and culture to the limited possibilities they face.

There are some that look admiringly to the primitive societies that still exist in pockets around the planet and state that these people are living in tune with their natural environment. They hold this out as an example modern society should emulate. This intellectual arrogance of radical environmentalism ignores the fact that most people in these "ideal" communities are not in tune with the environment but are trapped in their environment, unable to extricate themselves from poverty and hunger. Most of these people would dearly love to sip chardonnay and munch canapés while listening to elitist intellectuals expounding on the benefits of primitive society (except for the fact that they have no concept of what chardonnay is and canapés would make them vomit).

The free market system was not thought up in a university or in a revolutionary cell. It developed in an evolutionary process over many centuries. Theories and books about capitalism (many written by its opponents) are based on observation rather than armchair philosophical exercise. When philosophers and scientists try to develop ideal economic systems they usually make a mess of things. Plato's Republic would be an ideal society for Socrates; everybody else would hate living there. Marx wanted to create Socialist Man to live in his communist utopia. Of course Socialist Man does not exist, but Marx (and Lenin and Stalin and Mao) was going to make you into one whether you wanted to or not. Have you ever noticed that all of these "workers' paradises" are all led by authoritarian dictators? That's because no one would willingly comply with the requirements of such a society. "From each according to his ability, to each according to his need" may sound very altruistic; however, people (even altruistic people) still need a little something for themselves. While our self-interest may not be as enlightened as Adam Smith would have hoped, self-interest (some say greed - but they are wrong) is what drives economic activity.

Friedrich Hayek pointed out that socialism inevitably leads to authoritarianism. This is because economic activity is enormously complex as shown in Smith's example of the pin. From a central planning point of view this complexity is extremely difficult to manage so the answer is to eliminate choices and dictate prices, reduce the diversity of economic options so that the planners can deal with a limited number of variables (you don't need a staple, a pin will work just as well). This requirement to limit choice yields two results that doom the socialist exercise; people are forced to increasingly accept the economic decisions of the planners, limiting their freedoms step-by-step until ending in total dictatorship, and secondly there is no role for innovation in central planning such that the economy becomes stagnant and eventually collapses.

If the Free Market System is So Great – What Happened?

You would think that a good economic system would be good all the time, that everyone would have a job, that the economy would keep growing, that there would be no poverty, in short, that everybody would be happy. The problem is that free markets are made up of a bunch of people (actually all economic systems are). People screw up, they make mistakes, and they can be influenced by many factors including fear and greed. So a free market system can't be stronger than the people making the economic decisions (actually no economic system can be stronger than the people making decisions). What makes the free market system work is that millions of people are making the decisions by their choices of what they buy. A lot of people make bad decisions but usually, most people make okay (if not great) decisions. Adam Smith assumed that people made (rational) decisions in their own interest. We now know that these decisions are not always rational. Wouldn't it be easier to let someone else make those decisions – as long as they were rational about it?

Socialist systems assume that they (the government or its bureaucrats) know better than you do what you need and want. Maybe sometimes they do – but usually not. You know what you really want better than some bureaucrat a thousand miles away. Generally bureaucrats have no idea what you want. That doesn't matter, however, in a socialist system. The central planning bureaucrats don't really care what you want but rather what the system wants you to want (or what's easiest for the central planners to produce). They determine what you want and what you will get. They give you ration cards. They give you one kind of car (remember the Trabant?) except for the fancy ones for senior government officials.

But because people are a bit ornery, they don't like other people telling them what to do. When the official store is short of milk or eggs, the black market around the corner has an ample supply – for a price. You have to pay extra to get someone to break the law in order to get you the goods you want. The socialist officials accuse these traffickers of hoarding or economic crimes – you know the rhetoric. But the black marketers are just doing what comes naturally. You've got something they want. They've got something you want. Let's trade – we'll figure out what's a fair exchange. That's the free market.

So you want the simple explanation for what went wrong in the Great Recession of 2008? Greed – plain and simple greed. But before you get on your high horse and start raging about the fat cats on Wall Street think back and remember if you were one of the many thousands that thought the 50 percent increase in the your house value made you rich and you deserved the vacation to Cancun paid for by the second mortgage. You and practically everyone else in the world borrowed to the hilt to finance a life style you could ill afford.

Reinhart and Rogoff, in their book, This Time is Different, point out that the Great Recession differed little from many other previous financial crises over hundreds of years. Each crisis featured asset inflation (housing prices that increased 10 to 15 percent a year while inflation was 2 to 4 percent), high leverage (mortgages available at 102 percent of the valuation of the house), etc. The feeling of gloom and doom that you felt in the aftermath was very similar to the gloom and doom felt by your parents, and grandparents and great grandparents when they were hit by financial crises.

Financial crises are caused by human nature not by some wormy troll in a cubicle on Wall Street (although he or she certainly played their part this time). The real question is whether there is some method of regulation that government can impose on banks and financiers to stop these abuses. And the answer is .....no. If you think the trolls on Wall Street are bad, wait until you get down to K Street. Akerlof and Shiller, noted in their book, Animal Spirits, that government regulation was needed to control the animal spirits of human nature that lead to an endless cycle of booms and busts. In their fawning obeisance to Keynes, they neglect to also note that government and legislators are also driven by the same animal spirits that morphed the rationality of Wall Streeters into irrational exuberance. As Lord Acton noted, power corrupts; he could have said the same nothing of greed. Greed is a rather commonplace moderate sin when set next to the lust for power. Legislators are at the very least facilitators to the money addicts of Wall Street with more in common with street pimps than the Solon of legend.

The Great Recession of 2008-2009 is not the root cause of the pervasive economic malaise we live in. Nor is it the free market system that needs fundamental change (although it could use some fine tuning from time to time). The Great Recession is more of a catalytic agent: something that causes or accelerates change but is not directly affected by the change. The true factors that are affecting change are: leverage (the ratio of debts to capital and income), Black Swans (unpredictable events), financial strength (the ability to survive or take advantage of unpredictable events), the structure of our democracy (the bargain we make with politics to put our interest above those of the country) and the structure of our society (demographically, ethically and morally we are constantly changing – how do we make sure we are going in the right direction?).

But like the staffers in the Obama White House, we mustn't let a good crisis go to waste. I do believe that the United States (and what it stands for) is at a crossroads, and that what we do in the next few decades will have a defining impact on the course of history for centuries to come. A relatively few leaders and thinkers can reshape the course of future events. As a consequence of the devastation of the Great Depression, Roosevelt and his coterie of advisors set the United States on a new course that is now leading to its gradual decline and eclipse. I don't know if they could envision how things would turn out. They were facing a financial crisis that dwarfed historical experience, greater than a tsunami – it was a planet killing asteroid impact of a crisis. They did what they felt they had to do and it would be intellectual hubris to look back on the trajectory of history and say they were ill intentioned or wicked. Nevertheless, the New Deal really was too good to be true and never really worked anyway - it took World War II to get us out of the Depression. We need to take hold of our own future as did the founders of this great nation, with the vision, energy and plain old hard work and sacrifice to put us back on the right course. It was a tax on tea, of all things, that served as the catalyst for a revolution that changed not only America, but the world.

Without going into the why (we can speculate forever on the motives of historical figures) I will try and focus on the impact of their actions and leave their motivations to others. We can safely assert that Roosevelt introduced the concept of the government as the guardian of the people (some would say Nanny). This is a very different and expanded concept of government compared to what the Founders conceived. The Founders believed in freedom of the individual and viewed government (especially the federal government) as a potential enemy to that freedom. The Constitution was clearly designed to limit the power of the federal government stating clearly that powers not granted to the federal government in the constitution are retained by the States or the People.

In the depths of the Depression, Roosevelt obviously felt that the federal government had to do more. Do more to alleviate the suffering of the people. Freedom means little when you are starving (you can ask anyone in the Sahel or Somalia). Roosevelt wanted people to look at the government as a helpful friend, not with suspicion (he obviously wasn't listening to Lord Acton). The people deserved better. They deserved a secure future; they deserved Social Security. They deserved jobs; they deserved the WPA. The government could do this. Keynes told them it could. Not only could government do all this, this new activism could do something even better. It could get politicians reelected.

Adam Smith was too kind when he said that people would act within their rational self-interest. Any graduate student studying marketing in business school knows that consumers are rarely rational (if people were rational advertisements would be useless). Businessmen know this when they design their advertising programs to appeal to people's emotions to get them to want something that they previously had no knowledge of. Politicians are equally as adept as anyone on Madison Avenue in such pandering. Another example of illogical thinking is the desire of some to increase the power of the federal government in order to protect consumers from shifty businessmen but without an equivalent concern regarding the deficit bulging programs from shifty politicians.

Roosevelt taught us to look to government for answers instead of to ourselves. Succeeding administrations learned from Roosevelt and kept upping the ante of government benefits. Program piled on top of program until we have become almost totally dependent on government for our daily bread. How is this different from Socialism? The answer is...not much.

The problem is that the federal government has promised more than it can ever deliver. Despite an opaque accounting system designed to obscure rather than illuminate, people from Wall Street to Main Street are beginning to realize that there is no way the government can fulfill its promises (even as politicians from both political parties continue to add on program after program). This is why the doom and gloom of the Great Recession is a bit more profound than its predecessors. People foresee a diminished America. The United States is taking on many aspects similar to third world countries. While still a powerful industrialized country, each passing year it becomes a bit less so. We focus on our health care benefits and social security instead of industrialization and military power (for God's sake we have to depend on the Russians to take us into outer space!).

You know this isn't our destiny. You know that the final chapter of US history remains to be written; that there are many more chapters to come. What do we need to do to reclaim our rightful place? Read on.

Leverage And How It Precipitated The Great Recession

You know, we should have seen it coming. There were lots of warning signs. There were a lot of Cassandras pointing to the warning signs. None of us listened.

The Lost Decade of Latin America

Back in the seventies and early eighties, the rise of oil prices was transferring a lot of wealth from developing countries (as well as developed countries) to the Middle East. These oil producing countries, lacking investment opportunities of their own, deposited their new wealth in international banks around the world. This created a problem for the banks. There was nowhere for the banks to lend all the money they had received. Here's an idea; they could lend the money to countries that had structural deficits because of the increasing cost of oil.

Latin America at the time had, in general, a sclerotic economic system based import substitution where countries maintained high tariff barriers in order to promote domestic production. These systems were often buttressed by interest rate, capital and currency controls. The interest rate controls discouraged the growth of domestic financial markets, capital controls turned away foreign investors, and hard currency controls inflated local currency and promoted capital flight. Into this morass international banks boldly went where no (sane) man had gone before.

I was actually present at the start of what came to be known as the Lost Decade of Latin America. At the time I was part of a team at Citibank that had just raised $2 billion (back in 1982 when $2 billion was a lot of money) for Petróleos Mexicanos or PEMEX, the giant Mexican government-owned oil company. In those years the government of Mexico did not borrow as a sovereign entity but used a group of huge parastatal companies like PEMEX as vehicles to finance their budget deficits. Citibank and nine other huge banks had underwritten the loan to Mexico to the tune of $200 million each in the hopes that they could convince other banks around the world to join a syndicate to fund the loan. Eventually 132 banks joined the lead underwriters and Citibank funded only a small portion of their original commitments. Walter Wriston, the famed CEO of Citibank, attended the signing ceremony. Wriston is best known for saying, "countries don't go bust". They may not go bust, but unfortunately they often don't repay their debts.

This was during the time of the Falklands War between the United Kingdom and Argentina and markets were very nervous. Nevertheless, the Citibank team was able to do a very successful supplemental Eurobond offering for PEMEX for $150 million (this amount was actually going to be used by Pemex for its business operations and not transferred to the national government). The next round of financing for Mexico was another $2 billion syndicated loan this time ostensibly for Nacional Financiera or Nafinsa. The pre-offering telex sent out by Bank of America, the lead manager of the new deal, invited Citibank to send a representative to an initial meeting of lead underwriters but included very aggressive terms favoring Mexico which were not in line with market sentiment. The Senior Vice President of our team at Citi looked at his two Vice Presidents and said, "I'm not going, you go". The two VPs on our team turned to me and said, "We're not going, you go". Guess who got to go (because there was nobody junior on the team I could turn to and say, "I'm not going"). The meeting did not go well and the representative of JP Morgan stormed out on the Mexican Minister of Finance. I just kept quiet and reported back to the team – Mexico was not going to back down on the terms of the deal. The Senior Vice President said something to the effect, "this deal is going to crater". Citi declined to participate in the loan as a lead underwriter.

The lead underwriters took a bath and had to swallow the bulk of the underwritten loan. At that instant everyone knew that Mexico would not be able to raise any more money that year – even though Mexico still needed another $2 billion to close its fiscal gap for 1982. In August, the Finance Minister announced that Mexico could no longer service its debt. The telex (yes, we actually used those back then) from the creditors' committee to bank creditors trying to organize a restructuring of the massive Mexican debts was over 100 feet long - mostly of the addresses of the creditors (including the 132 banks in the syndicate we had done only a few months before). The rest of the dominoes in Latin America followed suit in the following months and years.

Looking back, any fool can see that Latin America was on an unsustainable course but at the time the bankers were slapping themselves on the back for having resolved the issue of recycling petro-dollars. But Mexico and much of the rest of Latin America had used the recycled petro-dollars to prop up antiquated and increasingly unproductive economic systems, constantly increasing their amount of loans in relation to their resources.

Leverage

The amount of debt a corporation has in relation to capital is known as leverage (the notion is slightly different for individuals but we know when we are in over our heads). The question is, why do corporations and banks (and even regular people) always seem to be getting into problems with debt because they have too much leverage? The answer is that if a corporation can use a loan to purchase an asset that provides a return greater than the interest paid on the loan, it will borrow the money and invest it in the higher earning asset.

For example if a company has 50 in equity and can borrow 50 more it can buy 100 of productive assets. If the assets earn 15% and the loans cost 7% the company can earn 11.5 ((100 X 15%)-(50 X 7%)). If we assume that fixed costs (like salaries and rent) are 5% of assets, then operating earnings (before tax) would be 6.5 (11.5-(100 x 5%)). This represents a return of 13% (6.5/50) on the capital (more commonly called return on equity or ROE). However if the same company can borrow 100 with the same amount of capital it will earn 8 before taxes ((150 X 15%) – (100 X 7%) – (150 X 5%)) and ROE goes up to 16% (8.0/50). Increasing ROE from 13% to 16% means stock prices go up which means bonuses and a luxury box at Giants Stadium. Companies are always motivated to push the leverage envelope in order to increase their return on equity.

Great! There is just one thing to keep in mind. If the return on the assets falls to 10% then the operating earnings of the highly leveraged company fall to 0.5 while the earnings of the less leveraged company only fall to 1.5. Worse if the return falls to only 8% the leveraged company will have a loss of 2.5 while the loss for the less leveraged company is only 0.5. Earnings of leveraged companies are more volatile than less leveraged companies and in finance volatility means risk. Leverage is risky.

Leverage affects the credit quality of companies because the earnings of highly leveraged companies are more volatile. In our example the losses are not too troubling since a loss of .5 or even 2.5 for the more highly leveraged company will only put a small dent in the equity of 50. But in our example the less leveraged company had a leverage ratio of 1/1 (50 debt/50 equity) and even the more highly leveraged company had a ratio of 2/1 (100 debt/50 equity). Many banks have leverage ratios of more than 10/1 while hedge funds are even more highly leveraged than that. Prior to its collapse, the infamous hedge fund Long Term Capital management had a leverage ratio of twenty-five to one.

Leverage with Volatile Assets

Leverage alone did not, however, cause the Great Recession of 2008/2009. In our example above we assumed that the value of the assets was stable. Any observer of stock or bond markets knows that this is not always the case. If a company has 2 to 1 leverage, its assets would have to decline in value by 33% before the equity in the firm was eaten up. But if a bank has 10/1 leverage assets would only have to decline 9% to eat up all the equity. In the case of Long Term Capital Management, the hedge fund had debts of $124.5 billion backed by only $4.72 billion of equity. A mere 3.8% decline in the value of their assets would wipe them out. And it did. LTCM went bankrupt in September 1998 and had to be bailed out in a deal brokered by the New York Fed.

How leverage and volatile assets precipitated the first phase of the Great Recession

Leading up to the Great Recession, Wall Street was getting fat bundling up packages of loans and selling them to hedge funds. Many of these transactions were sold as mortgaged backed securities (MBS) and in theory they can be great deals. I looked at one of these for the investment bank I worked for at the time to try and determine if we should invest in these securities. I think I am a pretty smart guy, but to analyze these babies takes special skills and training most people don't have. The idea that the cash flowing from thousands of people paying their mortgages can be analyzed statistically for different scenarios is theoretically sound but horribly difficult. Within those thousands of payers there are those that pay on time (the majority) but also those that pay late, those that pay early and those that don't pay at all. A certain default rate has to be included in the considerations but that rate can vary according to the quality of the mortgages and the state of the economy. Then there are the people that pre-pay their mortgages either from selling their house, re-financing or just being frugal. Although most mortgages are for either 15 or 30 years, the average mortgage is repaid in about 7 years. So once packaged, the MBS is a diminishing asset as loans get repaid.

In order to take into account the problems of default and pre-payment, the MBS is carved up into several segments called tranches. Each tranche has a different priority of payment from the cash flows of the bundled securities. Investors in tranche A receive money first; those in tranche B receive their money after the investors in tranche A have been paid. A single MBS deal can have many tranches and each will have a different credit and prepayment risk. And then comes the X tranche or residual; someone has to be at the end of the line. The investor in tranche X absorbs the losses from defaults but has the underlying property as collateral. Investors in X tranches are usually firms (often the banks who originated the mortgages) specialized in collections and liquidating real estate.

In normal times, a security backed by qualified mortgages (based on the quaint notion that mortgages with a 20% down payment and certain other credit factors qualified to be purchased by Fannie Mae or Freddie Mac, the government sponsored mortgage discount houses) could be a decent investment. Tranche A of a MBS backed by qualified mortgages would normally be rated AAA by the rating agencies which meant that it could be purchased by your retirement fund. In a well-structured deal several tranches could be rated investment grade while others were rated speculative. The X tranche was not rated. These transactions were usually over collateralized (i.e.; $110 million in mortgages for a $100 million MBS sale) in order to protect the investors in the x tranche.

Ah, yes. Life was good on Wall Street. But that was before sub-prime mortgages. Subprime mortgages are an unintended consequence of government rules and regulations that attempted to put an end to redlining. Redlining was the practice banks had of not lending money for mortgages in certain sections of town. These redlined areas were usually in the poorer sections of town and made up to a large extent by minorities. Although many in these poorer communities were decent hard-working folk that would make good mortgagees, banks were too lazy or too discriminatory to put the time and effort into sifting out the good ones from the bad. The Community Reinvestment Act of 1977 changed all that. The CRA required banks to reinvest in those communities where its depositors lived. Community activists will point out that the CRA does not require banks to make unsafe loans, only to make the effort to search out good loans within those communities. True, but banks were under a lot of pressure to make those loans and the community activists would run to regulators if they thought the banks were not doing what they thought was enough (or giving enough donations to the community activist groups – but that's another story).

Banks had a tough time finding enough people to make qualifying loans to. People in poorer communities often didn't have enough savings to make the 20% down payment. Back in those days most non-qualifying loans were large mortgages (over $400,000 if I recall correctly) that could not be purchased by Fannie Mae and Freddie Mac. Making qualifying loans to poor people couldn't justify the extra time and expense involved in finding the good credits because they had to charge the same rates for all qualifying mortgages. Applying the same logic as used for the wealthy, banks found that making non-qualifying (sub-prime) loans to the poor would allow them to charge different (higher) rates than for the qualifying (prime) loans. Not only that, these sub-prime loans could also be bundled into a MBS and sold off. Banks originated and then quickly ditched the paper. Investors got juicier returns. Investment banks made oodles of commission and fees. Poor people got loans to buy houses. What could be better than that!?

Welllllll... Bankers on Main Street as well as Wall Street so loved sub-prime mortgages that they started making them all over the place – and not just to poor people. Anyone and everyone could have a sub-prime mortgage. Eventually sub-prime mortgages became 40% of the entire mortgage market. Mortgages with 5% down, zero down, even mortgages at 102% of appraised value. People with good credit, people with bad credit, even people with no credit, no verified income and no documents. And people started buying houses. Man did they ever buy houses. And not to buy and live in for 7-30 years, but to resell ("flip") in a year or two after the price went up another 25%. Guys with a mechanic's salary were flipping million dollar houses. And housing prices skyrocketed. But what's to worry? Housing prices always go up (just don't tell Reinhart and Rogoff).

What I really don't get is how the rating agencies kept rating this stuff as investment grade. The sub-prime mortgages that were the underlying collateral kept getting more highly leveraged and higher leverage as we noted above increases financial risk. Housing prices were going up many times faster than the inflation rate such that even a slowdown in price increases would crater the house of cards.

But in 2006 prices did start to come down. Sub-prime mortgages were underwater because the owners had no equity in the houses – nothing to lose. MBSs backed by sub-prime mortgages became toxic assets. Investment banks, lured by easy money, kept trying to bundle these assets into MBSs but investors stopped buying. Investment banks, through stupidity (they actually bought some of their own garbage on purpose) or greed, were stuffed to the gills with toxic assets. There was only one thing to do......SELL!!!!!

Do you know what happens to the price of something that everybody has and wants to sell and no one wants to buy? Of course you do, it plummets. There is another thing you may not be aware of, investment banks have to mark to market (it may not be so little known if you have been checking the asset values in your 401k as they are also marked to market every day). This means they have to revalue their assets based on the market price so even somebody else's selling meant they were losing money (on an accounting and regulatory level anyway). Here's another little known concept: redemption. This kind of redemption doesn't save your soul. It sends you straight to hell.

Hedge funds (many of them started up by investment banks to hold the assets they were creating) had tons of these toxic assets on the books. And their investment clients knew it. When real estate prices started to fall these clients asked for their money back (a redemption). So the hedge funds started selling their assets in order to have money to pay to their redeeming clients. Prices really started to fall. Assets that had been very difficult to evaluate (MBSs backed by sub-prime mortgages) became impossible to value. No one was willing to buy these toxic assets at any price. The hedge funds had to sell their good assets to repay clients and hold the toxic ones.

In times of uncertainty the values of speculative assets can drop precipitously. I have seen Brazilian and Argentine bonds trading in the teens (e.g. 15% of their face value) only to come back later (the Brazilian bonds anyway). If the investment banks and hedge funds could just sit tight they might be able to ride out the storm. Redemptions (like a bank run) and mark-to-market doomed them. Investment banks dependent on short-term loans (broker loans and repurchase agreements (repos)) saw these sources dry up. LIBOR (the London Interbank Offer Rate – the rate at which banks lend to each other) spiked and then virtually disappeared, as banks were afraid on of lending to one another because they didn't know their counterparts' exposure to toxic assets or to financial institutions holding toxic assets.

This liquidity crisis was the first phase of the Great Recession 2008/2009. Banks hoarded whatever cash they could find. Lending stopped.

The Role of TARP and Other Bailouts

In theory bailouts are bad. They create moral hazard and bail out fat cats who took unreasonable risks with other peoples' money. But what's a little moral hazard when compared to financial Armageddon? Refusing to bailout Wall Street would have hurt the fat cats but it would have devastated everyone else. The collapse of Wall Street Banks would have cascaded through the financial system as depositors tried to extract money from good and bad banks alike.

Even the best-capitalized banks can quickly become insolvent because there is an inherent mismatch between their assets and their liabilities. A bank's liabilities are the deposits and the checking accounts of its customers, which tend to be very short term. A bank's assets tend to be "sticky" – that is, longer term and harder to renegotiate. Even if a bank is making call loans (loans that can be called back at any time), businesses often lack the ability to immediately liquidate these loans because they have to sell their inventory to get the necessary cash to pay off the loan. A bank's cash reserves that it can use to pay off depositors is usually only a fraction of thepotential demand because cash reserves earn little or no return and banks need to generate earnings to support their infrastructures and to pay their employees. But just because a bank may be insolvent, it doesn't follow that the bank is bankrupt. Given the time to turn the assets that are in the form of loans into cash, most banks would be able to repay their depositors.

To quote the Treasury Department:

The Department of the Treasury established the Troubled Asset Relief Program (TARP), pursuant to the Emergency Economic Stabilization Act of 2008 (EESA), which was passed by Congress with bipartisan support in October 2008. In conjunction with other federal government actions, TAR P enabled us to avoid a catastrophic collapse of our financial system. TARP helped to stabilize the system and unfreeze the markets for credit and capital, which brought down the cost of borrowing for businesses, individuals, and state and local governments. This in turn helped restore confidence in the financial system and restart economic growth. And, TARP did so faster and at a much lower cost than anyone anticipated.

The TARP was, and is, an enormous commitment of taxpayer money. And it has been unpopular for good reason — no one likes using taxpayer dollars to rescue financial institutions. However, by any objective measure, TARP worked. It helped stop the widespread financial panic we faced in the fall of 2008 and helped prevent what could have been a second Great Depression. Moreover, it did so at a cost that is far less than what most people expected at the time the law was passed.

ESA provided the Secretary of the Treasury with the authority to purchase or guarantee $700 billion in troubled assets, but it has been clear for some time that TARP will cost taxpayers substantially less than the $700 billion allocated for programs. In December 2009, the Secretary of the Treasury announced that no more than $550 billion of the authority would be used. In July 2010, the Dodd-Frank Wall Street Reform and Consumer Protection Act (Dodd-Frank Act) reduced

Treasury's cumulative spending authority to $475 billion, in line with expected investment amounts.

Our most recent analysis of the potential lifetime cost of TARP, based on November 30, 2010 data, suggests that the lifetime cost of TARP could be less than $50 billion, and less than $30 billion when considering the entire investment in AIG held by the Treasury. Many of the investments under the program, particularly those aimed at stabilizing banks, have thus far delivered positive returns for taxpayers. The costs of the program are expected to come primarily from the initiatives to help responsible homeowners avoid foreclosure. All other programs and investments, considered as a whole, are likely to result in little or no cost.

US Treasury Department, Citizen's Report of the Troubled Asset Relief Program

Of the $700 billion originally authorized for TARP only around $418 billion was used and most of that has already been repaid. The US Treasury Department states that, through repayments and the sale of assets, the Treasury has collected more than the amount of money disbursed. TARP was basically a line of credit giving the banks time to get their houses in order. The line of credit was effective because the initial onset of the crisis was a liquidity problem, not a credit problem. Once the liquidity pressure was off, the banks did not have to sell off good assets to save bad assets and didn't have to sell the bad assets at fire sale prices. Most of the MBSs weren't worthless, just a pain in the butt. Over 50% of sub-prime loans were current and less than 20% were more than 90 days past due. That sucks; but it's better than nothing – plus there is still the house as collateral (it may be under the water but it's not at the bottom of the ocean).

The Role of Stimulus

Generally, bailouts are very unpopular while stimulus is much more popular (everyone wants the government to do something and stimulus is at least something). This is despite the fact that the final cost of the TARP bailout (which stopped a systemic catastrophe in the banking industry) was low, while the very costly stimulus package has not proven to be very effective in getting the economy jumped started.

Stimulation of the economy by government is based on the work of John Maynard Keynes and people who subscribe to his theories are known as Keynesians. Keynes felt that in a recession demand would drop resulting in reduced production that would create layoffs further reducing demand and thus creating a vicious circle deepening the recession. Keynes stated that government spending would support demand, maintain production and uphold employment.

Milton Friedman (a conservative economist whose followers are known as Monetarists) countered that people realize that government spending would result in higher taxes to pay for the spending spree or in borrowing (that would be repaid by higher taxes in the future) and that people would reduce consumption (and thus demand) to be able to absorb the higher taxes, thus blunting the impact of the stimulus.

The Keynesians counter Friedman by averring that the stimulus will help the poor who are hardest hit in a recession while the rich who can afford it and consume less of their income than the poor will pay the taxes. Ah, but there is another problem here. If the rich pay the higher taxes then they have less to save and invest. These savings are needed to provide capital for the economy to grow. Thus, under the Keynesian model each recovery from recession leaves the private sector more debilitated with the government taking a bigger share of the economy in order to redistribute the wealth.

The benefits of stimulus have not been very clearly demonstrated. The grandest stimulus package ever conceived, the New Deal of President Franklin D. Roosevelt, was designed to end the Great Depression, but the economy continued to stagnate after the New Deal with low growth and 25% unemployment. It took World War II to drag the US out of the Depression. Of course it is impossible to state that stimulus has never worked as intended, because we do not have a control in the experiment showing what the results would be if no stimulus had been applied. All we can say for certain is that the benefits of government stimulation of the economy are limited at best. If the granddaddy of all stimulus plans - the New Deal - was only of doubtful utility, then what can we say about recent efforts?).

Unfortunately, even the limited positive impact of the recent government stimulus was blunted by the hodgepodge of legislation approved in 2009. Even if we assume that government spending stimulates the economy (a point not yet conceded), we would also have to assume that different types of spending would affect the economy differently. The Cash for Clunkers program stimulated car sales although many of those car sales would have occurred anyway without the program. With an average savings of only around $2,000 anybody who really needed a car could have afforded a purchase without the discount. But if you were going to buy a car anyway and there was a pot of money that was quickly disappearing before your eyes, you would want to rush out a buy a car right away. But this is just a timing difference more than a stimulus (we haven't considered the unintended consequences for this promotion which may have resulted in people purchasing cars before they were ready to afford them, resulting in an increase in repossessions).

The crash in home sales in the months following the expiration of the first time home buyers credit is another indication that we are spending dollars to create only timing differences rather than real growth.

Reinhart and Rogoff postulate that at certain levels of indebtedness, additional stimulus is, at best, ineffective. Increasing public debt required to generate stimulus increases the debt service of government, diverting what might be considered beneficial spending toward higher interest and amortization payments. Their analysis was based on the statistical analysis of 800 years of debt crises. At some point, stimulus is the equivalent to going on a shopping spree because you are depressed about your credit card bills – it just doesn't work anymore.

Even tax rebates (just stuffing money into peoples' pockets) have limited benefits. The 2008 tax rebate (under the Bush administration – all political affiliations believed in stimulus) cost $158 billion, but much of the money went to savings or paying off debt. People don't get much of a lift from shopping if they are afraid of losing their jobs and are deep in debt. The rational thing to do with a one-time windfall is to reduce the debt. Even the average consumer understands that excessive leverage increases risk: the risk of losing your house, your car, everything. If only government could arrive at the same conclusion.

The Role of Confidence (or the lack thereof)

Even during a recession with a fall in GDP of 2 or 3 percent, the economy is still producing at a rate of 97 to 98 percent of the previous year. Not great, but it could be worse. I wish my income would go up every year but, unfortunately it hasn't always performed as expected. But if you have savings and are not excessively in debt you can weather the storm with a little belt tightening. But if you have no savings to fall back on, and are way over your head in debt, you're going to be pretty worried (if not panicked) about the future, especially if you have to borrow more in order to pay the interest on your debts.

For all the economic factoids discussed on the television, the classrooms and the op-ed pages, economic performance boils down to one psychological factor – confidence.

On the individual level, if you are confident that you will remain employed you will not hesitate to buy a new car or a new home. You can buy that new flat panel television to watch the Super Bowl. You can afford to get married and have kids. You may even have enough confidence to change jobs or start a new business to try to improve your economic circumstances. Lacking that confidence you won't do any of those things. You will hunker down and try to make it through the next day, week, month ...until things get better.

On the micro-economic level, small businessmen that are confident will try and expand their businesses and hire more folks to help them. If they have confident community bankers they will be able to get a loan to buy new equipment, finance inventory or open up a new operation. Without confidence, none of these things happen.

The importance of confidence is also apparent at the macro level: faced with a lack of confidence consumption declines, production declines and unemployment increases. To the extent that policy actions (such as quantitative easing, fiscal stimulus or tax cuts) do not increase confidence, they will prove ineffective.

Economic activity is human activity. Economics is the quantification and the placing of value on what we do. If we do work or build something we know that we have created value. But how does someone else, a third party, know the value of what we have done? If we have to trade our labor or our products in order to obtain something we don't have or can't produce, how do we determine the value of my labor or product compared to the product or service I wish to receive? We do this by setting a numeric value on my labor or product and also on the product or service I wish to receive. These numeric values or units can be added up or subtracted, divided or otherwise manipulated in many ways. This tracking of what we do or make is called economic activity but in reality it is just a representation (and some could say a poor or inaccurate representation) of the value of what we do or make.

Sometimes I think we get lost in the numbers and forget the humanness behind the figures. You can do a lot with numbers and you can use numbers in big fancy formulas. But economics is the aggregate of the activity of many individual humans. We use machines and computers to multiply our basic human powers but machines don't build themselves (at least not yet).

All economic theories make a set of simplifying assumptions in order to reduce the innumerable variables of human activity down to a manageable level. But in doing so, the theories are taking the humanness out of the activity we do. Humans are much more complex than the economic theories can allow. This humanness is compounded by the fact that humans do not always act rationally. In fact, as mentioned before Dr. Kahneman, in his book Thinking Fast and Slow, asserts that we usually don't act rationally. Rationality requires effort and, being human, we usually don't want to go to that effort. We usually go around on a sort of non-rational autopilot. Economists choose to ignore the autopilot but advertisers certainly don't.

We often make economic decisions on autopilot. This drives economists nuts, because it doesn't fit into their formulas.

In the world of risk management, where I operate, we say that correlation does not imply causality. By this we mean that just because the movements of two variables appear to be correlated (i.e. move in more or less the same direction at the same time) does not mean that one causes the reaction of the other, or even that a third factor affects both variables. The PhDs at Long Term Capital Management (one of them a Nobel Prize winner in economics) found this out in the late nineties much to their dismay when all their arbitrage transactions fell apart when all the correlations behind their diversification strategies went awry.

Most economic theories are based on a system of cause and effect (an increase in price will reduce demand and an increase in supply will reduce price). Many economic formulas are based on observed economic activity but the causality behind these observations is often confused with correlation. These correlations operate much like the formulas within a certain range (for example within two standard deviations from the mean) but change at more extreme values (outliers, black swans, crises). Things move in tandem until they do not.

That's because in normal times, the human beings that originate economic activity act within a normal and predictable range. In these cases the causality and the correlation are in sync. At extreme values or in crisis events, human beings react differently and, as a result, the correlations change. In order to predict economic activity you have to be able to predict human activity (a notoriously difficult thing to do). These are the skills of a psychologist or a sociologist. Dr. Kahneman, who won the Nobel Prize in Economics in 2002, is a psychologist.

This is the reason that Keynesian economic prescriptions, which appear to work during the routine fluctuations of an economy, were of little value in easing the pain of the Great Recession of 2008/09. And while the monetarist theories of Milton Friedman (that the impact of increased government spending during a recession is offset by the realization that the spending will have to be repaid through increased taxes) appears to be a bit of a stretch in normal times, becomes more relevant when faced with a $17 trillion (and constantly increasing) national debt.

Economists have been scratching their heads wondering why deficit spending and the wildly accommodative policies of the Fed (short term interest rates have been basically at zero for six years) had such little impact. Banks were (and still are) stuffed with cash but lending was stagnant. Everyone blamed the banks (which was partly true as banks rediscovered that the application of reasonable credit standards reduced losses), but the basic underlying cause was that companies and individuals didn't want to borrow money: there was no loan demand.

Given these circumstances, people were not confident that government actions would work. Therefore, they didn't. It is the confidence of the people that drives the economy: the confidence to invest in a company or start a new business, the confidence to look for a new and better job, the confidence that getting your college degree will make your life better. It is the confidence of the people that will end the lingering effects of the Great Recession.

Confidence is a lot like trust (because trust is part of confidence): it is hard to get and easily lost. Confidence in government is equally hard to get. Populist programs may have a short-term impact, but their unsustainability usually ends up with a loss of confidence resulting in economic malaise. Entitlement programs are equally hard to sustain over the long run as many of the renowned welfare states of Europe are finding out.

Good governance generates confidence in government; but good governance is not an easy path. Good governance requires some difficult (and many times unpopular) decisions. Big wage increases and cushy pensions are always popular but can't be delivered on empty promises and borrowed funds. Eventually cold hard cash is required and this comes out of the pockets of taxpayers.

Many progressive commentators and economists have railed against austerity policies being pushed by the IMF and others. And it's true that draconian austerity measures cause harm to many people and foster social unrest. But simply spending more borrowed money is no solution either. It takes the consistent application of safe and sound policy measures over many years to foster the level of confidence needed to turn a vicious downward cycle into a virtuous upward cycle.

Employment as a Derivative Function

Has anyone noticed that while the economy declined 2 or 3 percent, unemployment doubled? Why was that?

I believe that many economists misunderstand the role of labor in a modern economy. Marxian economics defined the value of a product based on its inputs; i.e., capital (in the form of machinery and equipment) and labor (in the form of hours worked). This differs from classical economics that states the value of a product is based on supply and demand. But supply is based on the confidence of producers in future demand and demand is based on the confidence of consumers of future income (in the forms of salary or credit). Fluctuations in confidence will affect supply and demand irrespective of Marxian equivalency of capital and labor inputs.

There is a further aspect that is not usually included in these equations and that is innovation. Innovation can be in the form of Process improvement (increased productivity) or in new products (increasing demand). If confidence and innovation are the key drivers of the economy then capital and labor are secondary or derivative inputs. It is innovation that drives investment in new equipment and machinery. Most economic equations assume a static level of development because innovation is hard to quantify (in other words economic formulas assume more and more of the same machines rather than new and different machines).

This is why investment in capital goods and the level of unemployment are so volatile in economic downturns. If capital goods and employment are derivative functions of the underlying causes of economic growth it is no wonder that they are so volatile (this is basic calculus but please ask someone else to explain – it's been over thirty years since my last calculus class). It's why equity options are more volatile than the underlying stocks. It is why most fiscal and monetary policy actions (such as quantitative easing, increased government spending and tax cuts) are often ineffective in ameliorating these symptoms of economic malaise. If you want to reduce unemployment, then you must increase confidence. Much of government fiscal and monetary action is just so much make work, the semblance of taking action in the hopes that the placebo effect will prove palliative to the underlying causes.

Jobs, Jobs, Jobs

I could fill this space with myriad quotes from politicians of all stripes about how they are (or will be) the Jobs President, that their primary focus will be jobs, that they will not rest until everyone has a job, etc. etc. etc. Here is the truth in a straight shot – there is very little that the President or Congress can do to create jobs. I almost said there is nothing they can do to create jobs but that is not true. There is ONE thing they can do to help create jobs; they can increase confidence. When there is confidence in political leadership and in the economy jobs will be created. Unfortunately, most of what our representatives in Washington do, from the President on down, undermines confidence. From increased debt, political deadlock, poisonous language and defamation of motives and character, these are all buzz killers.

The government could, of course, hire more government workers. But to do what? Shuffling papers or running new government programs will only increase the deficit, which will further undermine the general confidence of the people. Reopening bankrupt factories will only block the force of creative destruction that is necessary for the eventual recovery. They could hire workers to build infrastructure. This is more reasonable however logical analysis would indicate that there is a greater need for more or better infrastructure in an expansion than in a recession (i.e.; if government wasn't wasting money on entitlement programs they would have had enough money to keep our infrastructure up-to-date). But infrastructure is a facilitator of growth, not a producer of growth. For growth you need demand and new products.

Keynes, Keynes, Keynes

Politicians love John Maynard Keynes. They love him because he encouraged them to do what they love to do. Spend money. Politicians don't like to be told that they are not able to do something. When constituents say they need jobs, politicians have got to deliver. But how? Keynes told them they could do it by spending money. The money the government spent (whether through tax cuts, purchases or programs) would put money in people's hands, thinking that they would immediately go out and buy stuff. All this buying stuff would kick start the economy and employers would immediately begin hiring all the people pestering politicians for jobs. The fact that all that spending was ineffective and that people kept pestering politicians for jobs just led them to spend even more. Something they love to do.

Keynes was a smart guy. He knew that you can't just keep spending and spending. He theorized that spending in a recession would lessen the impact of the recession and maybe help initiate the recovery. But he also stated that after the recession, government should spend less and operate at a surplus to reduce the debt accumulated during the recession. Keynes didn't realize (or if he did realize it he didn't include in his theory) the fact that, politically, there can never be enough jobs. From the perspective of the politician paying off the public debt is a job killer (principally his or hers). Every politician knows that, given economic cyclicality, there will be another recession at some point of time in the future and also that, if he or she had supported financial austerity, his or her opponent would blanket the airwaves with attack ads blaming him for the loss of your job. Talk about job killers.

After the Great Recession confidence was hard to come by. Unemployment remained stubbornly high. Economic growth was tepid. Normally after a recession, economic growth charges back. But after the Great Recession confidence was low and the recovery could barely stagger forward. The passage of time and fading memories probably account more for getting America back on its feet more than all the stimulus programs and targeted tax cuts.

Facilitators of Malaise

When I came back from my first stint overseas, it was just in time for the 1992 elections. After having watched Gulf War I on live television, George H.W. Bush was at the pinnacle of popularity. From the close of the war on February 28, 1991 until the presidential election in November 1992 Bush's popularity fell from the incredible level of 90% to an abysmal 37% approval rating. While there were many factors that contributed to his slide in popularity, chief among them, in my mind at least, was the pounding he received on the economy. Day in and day out, the television blared lurid stories of people lining up in the snow for hours just to get an application for a few scarce jobs. This was the worst recession since the Great Depression the newspapers screamed. Only after the election did the measured analysis show that, in fact, the recession had been quite mild and by some standards did not even qualify as a recession.

But what causes these woeful expressions of malaise? What or who causes the confidence-sapping litany of problems to be aired on a daily basis? I think there are a few places we can look to for answers.

If it Bleeds it Leads

The media has always specialized in lurid headlines. We all know that but are all still drawn to the photos of bloody corpses or the juicy details of a Hollywood breakup. Good news is boring, and good economic news doesn't even qualify as news. So it's normal that the economic news is mostly bad. It is called the dismal science (a derogatory name for economics first used by Thomas Carlyle, 1849, in his book Occasional Discourse on the Negro Question). Although that's crazy talk – economics isn't a science – it is, however, dismal. Even in the good times, reporters will search out stories that show the economy in a bad light. This is especially true if the stories create a feedback loop of serotonin in the biased brains of the mainstream media (if you don't already know that the mainstream media is biased then you are reading the wrong book!).

I'm not a Jerk, You're a Jerk

It's been a long time since any politician has had something nice to say about a fellow pol from the opposite side of the aisle. That goes doubly true for any policy recommendation or draft bill. There is nothing in my bill that I am willing to forego and nothing in yours I am willing to accept. One side is stupid and the other side is evil.

I don't care how it looks, I'm gonna get mine while the getting's good

On top of everything else, there are people who are tone deaf to the mood of the people. In 2011 Wall Street bonuses were back at pre-recession levels while unemployment was still around 9 percent. This was just pouring salt into the wounds of people that already had a pretty low opinion of the greedy bastards.

The problem with all these histrionics is that they sap the confidence of the people. That just makes it harder to dig out of a recession. I am not saying we should all go Pollyanna and ignore the real problems that do exist. But all this doom-saying that undermines economic recovery is done based on the personal agendas of the doomsayers.

Keynesianism's Fatal Flaw

The fatal flaw of Keynesianism is that it assumes that government can manage the economy. It assumes that the economy is like a big machine and that the government can influence this machine through the application of enlightened policy decisions. This leads to three fatal errors; 1) that government, or more precisely a small group within government or even one person, can manage the direction of the economy, 2) that the decisions

made by this small group or single person are superior to the economic decisions made by millions of citizens every day, and 3) that this group or single person is somehow immune to the basic flaws of human nature that afflict the free market system.

Keynes assumed that if you add up millions of people you got a machine and the operation of a machine could be managed by changing its inputs. Keynes viewed the economy as a formula: if you changed one of the variables in the formula you would change the results (economists love these formulas). I just assume that the economy has millions of people that make billions of economic decisions a year. Some of these decisions are rational and some are not. Keynesian policies from the New Deal to the Stimulus Plan of 2009 have always come up short. If you want to change how the economy is functioning you have to change the minds of millions of people - not fiddle with some Keynesian formula. That's called leadership not economics.

Under Keynesianism and other even more leftist theories such as socialism and communism there is a basic arrogance that the decisions of a small group or even one person in government are superior to the decisions of millions of citizen consumers.

Finally, there is an assumption by this small elite group or single person, that their decisions are morally superior to those of millions of economic decision makers. Akerlof and Schiller in their book *Animal Spirits* lament the free market's subjection to the base nature of human beings but are blind to the fact that government is made up of (basically) the same people. Keynesian meddling with the economy is based on the false assumption that government is morally superior to the free market.

Keynesianism has been the dominant economic theory for most of the Twentieth Century and for many years it appeared to work. The appearance of efficacy of government actions implementing Keynesian theory played well to politicians, bureaucrats and progressives who all benefited from the government taking on this (unconstitutional) role. But the efficacy of Keynesian solutions in the aftermath of the Great Depression was unproven when the experiment was interrupted by World War II. It has also proved ineffective is resolving the Great Recession. As noted previously, correlation is not causality. The fact that Keynes' theory appears to work in good times does not imply that it works during crises. Further, by ignoring Keynes recommendation to rebalance after a recession sets the stage for greater crises in the future.

It is quite clear that both government and market participants have a role to play in the political economy. However, it is this presumption of the moral superiority of government that has led us to the precipice of default and a potentially diminished future.

Is the Cure Worse than the Disease?

If leverage is the problem (or at least one of them) then why not just reduce leverage. Are there any drawbacks to reducing leverage? Wouldn't reducing leverage (government and private) result in lower consumption, reduced governmental services, increased taxes or all of the above? The answer is, of course, D – all of the above. But wouldn't lower consumption, reduced services and higher taxes aggravate an already bad economic situation? (The Keynesians are shouting YES, YES, YES!!!) But we have already shown that Keynesian solutions are ineffective, principally because they do not substantially change the level of confidence of the public.

Keynesian solutions also have a more insidious impact on the economy. They delude at least a portion of the population into thinking that government can actually do something about the recession and unemployment. Presidents and their administrations like to take credit when things are going well and blame their predecessors when they are not. The truth is that government actions have little direct impact on the behavior of the economy. However, when the government focuses on burdensome regulations and income redistribution instead of the proper business of government (maintaining the social contract through the rule of law and the level playing field) it drags down economic activity. When Keynesian solutions such as deficit spending or taxing the wealthy don't have the desired result, confidence is further undermined. Even worse, people become conditioned (is brainwashed too strong a word?) to look to the government for solutions instead of themselves.

In every recession including the recent one, reporters from the TV stations fan out across the country looking for the most pathetic stories of people being hard hit by the recession. Inevitably they turn to the cameras and plead that the government to solve their problems whether it be extended unemployment benefits, more food stamps, a government jobs program like the WPA, etc. (Please don't think I am hard hearted because I don't feel their pain – I do! It's just that I don't think these programs are the solution to their problems). As an employer I wouldn't be highly motivated to hire these pathetic souls. I would want to hire someone who has the gumption to make something of the job and to help me advance my business – not someone who is going to treat a job in my business as another form of welfare (or worse, a right instead of an opportunity).

If the solution to the current economic malaise involved cutting public expenses and even increasing taxes but was done in such a way as to increase the general confidence of the population, it would be the first step toward a sustainable recovery of the economy. Ultimately, the best source of confidence comes from within: from being able to stand on your own two feet and get the job done. Reliance on the government to resolve all your problem increases dependence and it's hard to feel confident when you are dependent. This is why the free market system and personal liberty are so closely linked. In the coming chapters we will discuss how we can reduce our dependency on government, revive the economy and increase our liberty – all at the same time.

Social Security is Un-American

Social Security has always been called the third rail of politics (although we seem to have more third rails than tracks leading us somewhere). Efforts to reform Social Security are thought to be deadly to the political aspirations of any politico who dares bring up the subject. Efforts to make even modest reforms in France by increasing the retirement age from 60 to 62 (in the US its 66) turned out tens of thousands of protestors into the street. I have a better idea – GET RID OF IT!!!!!! (Immediate shouts of what? This guy's crazy. Don't you dare touch my Social Security!!)

Economics is only one of the reasons to get rid of Social Security, but let's start there anyway. Social Security does not make economic sense. It is portrayed as an insurance policy just in case we are so unlucky to live long enough to retire. When FDR thought up Social Security he (or his minions) structured it to provide pension benefits starting when a person retired at age 65. Question: What was the average life span of Americans in 1932? Answer: 65! Social Security worked because approximately half the people contributing to it wouldn't live to collect. Or so they thought. The average life span of Americans is now 79. Imagine how many people would turn out into the streets if they proposed raising the retirement age to 79 (Heck, I'd roll my wheelchair out there too!).

Kick the Bucket

Wait a minute! Some will say, What about the Social Security Trust Fund? The Social Security Trust Fund is supposed to supply a fund of money to cover the benefits to be provided. But there are several layers of flaws in this way of understanding just how Social Security actually works. Think of the Social Security Trust Fund as a big bucket and the Social Security deductions from our paycheck as a lot of little spigots of water from each individual contributor pouring into the bucket. Think of the Social Security checks to our seniors as holes in the bucket that drizzle some of the water out of the bucket. The Social Security Trust Fund is the water that stays in the bucket, i.e., the difference between what comes in and what goes out). Good! You say. As long as there is enough water in the bucket, I can be reasonably assured that I will get my drizzle of water when I retire. A couple of problems. One, that water in the bucket? Your government needs that water for other programs so they are ladling out water to feed various other government programs. In fact they have ladled out almost all the water from the bucket and replaced it with IOUs (think of the IOUs as rocks in your bucket). So although the water level in the bucket (the balance of the trust fund) seems pretty high there is very little water actually in the bucket after you take the rocks out.

There's another little problem. While the number of little spigots pouring water into the bucket continues to grow for now, the number of little drizzles draining water out of the bucket is growing even faster (us Baby Boomers). So while the water level in the bucket keeps increasing, the actual amount of water in the bucket is now going down due to demographic changes over the last eighty years. The government has to take the rocks out and replace them with water to keep the water flowing.

But the amount of water in the bucket keeps on going down and soon the government will have to find another way to put more water in bucket. I can think of three ways: 1) open up the spigots of all you little spigoteers (i.e.; increase your Social Security contributions), 2) plug up some of the holes in the bucket (reduce benefits by various means -- institute means testing, raise the retirement age or create some other mechanism to reduce the outflow) or 3) borrow more money from China and others.

Obviously the bucket, I mean the Social Security Trust Fund, is nothing more than a ruse used to deceive you into believing that the government is being a good steward of your money and thus is setting you up for a safe and secure retirement. It's setting you up all right!

The Government as Bernie Madoff

There is no other way to say it. If a private individual or a private corporation tried to do what your federal government is doing with Social Security, the individuals would be thrown in jail. They would be prosecuted under a wide range of laws including money laundering, operating a corrupt enterprise, fraud, etc. Many of the problems afflicting the Social Security System are the same problems that happen to Ponzi schemes. Ponzi schemes pay out benefits to old investors from the investments of new investor. Meanwhile the perpetrators of the scheme live lavishly. When new investors dry up, there is no money to pay the investors, old or new, and the Ponzi scheme collapses.

What did Bernie Madoff do that Social Security isn't doing as well? He took money from investors and used it to pay off other investors. Meanwhile he was living the high life. He cooked the books by using an obscure (and obviously corrupt) accounting firm (sound familiar? Well no, the government doesn't use any accounting firm). He lied to the Security and Exchange Commission (that's like lying to the American people, isn't it?).

The truth is we should expect more from our government. We deserve it.

Un-American Activities

But the real disservice perpetrated upon us by Roosevelt was the corruption of the American spirit fostered by Social Security and other entitlement programs. But Social Security was the first and it laid the foundation for the other corrupting programs that came later.

The insult is that Social Security assumes that no one (let me repeat, no one) in America is capable of adequately preparing for their retirement. That everyone must be dependent on the government for financial security (where is that in the Constitution?). Social Security is not a safety net for just the poorest segments of society or for those that have had financial reverses affecting their retirement plans. It isn't for folks who have seen their private sector retirement plans go up in smoke when they find out their pensions were underfunded or funded with company stock and their company is now bankrupt (sounds a lot like the bucket plan, doesn't it?). No, Social Security is for everyone. Everyone is entitled.

During the Depression, when just about everyone was either unemployed, had seen their portfolio wiped out or their employer go bankrupt or disappear altogether, creating a social safety net might have been considered a justifiable measure to deal with the dire circumstances of the times. But there was no way to wean the financially sound citizens off the government largesse once the economy rebounded. Some folks might consider that this was part of a left wing plot to bring socialism to the US and sap the vitality of the capitalist system. I'll leave that for others to debate. The motivation doesn't matter. The result is the same.

Social Security is the foundation of the entitlement mentality. What is the entitlement mentality? It's the concept that the government is there to give us something: social security, medical care, food stamps, jobs (or unemployment payments), you name it. If the government hasn't offered it, it's only because they haven't thought of it yet. This is a far cry from the concept of government envisioned by the Founders. They wanted to get government off their backs (and the backs of their posterity). That government is best which governs least – Henry David Thoreau. The Bill of Rights aren't rights for stuff, they are rights from stuff (primarily governmental oppression).

Well, you might say. Why can't a government give us stuff? We need stuff like pensions, jobs, prescriptions, health care, job training, farm subsidies, aid to dependent children, WIC, mortgage deductions, the list can go on for practically forever. We want this stuff whether we have earned it or not. The government ought to give us this stuff.

But where is the government going to get the money for all this stuff? It could just print the money - print all the money it needed. Of course, governments have tried this in the past and the result has been inflation in the thousands of percent (think Argentina – do you want the US to be like Argentina? The Argentines have the entitlement mentality in spades.). The government could borrow the money, but then it would need a way to pay back the lenders. The government could raise taxes to pay for these benefits, but hey, wait a minute we pay the taxes. Wouldn't we be just shuffling money around with the government taking a cut for administrative expenses? Well then let's just tax the rich and let them pay for the rest of us.

This is just so wrong on so many levels; it pits citizens against one another, it saps productivity, it creates the free rider problem, and it accretes economic power to the government – extra Constitutionally.

From Each According to his Ability
The poor have votes and the rich have money.

This creates an unholy alliance of forces affecting our democracy. The votes of the poor elect our politicians whose principle avocation is staying elected. Supposedly they can earn those votes by working for the good of the nation, but in fact they usually just try to bribe voters by offering them benefits. In order to do this, they first must convince the voters that they (the voters) not only need those benefits but, in fact, deserve them, and that anyone who doesn't give you those benefits doesn't deserve your votes. In order to convince you of this ineluctable fact, they need money. They need money for their campaigns and that's where the rich come in. As much as you need the taxes of the rich in order to pay for the benefits you feel you deserve, the politicians need their campaign contributions more.

There may be some that have great wealth that don't mind paying huge amounts to the government so that it can hand it out to other citizens based on formulas developed in the maze of Washington (trust fund babies, Hollywood stars, Warren Buffet) but most wealthy people fought hard to get rich and will fight hard to keep it. You don't need 77,000 pages of gibberish to extract taxes from people. Most of those pages are written to give someone a break on his taxes.

Free Riders and the Problem of the Commons

Back in England during the sixteenth and seventeenth centuries, much of the land was held in common. People in the village could use the common to graze their flocks of sheep or herds of cattle, but the land wasn't much good for anything else. Holding land in common is very unproductive and the land is usually only marginally improved. Let's say that land in a particular village is held in common by 50 families and let's say further that one of the families builds a shelter on the common land for the herders and shepherds. Because the land is held in common, the improvement on the land (the hut) is also held in common. Some (maybe even most) of the other families will help out in the construction of the little shelter that will be used by everyone. But there will also be some that don't help out but will still use the hut in the rain and the fog. Some of them will even complain that the hut isn't big enough (for all 50 families) or nice enough. They won't even maintain the hut or repair something that they broke. Not much motivation for that first family to take the initiative to go out and build the hut in the first place. This is why common land is usually very unproductive and why the remaining common land societies are usually very poor.

Entitled people are free riders. If you feel that you are entitled to something more than you produced then you are saying that the product of the work done by the people is held in common and must be shared among the hard workers, the unproductive workers, the lazy and the non-workers. Social Security was the first big entitlement program and it launched the beginning of the entitlement society that we now live in. Social Security is very insidious. By delinking the taxes you pay into Social Security (deceptively called contributions) from the amount of your benefits (entitlement) you have lost the sense of ownership of the money you "contributed". If you had ownership over your "contributions" like you have ownership over your 401(k) you would treat it very differently. Social Security is held in common and everyone is entitled to the benefits.

Insult to Americans

If you think about it, Social Security is an insult to you, to me, to all Americans. Social Security basically says that Americans are not competent to provide for their own future. That left to their own devices they would fritter away their hard earned paychecks like so many grasshoppers. There is only one thing worse than this insult: many (if not most) Americans have bought into this notion. They seem to agree that they're incompetent and that they need the government to give them a program to make up for their lack of backbone. If that's the future of America we might just as well hand the keys over to the Chinese right now.

Who Really Pays?

The way Social Security is structured, current workers pay for the retired workers. We pay for our parents and our kids will pay for us. Except that we have had a lot less kids than our parents did and there are less of them to support us when we (the baby boomers) retire. As with other entitlement programs, it is the next generation that is supposed to support us. Not only will the kids of the upcoming generation have little inheritance from their parents and grandparents, they will inherit an enormous load of debt from their Uncle Sam (who gave the money to their parents and grandparents).

Social Security is not the greatest problem facing America (we're coming to that), but it is one of the problems and any solution to America's problems must include fixing Social Security. To me, the big problem with Social Security is its lack of economic viability since continuing Social Security in its present form will place enormous economic burdens on our progeny. Right now, experts project that beginning as soon as 2014 there will be more money flowing out of the Social Security Trust Fund (the bucket, remember?) than coming in which means that the government will begin having to borrow funds to pay benefits. Are you aware that the rating agencies have already downgraded the US' credit rating? Are you aware that rising interest costs could compound government costs leading further credit downgrades? Are you aware that Greece went from a credit rating by Moody's of A1 (Investment Grade) down six levels to Ba1 (Junk) in less than a year? That Greece was frozen out of credit markets and had to beg the IMF and the Germans to bail them out? And the cost? Layoffs, cuts in benefits and riots in the streets. Oh, you might say, we're not Greece. Well we think we're not Greece, but what do the Chinese think about us? They are (or at least, were) the ones buying our bonds. Do they think of us as Greece? They might if we don't change our ways. But like I said, economics is not the biggest problem with Social Security.

The biggest problem with Social Security is the way it has undermined the American Spirit. It has gotten us lining up to the trough like pigs waiting to be slaughtered.

Yes we could jury rig a fix to the economic problems of Social Security (assuming we resolved all the other intermingled economic problems we have as well), but that would not solve the real problem of Social Security. So what is the solution? **GET RID OF IT!!!!**

Don't emulate Greece – emulate Chile

No matter what you think about Pinochet as a dictator, he did a pretty good job fixing Chile's economy. So good that 20 years of subsequent left-wing Concertación governments kept the basic structure of his reforms in place. Pinochet brought in leading economists from the University of Chicago (the "Chicago Boys") who had studied under Milton Friedman who, in turn, was a student of Freidrich Hayek. They were all major proponents of free market economic theory. The Chicago Boys prescription for Chile was a strong dose of free market capitalism and monetarist economic policies. One of their key reforms was to privatize the Chilean equivalent of Social Security. While not perfect, it was a great improvement over the old system. Instead of having social security payments go to already retired folks, their payments went into a special account like a 401(k). The funds are managed by special government approved administrators who offer a variety of investment plans. Although people can't touch the money, it is theirs. At retirement the funds will be there. If they die, the money will go to their heirs.

The biggest problem, which is also one that would also be faced by the US, is the cost of the conversion. While workers under the new system contribute to their own pension fund and do not pay Social Security taxes, the government must continue paying benefits, not only current retirees, but also people who do not join the new system and people that are only partially covered by the new system. Why, you might ask, if the new system is so great doesn't everyone join? Well, some people have been paying Social Security taxes for many years and would not be able to accumulate enough under the new system before they retire. Others may convert but still have a claim for substantial payments under the old system arising from the many years that they paid into it. The difference between the amount of benefits paid out and the amount taxes coming in (effectively zero) can run into a substantial percent of GDP (in the case of Chile it ranged from between 3 and 5 percent). This obligation will continue for decades until all the people due money under the old system have died off although as the number of people decrease and the economy grows the burden will become less significant over time. Nevertheless, we are talking about a very significant amount of money.

For the US, such a changeover would cost many trillions of dollars. But if you think about it, this money is really the money that the government has taken from us and used for other things (it should be in the bucket, but isn't). These trillions of dollars represent the net present value of the unfunded pension liability (the rocks, remember?) of the Social Security System. The cost to convert to a privatized system represents the monetization of those unfunded benefits over time. The impact on the annual deficit will be gut wrenching but is essentially reporting the true impact of the Social Security pension plan which is currently not reported at all.

The Fallacy of Security

Many of the opponents to privatizing Social Security will point to fluctuations in the stock market and state that pensioners should not subject their retirement to the machinations of greedy Wall Streeters. To them, the security of the payments from the government trumps the higher potential gains from the market. While it is true that the stock market (although under a privatized system participants could choose from a variety of securities to invest in including government bonds) goes down during recessions, so do government revenues in the form of reduced taxes and reduced contributions to the Social Security system. This would force the government to increase taxes or borrow the money needed to pay social Security benefits (they could also reduce benefits but that would be the same as the scenario under the privatized scheme). So in the short-term the government's ability to borrow would make it appear to be superior to a privatized retirement program.

In the medium to long term, however, the stock market has shown a resounding ability to bounce back and return to its long-term growth pattern. So despite its short-term volatility, a privatized program would prove a superior option to a government one.

Well, one might counter, what if the market didn't bounce back? And therefore seniors should be protected from this risk by a benevolent government retirement program. Certainly this sense of security is worth more than a few percentage points of additional gains? But this is a false sense of security. The stock market broadly reflects the performance of the US economy and for the market to have a prolonged swan dive, the overall economy would have to be equally lackluster. But the implication to the government if the US economy was debilitated for an extended period would be reduced tax revenue and a reduced ability to borrow funds (because the ability to borrow is based on future tax inflows). This would leave the government no option but to reduce benefits – the same result that would occur under a privatized system.

Will ending Social Security end the illness of the entitlement mentality? No, but it would be a start. We are like addicts hooked on multiple drugs and the process of drying out will be very uncomfortable and drawn out. Financially

Social Security could probably be fixed, some sort of jury-rigged system that will kick the can far enough down the road that we need not worry about it. The real reason that we should get rid of Social Security is that it is morally repugnant. Reliance on an enormous government pension program may have appeal in Europe, but Americans must choose between being dependent (on government) or self-reliant. Social Security is un-American.

Hypochondriac Nation

Our addiction to entitlements found its fullest expression in healthcare. Before we get too deep into this, as an exercise, let's go back and take a look at the good ol' US Constitution and find out where it says we have a right to healthcare. Back already? What! You couldn't find it anywhere in the Constitution? I'm shocked. SHOCKED!

The US Constitution, for the most part, is a simple and elegant document. It says what it means and means what it says. If the Founders had thought that medical care was a right they would have put it in. It's not there.

The Founders felt that some rights should be specifically enumerated and so the Bill of Rights and subsequent Amendments have clarified the rights retained by American citizens. There is no healthcare amendment.

More specifically, as we have discussed previously, the Founders assumed that we all have natural rights. The government only has the powers that we give to it, ceding some of our rights and freedoms so that the government can fulfill its duties. The government lacks the authority to grant us rights since, by definition it only has the powers ceded to it by us: granting us rights (especially economic rights) can only be done by giving us back the rights we ceded to the government in the Constitution.

One of the powers ceded to the federal government is the power to tax. The government needs the ability to tax us in order to fulfill its functions and can use its coercive power in order to do this. These tax monies extracted from us can then be used for the common defense, to insure domestic tranquility and the other duties of the government including promoting the general welfare.

The questions we are then faced with are: Does the government have the authority to use its coercive power to pay for healthcare in the name of promoting the general welfare? Does the government have the power to force us to provide healthcare not only for ourselves but also for others (i.e.; force us to make economic decisions against our will)? And finally, does it make economic sense for the government to create and regulate a healthcare system?

Why in the world do so many people think they have a "right" to healthcare? The right to receive healthcare without the obligation to pay for it. Everyone needs healthcare, but they also need food and shelter as well: and the need for food and shelter is, in most cases, more urgent than the need for healthcare. It's true that healthcare is very expensive. But food and shelter are also expensive. Couldn't we could come up with a system that would also pay for food and shelter. Yes, we can! Oops, that's socialism.

What is it about healthcare that requires government intervention as compared to the other requirements of day-to-day living? It's true, as noted above, that healthcare is very expensive. The cost of healthcare is about 17% of GDP and it is rising faster than inflation – quickly approaching 20% of GDP. Would you want to spend one fifth of your personal income on healthcare? No way! You'd say. But that's what you're paying. There's no way around it. Some may pay a bit more; some may pay a bit less. That's what insurance is all about. But on average we are all paying almost one fifth of our income on healthcare (actually we are borrowing to pay for this increasingly expensive service with little hope of generating the additional income to pay off this debt).

The problem with healthcare isn't availability. It's the cost. We cannot afford, as a nation or as individuals, this level of healthcare cost. And with Obamacare adding millions of new beneficiaries, these costs can't help but go up. One can easily see that a nation that is so preoccupied with health and retirement is not focused on producing anything. That is not....well...it's not healthy.

Some people say that we have the best healthcare in the world (only the most costly). The statistics, however, do not bear this out. Out healthcare statistics are mediocre at best. Other nations do better with less. Is it due to government run healthcare? I don't think so. Let's take a closer look.

How did we get in this situation? It started back in World War II when most of America's finest were busy fighting the Nazis and the Japs (well that's what we called them back then – it was a different world). Companies were competing to hire the few non-combatants and offered attractive benefits to get the best people. One of those benefits was a company healthcare plan. There is nothing wrong with offering benefits to hire the best talent (some companies offer free popcorn or massage therapists). But then somebody got the bright idea that government could help in this process by offering a double tax deduction for healthcare benefits. Companies could deduct the cost of healthcare benefits for its employees but the employees did not have the cost of those benefits added to their taxable compensation. What a great idea! Everybody benefitted.

Well there were a few problems with this idea. And these few problems, as they have compounded over the years, have totally screwed up health care in America. One, employer based healthcare assumes an America from the Donna Reed idyll of America of the 1950s, where the man in the grey flannel suit worked for the corporation his entire life (my older brother joined GM right out of college and stayed there until he retired). Unionized factory workers likewise were assumed to work on the line for the same employer for their entire life. These demographic assumptions didn't hold up as our economy and workforce changed. People today bounce around from job to job, unionization is way down and more and more people are self-employed, part-time employed or contractors (even more so thanks to Obamacare). The employer based healthcare plan is fatally flawed because it doesn't match the ebb and flow of employment as people move (by choice or necessity) from job to job. Conversely, people with "prior existing conditions" became trapped at their current jobs, since a new insurer at a new employer wouldn't want to cover the existing condition at a loss. This is one of the principal reasons that there are so many people without healthcare coverage in America. What started out as a perk has become a requirement (thanks to the employer mandate that is part of Obamacare) and a right that locked us into a healthcare system that grows more unwieldy and complex by the day.

But that's only the start of it. Under the double tax benefit, it made sense to pass as much of the cost of healthcare through the insurance plan as possible, even things that would not normally be considered as needing insurance, such as well baby visits and annual check-ups. Insurance is designed for catastrophic coverage, not routine expenses. You don't use your car insurance when you go in for an oil change. You use your car insurance for catastrophes, accidents that you hope will never happen but sometimes do. But if you could include the cost of your oil change as a tax deduction, you would do it in a heartbeat. But that's not insurance. That's playing the tax avoidance game (which means your lack of tax payment falls to someone else or must be borrowed by the government).

But this mechanism to avoid taxes had two consequences (everything has consequences): 1) the cost of healthcare services was divorced from the consumers of healthcare services, and 2) people (because they no longer felt the full burden of their healthcare costs) came to feel entitled to healthcare no matter what the cost. I believe (because I am a bit of a Pollyanna) that our legislators were well intentioned and that they did not realize the unintended consequences that would swell up as a result of their largesse. But they might as well have been evil gnomes plotting our destruction because the result is the same.

The Missing Invisible Hand

Here's a riddle. How do you know if an invisible hand is missing? Adam Smith (remember him?) felt that people acting in their own enlightened self-interest (Enlightened? That's a bit of a stretch but we'll deal with that later) would interact with other people in such a way that the laws of supply and demand would be in equilibrium at a price: that it would be as if an invisible hand would be guiding the economy. Arriving at this price requires an interaction among people: the producer and the consumer. If the beefsteak at one butcher is too expensive you can go to another butcher to see if you can get a better price (assuming there is no monopoly price setting – but let's not get into conspiracy theory at this point). It is in the enlightened self-interest of the first butcher to offer you a price you consider to be fair to keep you from going to the second butcher, just as it is in the interest of the second butcher to offer you a competitive price to attract your business. It is in your interest to pay the lowest price for beef (assuming quality and all other factors the same) so that you will have some money left over for a pint or two of beer to go with your beef. This is in essence how competition increases the price efficiency of an economy. Multiply these price decisions millions of times for all the consumers in the economy and you have a powerful mechanism to not only obtain the best prices but also the best products as producers vie for your business.

The healthcare system in America breaks this basic economic relationship. It divorces consumers (patients) from the producers (doctors and hospitals) and puts a bureaucracy (whether an insurance company or a government institution) in the middle. As a consumer you don't care about the cost effectiveness of your healthcare because that has no impact on you. Your costs are the same no matter what. You (and millions of others) complain when your co-payment goes from $15 to $25 but could care less if the actual charged cost of the medical service is $150 or $250 or $2500. When price is not a factor, people demand the best. You're probably not going to have Kobe beef or lobster tonight — it's too expensive. But when it comes to healthcare — nothing but the best.

Doctors and hospitals are motivated to raise costs because they can (that doesn't make them bad people — they're just acting in their own enlightened self-interest given the economic framework they are living in). Have you ever wondered why there are so many advertisements for prescriptions drugs on TV? It's not to convince doctors that that this is a good drug for what ails you, it's to convince you to demand the drug from your doctor whether it's what you need or not. And the cost doesn't matter because you are not going to pay the cost. Drug companies tinker with their formulas not to make them better but to qualify for a new period of patent exclusivity where they can keep their patent in force longer and charge higher prices than generic medicines (and then convince you to ask for these new medicines through advertisements even though the now generic medicine is equally beneficial and now much cheaper).

So the answer to my riddle of how to tell when an invisible hand is missing is to look at prices. If the prices are going up faster than incomes or anything else, the hand is missing. That is what's happening to healthcare.

The Right to Healthcare

How did access to healthcare become a right? A right is something that I consider of great significance and not easily obtained. Compassion tells us that sick people should be treated, just as homeless people should be sheltered and hungry people fed. But why is healthcare a right while homeless shelters and soup kitchens are mostly based on people's charity?

We might look to Europe to find an answer. Many European countries have extensive welfare systems that include free or highly subsidized healthcare. Progressive elements in the US political scene have looked to Europe as a paradigm for the US model. It matters little to them that Europe is in eclipse, or that its days of empire and greatness are behind them. Sure Europeans live very comfortably but where are they going? Oh! And by the way, they are going broke today paying for their welfare systems (which in fairness includes a lot more than healthcare). Country after country in Europe is cutting back on the nanny state, provoking street protests and riots, as people are enraged at losing what they think they are entitled to.

But where did people get this sense of entitlement? From shame! People are ashamed to accept charity but not to receive something they are entitled to. Politicians since the New Deal have been encouraging people to consider these kinds of benefits as rights and entitlements rather than handouts. People rationalize these redistributions of wealth in order to reduce their sense of shame. You say, I pay Medicare taxes so I feel no shame in receiving Medicare benefits. That's fine, except that the Medicare taxes you pay bear no resemblance to the benefits you receive. Where does the extra money come from? From the wealthy, foreigners buying our government debt, our children? It doesn't matter as long as I get more out than I put in.

The US healthcare system is a heavily subsidized mess that not only doesn't deliver superior service, it is costing more and more every year. Employers (especially small business) cannot afford to pay the enormous and ever increasing costs nor can they afford the additional burden of extra paperwork required to meet the bureaucratic requirements of the government. Our current healthcare system is like a cancer that is eating away at the healthy productive body of our economy, consuming more and more of our GDP each year. And what do you do with a cancer? You have to cut it out.

Well maybe we can't get rid of it, but we must reform it from top to bottom. It won't be easy because it is a complex mess that will take a lot of unraveling and we must do it in a way that doesn't leave people stranded without coverage. I am not a healthcare expert and I cannot provide all the details of how such a reform would look. But I do know some of the key elements that must be included in any such reform.

Eliminate Double Tax Exemption

It is obvious that the double tax exemption is one of the root causes underlying the healthcare mess in the United States. Congress uses tax policy to micromanage the motivations of taxpayers and citizens (like the mortgage deduction is designed to motivate people to purchase homes instead of renting). But the human psyche is even more complex than Congress and the double tax exemption has had the unintended consequence of divorcing consumers from the cost of the services provided with all the attendant problems outlined above.

Eliminate Company Healthcare Requirement

Why should your employer be responsible for providing your healthcare? Your employer is basically responsible for providing your paycheck. You use that paycheck to purchase the necessities of life such as food and shelter. Why isn't healthcare one of the necessities you need to purchase with your paycheck? And why isn't it your right to prioritize your own necessities and to determine how much you want to spend on them compared to other purchases?

There are two arguments for employer provided healthcare; 1) large employers can get a better deal from insurance companies, and 2) without employer healthcare individuals cannot afford health insurance. (Note: The tax benefit from employer provided health insurance would be eliminated in the first point above.)

Perhaps large employers can get a better deal from insurance companies but most of us don't work for large corporations. Most Americans work for small to medium-sized companies that have as much difficulty affording health insurance as do individuals. Many of us are self-employed or independent contractors who have even greater difficulty in getting affordable health insurance. But if employers and other large groups were eliminated from the picture, insurance companies would have to sell all their policies to individuals, leveling the playing field. Well, you might say, what's to keep the insurance companies from ripping me off? The same thing that keeps any goods or services provided by large corporations affordable. Competition. The key thing will be to make sure that consumers of health care services have the information necessary to make intelligent decisions about their healthcare insurance. We would also need to make sure that insurance companies couldn't abuse the system. The goal is not to give insurance companies free rein but to introduce competition to the system for the benefit of the consumer

Without employer paid medical insurance, how could we possibly afford health care? Well, for one, without the requirement of providing healthcare insurance, employers could (and should) raise your salaries, giving you more money to purchase your own medical insurance. Plus, you should be able to choose the type of coverage you need in the marketplace, rather than having to fit into a cookie cutter plan that your employer (or Obamacare) selects for you. If you have to go out a search for health insurance instead of ovinely accepting what is given to you, you are going to make sure you get the best deal. This will help to drive costs down.

(Note: Many people want to make employer provided insurance portable from employer to another, but the elimination of employer insurance would make this unnecessary.)

Transfer Costs to the Consumer
Hey, wait a minute, you might say. Why would I want to have healthcare costs put on my shoulders (other than the fact that it is your healthcare)? But if US consumers don't pay for their own healthcare, healthcare costs will continue rising (see Hayek for details). Healthcare represents almost a fifth of our gross national product. Almost a fifth of our national income! Would you want to spend a fifth of your gross income (not take home pay) on healthcare? Well that's what you're doing. Only, instead of coming out of your pocket the government is borrowing (from overseas or future generations) to pay for this current expense.

Think about it. When flat panel TVs first came out they were horribly expensive; about $5,000 for a 42" screen. If flat panel TVs were healthcare, that same 42" screen would now cost $10,000 (although it might have a few new features you don't really want in order to justify the higher price). In reality, flat panel TVs are cheap now; a 42" screen can be had for under $400 (I've seen 60" TVs for under $500). And the features and quality are better than ever. Competition is the way to control healthcare costs, not government mandates and bureaucracy.

Give Patients the Information they need to Make Decisions

What we really need to foster more competitive medical markets is access to information so that consumers can make rational choices (not that they always do but that is their choice – it's called freedom). There are already websites that rate doctors and provide information on the infection rates at certain hospitals but the coverage is spotty and prices are generally a no-no. One of the reasons for the healthcare mess is the toxic combination of government red tape and corporate bureaucracy that results in an incomprehensible healthcare system. Interesting, the hospitals and doctors have bent over backwards to make it really hard for you to have a copy of your own medical record.   The goal of government should be to make sure healthcare consumers have access to intelligible information so they can make rational healthcare decisions. If doctors, hospitals and other healthcare providers had to compete for your business on this basis, not only would prices go down but also the quality of the services would improve.

Give a Coup-de-Grace to Medicare and Obamacare

Even if these programs were good ideas, we can't afford them. But they're not good ideas. Like Social Security, Medicare is based on the assumption that we cannot take care of ourselves – that we

need a government program in order to afford healthcare (the healthcare made prohibitively expensive through government interference with the competitive process) Obamacare takes this thought process one step further: forcing us to pool our health care costs with other people who can't afford (or just don't want to pay for) insurance. The net present cost (the current value of future revenue streams less the current value of future expenses) has been calculated as much as between $36 trillion and $86 trillion. A Congressional Budget office study states that Medicaid and Medicare costs alone may be approaching 20% of GDP by 2082. Much of these exploding costs are caused by rising prices, which are generated by the Medicare system– a self-fulfilling prophecy.

The Transition to a Competitive Healthcare System

Certain people with socialist tendencies will claim that the profit motive is the bane of the US healthcare system and that, if we can just switch to government run healthcare everything will be right with the world and we will all live better lives (of course under socialized medicine you'll be getting Trabant healthcare instead of Cadillac healthcare). If only the world was so simple. The essence of competition that provides us with high-quality flat panel TVs for under $400 can also provides us with excellent healthcare services at affordable prices. The question is, how to do it? A cold turkey approach would have a devastating impact on individuals and the economy. Seniors, that have been paying into these programs for decades and are now totally dependent on these programs, must be protected. Alternatives to healthcare entitlements must be developed for those dependent on the current system. It will take decades to unwind this horrible mess. But that does not mean that we don't attempt it. It means that we have to get started now!

Free Market Tax Policy

I think I am going to shock you now. Tax cuts are not essential to promote economic growth.

Wait a minute, you might say. *I thought I knew where you were going in this book but now you're telling me that tax cuts are not the answer and that confuses me.* You would say, *I don't know where you stand anymore.*

I've got another curve ball for you. Progressive taxation is not necessarily a bad thing. I know your head must be spinning by now. Let me explain.

The Purpose of Taxation

You might have thought that the purpose of taxation is to fund government operations but this is clearly wrong. Taxation isn't covering government operations because we are $17 trillion in debt from deficit spending by the government (we don't need to get into the unfunded liabilities of government programs such as Social Security and Medicare at this point of the discussion although those obligations far exceed the current debt).

I would contend that there are four purposes to the current tax regime; 1) micro-managing the private sector through various tax incentive programs, 2) income redistribution through highly progressive and punitive taxes, 3) providing tax benefits to specific industries, companies and other organizations in order to generate donations to political campaigns, and 4) reelecting Congressmen and Senators. I would further contend that points 3 and 4 are foremost in the minds of our legislators and that actually funding government operations is not a major consideration of our legislators.

I, for one, take offense at elected officials hijacking government finance for the promotion of their personal agenda. We need to bring the purpose of taxation back to funding government operations and eliminate the extraneous subjection of our taxes to the interests of others.

The Fallacy of Motivation through Taxes

It is very true that tax increases, tax cuts and other tax incentives can motivate people and companies to do things. The problem is that human motives are hard to control and legislation to motivate people to do things the government wants (whether through taxes or other programs) often suffer from unintended consequences. These unintended consequences can lessen the effect of the proposed motivating factor or even work against it.

The goal of trying to motivate people and businesses to do the "right" thing is one of the basic principles of our tax code and one of the reasons that the tax code is so complex. There are a couple of problems with this approach to taxation; 1) people try to game the system, and 2) many of the supposed gains are transitory.

Because people know that they can convince legislators to modify the tax code to grant certain benefits (for particular people), people and companies are motivated to hire lobbyists to try and influence legislation in their favor. In other words, they do it because they can. It works. It's profitable. If lobbying efforts didn't bring results, private individuals, unions and companies would not be willing to fork over millions of dollars to lobbyists to influence legislation. The question is: how can we make lobbying ineffective to rid us of this undue influence?

The second problem with trying to motivate people through modifying the tax code is that the changed behavior is transitory and that there is little economic benefit for the temporary tax policy. A good example of this type of fallacy was the first time homebuyer credit designed in 2009 as part of the economic stimulus bill, which was intended to promote the purchase of homes and slow the continuing fall in housing prices. The tax credit was worth up to $8,000 and, while the program lasted, it motivated homebuyers to accelerate the purchases of homes in order to take advantage of the tax break. But these were people who were already going to purchase a home. An $8,000 credit is not a sufficient inducement to affect the basic purchase decision of an asset that could easily cost $200,000 to $300,000. It can, however, affect the timing of the purchase. After the end of the program, house sales dropped as did home prices. The government had expended several billions of dollars that only motivated people to take advantage of government largesse without actually increasing home sales or prices. They only moved home sales to the period of the tax break from the period when there was no tax break. The end result was a reduction in government tax revenue with no offsetting growth in the economy.

The home mortgage interest deduction is another tax policy gone awry. The goal is to promote home ownership. This benefit, however, is only available to taxpayers who itemize their deductions. Only 70 percent of tax filers itemize deductions and most of them are in the higher tax brackets. It takes a lot of deductions to make itemization a feasible alternative. Only the relatively wealthy have enough deductions (including big mortgage payments) to make it worthwhile. So this tax policy, intended to promote home ownership, only benefits the wealthy who don't need additional motivation to purchase a home (although the tax subsidy will allow them to purchase a larger McMansion for the same cash outflow). Canada, a country that does not provide a mortgage interest deduction, has a higher percentage of home ownership than the US.

So the fallacy of motivating people through manipulations of the tax code is that it doesn't promote growth. The free market economic system is supposed to allocate capital efficiently. Tax policy to change the behavior of markets reallocates capital is ways preferred by the government, presumably to achieve goals counter to an efficient allocation of capital.

People often use these incentives for their own benefit but without changing their permanent behavior. Others game the system instead of investing productively. They take advantage of government tax policy but the government (and the people) gets little in return (the same cannot be said for our legislators who benefit by stuffing their campaign coffers from these shenanigans).

There is another problem with all these micro-management tax policies and that is an uncertainty of tax policy (depending on the whims to legislators or the changing of presidential administrations). Because tax policy changes from year to year, businesses focus more on trying to influence tax legislation rather than on their business. Tax policy can affect their bottom line more than sales volume and margins. A dollar spent on a lobbyist has a higher return than a dollar spent on capital expenditure or additional employment.

We need to develop a tax policy that promotes growth – not all this other stuff.

Tax Competitiveness

We need to have a tax policy that works for us as a nation but we also need a tax policy that works internationally. If our tax policy is out of sync with the other nations of the world, our companies will not be able to compete internationally and that will limit our economic growth and increase unemployment. The United States has the second highest corporate tax rate of developed countries in the OECD (the Japanese are first but they have been in a slump for two decades). However, according to the New York Times, after taking into account loopholes and subsidies the US rate is closer to the OECD average (although still above it).

Personally, I would be comfortable with eliminating corporate taxes. Corporate taxes are just passed on to the consumer and not paid by the corporation. I know that most of you would be outraged that corporate fat cats are not paying taxes but the truth is that you are paying those taxes in the price of the goods you purchase. If corporations in China or other countries have a lower corporate tax (i.e.; their national tax burden is skewed toward the citizens) their corporations will have a competitive advantage over our corporations in domestic and international markets.

I know that you all want to sock it to the corporations but in doing so you are only socking it to yourselves. To have a level playing field with our foreign competition, we can either have a zero corporate tax or work with our international partners to develop an international standard for corporate taxation.

Taxation of Global Income

The United States is one of only two countries in the world that taxes the worldwide income of its citizens and corporations. The other is Eritrea; a country whose principle export is refugees (which is probably why they want to tax them).

Being a strong believer in America exceptionalism, I normally don't mind if the US is not in sync with other countries on specific policies. However, in this case the policy is not only wrong-headed, it also stifles economic growth here in the US.

It is wrong-headed because it makes American companies less competitive overseas. American companies face stiff competition overseas, especially from companies immune from the Foreign Corrupt Practices Act. In the face of stiff competition, the burden of additional taxes makes it even more difficult for American companies. In the US, corporate taxes are transferred from producers to consumers. But in the US, all producers face the same tax burden. US companies cannot transfer these US taxes in foreign countries because of competition from companies not so constrained. You may not care that US corporations have to eat these taxes instead of passing them on to consumers. But the lower returns overseas discourages the expansion of US business overseas and that means less jobs in America.

In spite of global taxation, American corporations have invested over $6 trillion overseas and these investments have generated over $2 trillion in profits that have not been repatriated to the US because doing so would create a huge additional tax burden. Of course, some of this money will be reinvested back overseas to take advantage of opportunities there. However some of this accumulated horde could be reinvested in the US but is parked in banks overseas because paying additional taxes on these remittances (remember taxes have already been paid in the host country) makes many opportunities uneconomic.

Some progressives as well as conservative isolationists will tell you that this is precisely what they want. They will tell you that overseas investments by US corporations just sends US jobs overseas and these corporations should make their products in the good ole US of A and the golden age of blue collar middle class will return. If you believe this I have a bridge in Brooklyn I would like to sell you. Next they will try to tell you that high tariff barriers will protect US jobs and reduce our dependence on imports. (Two things to remember about golden ages: 1) the people at the time probably didn't think they were so golden, and 2) the circumstances of the age were specific to that time and do not exist now). I lived through the collapse of the import substitution economies of the 1980's and it wasn't pretty. Overseas investment and foreign trade has provided great benefits to the United States and to the rest of the world.

The Special Case of US Expats and the Impact of FATCA

Thanks to the Internet, cable TV and lower tariff barriers, living overseas is not as difficult as it was thirty or forty years ago. That is until tax time. US Expats are also exposed to global taxation. They have to pay taxes in their host countries and in the US as well. It is true that they get an exclusion of up to around $100,0000 in income to offset local taxes but living overseas in expensive and many expats exceed the exclusion limit. In order to encourage Americans to work overseas, my old employer, Citibank, or more likely their accountants, came up with a complex to offset the implications of global taxation. I would pay a hypothetical tax as if I had never left the States, and Citibank pay all the difference. The calculations to manage all this are so complex I gave up trying to understand it all (and I have a Masters in Finance).

Recently, the passage of FATCA (the Foreign Account Tax Compliance Act) had made life even more difficult for Expats. FATCA is an arrogant and intrusive law passed by the US to force foreign banks to disclose the names of Americans with accounts in their bank. Any bank that doesn't fork over this info is subject to fines and withholding taxes on all their clients. Of course the IRS doesn't trust these banks so they are required to divulge reams of information on all their clients or provide this information to their own tax collectors even if their country doesn't require this information. Many developing countries don't even have the capability to manage all this data. The net result has been that many of these banks are refusing to open accounts for Americans and directing the money of their domestic clients to other countries. It is not only inconvenient it is also dangerous because expats have to carry excess cash to pay routine obligations.

Tax "Fairness"

What is tax fairness? I suppose that it depends on how much money you make and how much tax you have to pay. Nobody likes to pay taxes; but we all have to pay our fair share of taxes. So what is fair?

The current mantra is for the rich to pay more. But how can we reasonably expect only the rich to pay and still have a system that functions for the benefit of the nation. If we try to skew the tax code to extract more from the rich they will be motivated to use a portion of their wealth to protect their wealth. They will hire lobbyists to provide them with exemptions and shelters to protect their wealth rather than to invest their wealth. The more we try to tax them, the more they will try and resist. This is the system we currently have and it is not working.

There is a line of thinking among progressives and other leftists that wealth is generated through exploitation of the poor. Based on this, any sort of punitive tax regime up to 100 percent (higher if possible) is justified because all that wealth was ill gotten. But this is socialism (which I have shown elsewhere in this book to be an unjust and totalitarian system) and such a regime cannot be justified in the free market economic system.

Taxation and Economic Growth

Much of the complexity of the current tax code has been justified (whether special interest tax treatment or government nudges for approved behaviors) as necessary to promote economic growth. Even more so, tax cuts have been pushed (especially by Republicans but by JFK who also cut taxes) as an engine for growth. The revival of the economy under President Reagan is often cited as due to his tax cuts. Contrariwise, Democrats have pointed to the very high marginal tax rates during the Eisenhower years as proof that high taxes do not restrain economic growth (despite the fact that actual taxes paid were far lower than the marginal rates).

There is a trade off between the level of taxation and the government's job as protector (and at times enforcer) of the social contract. A country where the government lacks the resources to maintain the social contract will see a deterioration of the rule of law (as has often been the case in Latin America). The rule of law is an essential element of the free market economic system. With a debilitated rule of law, the economy becomes distorted, poverty increases and the people lose their confidence in government. Conversely, a confiscatory tax regime will drive the wealthy from tax avoidance to tax evasion, corrupting the entire system. The free market system, based on trust and confidence, requires a balance between the revenue needed by government to maintain the rule of law and the ability of business to generate and retain profits which allows innovation to drive growth.

The Impact of Social Expenditures

The social welfare system changes this equation. Under a social welfare regime, the government must increase its revenue in order to provide more services and transfers while eroding the productive base from where these revenues are derived. In Europe, the people in many countries have become accustomed to very high taxes to pay for such a system (although the contention of this book is that such a system is unsustainable). The United States and its people have not made this adjustment: they want a strong social welfare system and low taxes. There has been no strong motivation to close the gap between increased expenditures and reduced revenues because the gap has been covered by debt. This has allowed Republicans to cut taxes and Democrats to spend for decades with no sense of urgency on how to resolve these differences. Time, however, is running out.

Economic growth will be maximized when trust and confidence in the social contract is high. The level of taxation is one factor in this equation but there are many other factors that must also be included in achieving this goal.

A Social Contract on Taxation – A Proposal

Given all the complexities above, how do we arrive at a tax regimen that is not only deemed fair, but is supported by the large majority of citizens? Not only must the majority of the people support it, it must be a plan that promotes growth within a sustainable framework.

The biggest problem we have with tax policy is uncertainty. Tax policy changes from year to year, with every change in the makeup of Congress, with every change of administration, with each change in the district representative. How are companies supposed to plan future investments in a system that is not only in constant flux, but that is capricious to the whims of politics and influence? A complex and constantly changing tax code is opaque and incomprehensible (on purpose) which leads to all the charges and countercharges regarding the effective tax burden of various segments of our society.

Our tax contract depends on five elements: 1) a national consensus of perceived fairness, 2) the belief that the money will be well used, 3) the tax regimen will be competitive with our major trading partners, 4) a more or less balanced budget (financing deficits with debt just transfers the tax burden to future generations) and 5) tax stability (incorporating the previous four requirements). A tax regimen that incorporates these elements will promote growth.

Perceived Fairness

You obviously have noted that I didn't say fairness but perceived fairness. Two people looking at the same thing will see two different things. (This basic human difference is what drives the free market economy). What one person perceives as fair may be perceived by another person as grossly unfair. Harken back to what I said about fairness in Part I and remember also what I said earlier about the key to economic growth being confidence. A system that is perceived as being unfair will sap confidence and undermine growth.

There are a number of key concepts that go into the perception of tax fairness: 1) burden sharing, 2) the overall level of the burden, and 3) transparency.

If we take a hypothetical example where 20% is considered the amount each citizen should pay to meet the obligations of the government and each citizen paid his or her 20%. This would seem fair would it not? Then further suppose that one of the citizens earned $1 million and another earned $10,000. The first would pay taxes of $200,000 and the second taxes of $2,000. Many would say that this seems imminently fair. But the sacrifice made by the wealthy citizen in order to pay his tax burden might mean buying a Cadillac instead of a

Bentley while for the poorer citizen it might be the difference between beans or meat for his kids. The equally weighted burdens are not deemed equally fair. By whom? you might say. Obviously the rich man feels the burdens are fair, but the poor man may not. In a democracy, where there are many more poor people than rich ones, this concept of fairness has little chance of working as a practical matter. The rich should pay a higher tax because the burden on them is less.

Wait a minute. Some of you, no doubt, are saying, the rich man wasn't really going to buy a Bentley with his income that was not paid as taxes, he was actually going to invest in his business and hire more people, which would make more people better off than by reducing their taxes.

This is a conundrum. But the conundrum is compounded by the fact that we don't know what the overall level of taxes that we pay should be; which makes the apportionment of the tax burden very difficult. What has happened in the United States is that, thanks to massive amounts of debt, no one, least of all government, has had to resolve this issue leading to the debilitated financial state we are currently in. The first step in determining tax fairness is not the arguing about who should pay what, but what amount should the nation pay as a whole in the form of taxes (and then trying to live within those means). Deficits should be relegated to the hard times while surpluses should repay debt during the good times (a strategy recommended by Keynes, as well). This is a basic formulation of our free market economy. This is also what we do when preparing our family budget. Its just good old common sense.

What is the appropriate role of the government and what is the role of the private sector? We need a national consensus as to what these levels should be.

In order to make that decision, we need to be able to see that what we take in and what we spend is fully accounted for. The current system obfuscates the true burden placed on citizens: on one hand, by the complexity of the system that obscures the tax burdens of various individuals and corporations; and on the other hand, by the use of debt and future (unfunded) promises to obscure the true cost of government. (You would be outraged if your brother-in-law had conned you into countersigning a car loan for his new Lexus and then drove off to Vegas with some bimbo, sticking you with the bill. Well, this is exactly what you are doing to your own kids and grandkids.)

A Progressive Tax that Works

There is a lot of controversy about the progressive tax system, that richer folk pay a higher percentage of tax than poorer folk. Progressives will state that the rich can afford to pay more (for some, much more) and that is true. But it is not true that the rich can pay all the taxes. All citizens have a duty to pay taxes. The question is; how do we develop a progressive tax system that is perceived by all parties as "fair" (or rather "not too unfair"). The key word here is perception. The current tax system is already progressive; yet Republicans rail that it is too progressive and Democrats rail that it is not progressive enough.

The numbers don't matter. Both sides can quote numbers until they are blue in the face. Each side of the argument can quote numbers to prove their points. In fact you can get numbers to prove almost anything. What we need is two things: 1) a consensus that the tax system is not too unfair, and 2) that the taxes raised are sufficient to cover the cost of government.

Building a Consensus

It is impossible to build a consensus with the current tax system because it is so complex that most people can't understand it (Thank God for Turbo Tax!). Complexity is the equivalent to opacity. Consensus can only be built upon understanding and understanding requires transparency and transparency is impossible under the current tax code. We need to cut down the tax code, strip out all the special interest deductions, all the well-intentioned tax breaks, everything! Throw out green incentives. Throw out mortgage interest deductions.

We have already talked about getting rid of Social Security and Medicare. These social insurance deductions distort the tax burden of the people. When conservatives say that the rich pay a disproportionate amount of income tax (and that poor people pay almost no income tax or have a negative tax) they are correct. And income tax is progressive. However, these figures don't include social insurance deductions (it's like they're pretending they're not really taxes). Social insurance deductions, on the other hand, are regressive.

Because the income subject to these deductions is capped, high-income earners pay less, as a percent of income, than do lower income earners. And although the poor indeed pay little or no income tax, they pay an inordinate proportion of their income to these social insurance deductions compared to the rest of us (or at least the wealthier among us). So it's a good thing that we are going to get rid of these deductions.

Because the new system will be greatly simplified, the tax burden of individuals and corporations will be much more apparent. Wealthy people will lose their deductions and will probably pay more taxes than they do now.

Listening to some of the national conversation on taxes there are some that think it is inherently wrong that some people in the population make more than others. They can justify the confiscation of at least a portion of these somehow tainted earnings – as if owning a corporate jet made you guilty of a criminal activity. This is mere pandering by politicians attempting to justify an inherently illegal confiscation by tainting the activity (equating the making of a profit the moral equivalent of drug dealing). This is free market capitalism! Some people make more than others. Live with it!

The other thing we need to do is to make these changes permanent, or at least as permanent as we can. That is the reason I recommend that the tax code be made an amendment to the Constitution (or some other immutable and hard-to-change law) – so that the next Congress can't come in and undo all this work. An amendment for the tax code will not only keep Congress from fiddling with the code, it will provide business and investors the certainty they need in order to help the economy grow. Although low taxes are always preferable to the businessman or investor, if possible, it is uncertainty that really restrains investment.

Covering the Cost of Government
There is, of course, a corollary to the concept of covering the cost of government, and that is that taxes be wisely spent. Eliminating entitlements is a big step in that direction. Some of my other recommendations will also help, such as the line item veto.

The cost of government should be borne by, and for the benefit of all citizens (and those who are lucky enough to be legal residents). Entitlements distort those benefits because their goal is income redistribution. However, it is impossible to level all the cost of some benefits provided by the government as some people will need more support than others. Elimination of entitlements does not mean that some old folks will have to eat dog food or that dying people will be turned away from hospitals. The problem with entitlements is not that of providing benefits for people truly in need; it's the totality of the programs and that they provide benefits for those not truly in need. Entitlements are about the government taking over our lives. Sometimes we forget who the boss is. We are!

It is possible (it has to be or we have lost our country) to have a civilized discussion about what should be the shared costs borne by government and what level of costs is reasonable. Right now government is composed of two basic forms of costs; 1) basic government operating expenses including such critical functions as national defense, domestic tranquility and justice, and 2) income redistribution, falsely labeled as entitlements. The current poisonous discussions in Washington have resulted in the starving of the government of the resources necessary to the delivery of its essential functions (curiously defined as discretionary expenses) in order to maintain and increase income redistribution (even more curiously defined as mandatory expenses). A recent report in the newspaper was noteworthy in that it stated the FDA was not able to implement a new program because after entitlement programs there was not enough funds to operate the government as mandated by Congress. This should not be allowed to happen.

What we are seeing is a government being starved of the resources needed to complete its Constitutionally mandated duties (insuring domestic tranquility, providing for the common defense, etc.) in order to redirect those resources to uses not mandated by the Constitution. To fulfill all these functions would require a level of taxation that most Americans would not support.

A more or less Balanced Budget
A budget deficit arises when government revenues (primarily taxes) are not sufficient to cover all of the government's expenses. The government must then borrow to have the money to cover those expenses. Problem solved, you

say! Problem deferred, I say! The cost of this debt and the interest payments on it are transferred to future generations who must pay higher taxes to cover these costs. These future generations, however, do not receive any benefit from these taxes as the benefits were consumed by their parents and grandparents. The borrowed money is spent on current consumption and not for building infrastructure or other investments that would provide a benefit to future generations. Furthermore, how can those future generations be perceived to have been part of the consensus on taxation and government expenses when they may not have even been born when the money flew out the door? How can deficit spending be justified under the American Social Contract when every deficit dollar spent tilts the playing field a bit more against our future generations? We are violating one of our most sacred obligations.

A Small Problem – Deductions

Deductions are a problem. Because they are sometimes complex, but more so because they apply to some and not all taxpayers. Deductions, at the very least, have an appearance of unfairness, and in the normal course of business are, in fact, unfair. Rich folk have a slew of deductions that lower their tax rate enormously. The poor have special deductions that only they qualify for, such that, in many cases, they have a negative tax rate. It is the middle class that doesn't qualify for the exemptions of the poor or the deductions of the wealthy, that pays the most. Unless you run your business as a sole proprietorship or are in a partnership, you will be hard pressed to come up with the deductions needed to exceed the standard deduction. Even relatively few get much benefit from the famous mortgage interest deduction.

At first I thought we should get rid of all deductions in order to simplify the tax code. Then I realized that a family of four with no deductions that earned x amount would pay the same tax as a single individual earning the same amount even though the average income for each person in that family of four was only a quarter that of the single individual. This would be considered too unfair and would, in fact, be counter-productive. Therefore, we should retain in the new simplified tax code, a standard deduction for dependents as in the current tax policy.

Other than that, there should be no deductions. Except, of course, business deductions.

Business Deductions

Businesses pay taxes on a net basis rather than a gross basis. This means that they deduct the expenses of operating the business, such as purchases of inventory or equipment, payment of salaries, etc. from the gross revenue received by the business. But businesses are often complex and a lot of the lobbying in Washington comes from businesses trying to get special treatment for their deductions. Add in the fact that many people are self-employed, personal services contractors or partners in a limited partnership and our goal of simplifying the tax code seems in danger of spinning horribly out of control. But we must try and stick to this goal. The goal of tax simplification is not to reduce the 77,000-page tax code down to one page. Our society is too complex for that. Further, such over simplification would actually result in unfairness rather than fairness.

One mechanism to achieve a tax system generally deemed to be fair (i.e.; not too unfair) would be through the process similar to amending the Constitution, which requires a broad consensus among a wide range of people. This would forestall, if not totally prevent, special interests from hijacking the tax code for their benefit. Making the tax code semi-permanent and difficult to modify would limit the ability of lobbyists to seek influence and the ability of legislators from peddling it.

The key factor in aligning tax policy to economic growth is not incentives that change from year to year but stability. With a stable tax policy people, companies and corporations can plan for the future and determine how to invest. As long as it is considered basically fair and competitive internationally, a stable tax policy will be the greatest promoter of growth we can employ. The question is: what is fair and competitive?

Estate Taxes

There was a lot of controversy about the inclusion of a deal on estate taxes in the deal to extend the Bush tax cuts to all taxpayers even the wealthy. The deal set the estate tax rate at 35% with an exclusion of $5,000,000 (the rate had been set to go up to 55% with an exclusion of only $1 million). This caused outrage among the liberal wing of Congress bemoaning the burden to future generations caused by letting the wealthy keep their own money (see comment on Thomas Piketty, above).

Truth be told, the estate tax violates the principal foundation on which we are trying to build a national consensus on taxation: that the principal purpose of taxation is to fund the government. The estate tax provides an insignificant portion of federal government revenue (less than 1%). Rather, the purpose of the estate tax is confiscatory. It is designed to take money from the wealthy and give it to someone else: to punish the wealthy for being wealthy. The tax is especially punishing to the wealthy because often their wealth is concentrated in assets that are not easily turned in to cash, such as ownership of a family company or large land holdings. To obtain the necessary cash to fork over to the government, the bereaved family may have to sell the family company, carve up their lands, and hawk family heirlooms (I can see all your crocodile tears). Without proper estate planning this can result in further losses because the value of these properties may be lost due to fire sale prices for large illiquid assets.

I have no qualm at taxing the wealthy but the estate tax is just mean. If we want to raise money there is a better way.

Dividend Taxes

We need to eliminate the double taxation of dividends. Just as the double tax exemption on medical benefits has caused havoc in the healthcare segment of the economy, the double taxation of dividends has messed up the productive sector of the economy. Again, I believe that the motivation for this policy is envy or meanness. What is the logical rationale for taxing profits at the corporate level and then again at the individual level except that they are profits? Profit, which is the energy driving our free market economy, is a code word for evil among some sectors of the polity.

We have seen in the healthcare industry that a double exemption drives revenue toward the exemption that causes a breakdown in the pricing mechanism by separating the consumer from the price paid for a service. In the case of double taxation, revenues are driven away from the double tax situation. This means that corporations retain earnings rather than pay out dividends. This is not a problem in fast growing industries that need additional capital. They would invest in new plant and equipment (and hire more workers) with or without the double tax on dividends because the returns on the investment are higher for shareholders than other alternatives (companies in tech industries rarely pay dividends). But in other industries, where the returns from new investment are not as high, the double taxation on dividends motivates companies to retain earnings when it would be more productive to distribute them to shareholders. The retained earnings are misallocated by these corporations to either investments in lower returning assets in their current industry, or to higher earning investments in other industries where management may have less experience and expertise.

It is impossible to calculate the cost of this misallocation of capital but it is certain that the result has been lower growth, less employment and a lower return to investors. Dividends should only be taxed at the individual level and at the same rate as ordinary income (which would eliminate the problem of the alternative minimum tax which castigates "passive" income such as dividends and interest).

Charge for Service
There is one more element to the revenue that government extracts from its citizens in charges for services rendered, but here we must tread carefully because of the potential of moral hazard. Corporations or individuals receive benefits from specific government services that they receive. In municipalities this could be for garbage pickup, sewerage, building permits, etc. In seems very clear that these services, which are in the public interest, often have specific benefits. In the national context, these services could be meat or agricultural inspections, customs inspections for imports, drilling permits for offshore oil exploration, etc. These services are necessary but are often the first ones to feel the budget cutter's ax, often to the detriment of the public. Departments such as the FDA and USDA should be able to recoup the cost of the services they provide. True, these costs will be passed on to the public, but principally to the public that benefits from these services (as opposed to the public in general: i.e.; vegetarians wouldn't have to pay for meat inspections because the cost of these services would be reflected in the price of the meat, and not vegetables).

Nevertheless, we must always be aware that bureaucracies tend to grow and never diminish (although most farms in the US had access to electricity by 1952 consumers continued to pay for rural electrification for many more years). Right now, the public is underserved in the areas of meat and agricultural inspections and many other services of government due to underfunding. We do not want to get into a situation where government bureaucrats charge industries more and more for services extraneous to those required for the public good but a fair charge to cover the cost of services seems reasonable.

How does a government agency determine the appropriate level of service? How many meat inspectors do we need? How often should meat packers be inspected? Too few inspections endangers public health but at some point the addition of more meat inspectors is of declining utility (the law of diminishing returns). The point where the public good is best served is difficult to determine. More inspections may reduce the chance of someone getting sick but will increase the cost. Reduction of risk to zero is impossible and even approaching that level of certainty would make meat (or any other service) outrageously expensive and unaffordable.

Why a Flat Tax won't Work
Although a flat tax (a single tax rate that is paid by all taxpayers) might seem imminently fair, it would be very difficult to implement and be ineffective in achieving the type of consensus we are talking about. Even though a flat tax would appear to be the same to everyone, it wouldn't be perceived to be fair by many, especially to low income earners. Giving up a yacht in order to pay taxes is very different from giving up food or clothing for your children to pay taxes. If the goal of a tax regime is to build a national consensus of perceived fairness, a flat tax must be left at the starting gate. Although there are mechanisms that could be put in place, to ease the inequities of a flat tax, the end result would be a (somewhat) progressive tax – so what's the point? I personally like the concept of a flat tax, but the bitter struggle to impose such a tax regime would preclude the ability to achieve a national consensus. Without a consensus, the tax regime would be changed by the next shift in power from one party to another. Thus it is clear, a flat tax cannot achieve the two principal goals we are seeking; 1) a national consensus, and 2) a stable tax regime.

A Value Added Tax won't Work Either

A value added (or sales) tax suffers from the same problems as a flat tax: it is regressive and would be perceived as unfair. A VAT also suffers from the problem that, in addition to already being charged by the states and municipalities, it could, as in the case of Europe, be added on to existing income tax, thus greatly increasing the overall level of taxation.

Conclusion

Taxation is a complex issue involving not only the differing situations related to tax affecting all citizens but, more importantly, it also underlies the ability of the nation to function and the sense of cohesion amongst citizens. People that try to twist the tax code to their benefit undermine the social contract that forms our nation. While this is a very natural and human response it must be resisted. Private action is always more focused than public action, which has resulted in the hyper-complex and inherently unfair tax code that currently exists. I must admit the current tax policy has achieved a form of national consensus. The consensus is that it sucks! Maybe everyone won't support the ideas listed above, but some type of major tax reform is essential for the revitalization of America.

The Regulatory Burden

Both the right and the left basically misunderstand the role of regulation. The right sees regulation as a mechanism to stifle the free market while the left sees regulation as the means to wreak vengeance on fat cats and robber barons.

Regulation is an essential part of the free market system and the American social contract. The true role of regulation is to assure the smooth functioning of the social contract and the free market system. It is one of the principal and most important functions of government.

The power to regulate commerce is the third power granted to the legislature (after collecting taxes and borrowing money) by the US constitution, signifying the importance to the Founders of regulation in the promotion of the general welfare. We the People granted the government the power to regulate our economic activities as part of the social contract among ourselves.

Economic interactions in the context of the free market system require a high level of trust. We need to know that economic exchanges between people are honest and open. It means that contracts will be honored. It means that goods and services provide the advertised benefits and are safe. It also means that labor given in return for salary fulfills the commitments under the terms of employment. It basically means we get what we pay for.

Shoddy or dangerous goods do not meet the test of trust. Reneging on contracts is a breach of trust. Sleeping on the job or working under the influence does not meet the terms of employment.

In any small Scottish village around the time Adam Smith wrote The Wealth of Nations, the villagers would know everyone in the village. They would, as commented earlier, know if someone delivered shoddy goods or spoiled vegetables. They would avoid purchasing goods from that person. In a small village there is no need for regulation.

In a huge country like the United States it is impossible to know all the inputs to the goods and services we consume on a daily basis. Recall Smith's analogy of the manufacture of a pin and all the thousands of inputs it required. Products today are much more complex as are their supply chains. How can we know that the quality of meat in our supermarket is as advertised? How do we know that our spinach is free from deadly microbes and safe to eat? How do we know that the toy we just purchased isn't made from lead?

The purpose of regulation is to assure the populace that they can trust their counterparts in economic interactions. Trust is also an essential element in the equality of opportunity. How can we know that the playing field is level (at least not too un-level)? How do we know that the price of a good or service, or the availability of an apartment, is not based on the color of my skin?

It is not the purpose of regulation to eliminate risk or to quell the booms and busts endemic to the free market system.

Risk and Regulation

Risk is part of life. Even staying in bed is risky; you could get bedsores or worse. The lack of exercise would kill you. Further, different people have different levels of risk tolerance. What one person deems risky (my wife, for example) another person might deem not that risky at all (me, for example). (Yes, we are talking about riding motorcycles.)

The danger lies in not knowing the risks that you are taking. If your car has a hidden defect, you are putting your life at risk driving it. Regulation can help reduce that risk by requiring manufacturers to meet certain standards such as requiring seatbelts or mandating recalls if defects are discovered. Regulation can also punish manufacturers who purposefully hide defects in their products that can endanger consumers. But driving a car is still risky; people die in car accidents every day.

I have always liked the Securities Act of 1933. The purpose of the Securities Act is not to eliminate the risk in making investments, but rather to make sure that investors have the information they need to evaluate the perceived risk of the investment (keeping in mind that different people have different levels of risk tolerance). New issues of securities must be registered and registration requires disclosure of all relevant information. Withholding of relevant information can result in sanctions. Investments that cannot meet these registration requirements cannot be sold to the general public but only to qualified institutional buyers (QIBs) who have the financial sophistication to analyze the risks involved.

In the case of foodstuffs, medicines and other similar products where people do not have the capability to test their safety and utility, we rely on government inspectors to perform those tests for us. They cannot perform inspections of every individual product, so we rely on a carefully controlled process for the development of new drugs, for example, and a level of inspections to assure that the manufacturing plant meets acceptable standards and ongoing random tests of the products to show they are safe.

So we have two types of regulatory frameworks to control risk depending on our ability to be informed. One form inspects products and services where we do not have the ability to evaluate risks independently and the other to make sure we have the information we need to evaluate risk (required labels on food, for example).

Booms and Busts

Regulations cannot eliminate the booms and busts of the free market system and shouldn't even try. I get chills up my spine every time I hear a politician say that they will make sure recessions or financial crises will "never happen again". Booms and busts are essential elements of the free market system. They are part of the creative destruction process described by Schumpeter, which we saw previously.

The expansions and recessions of the free market economy are inherently rooted in our human nature. We over-estimate or under-estimate, build too much of one thing and not enough of another. Recessions are the adjustments to these mis-estimations and as natural to the free market economy as breathing is to us. Irrational exuberance is not an anomaly, its just part of human nature.

Inappropriate Regulation

The 2007/2008 financial crisis was caused as much by Washington meddling as Wall Street greed and is a good example of what happens when regulations are not well thought out or go too far. You may recall from our discussion of the crisis that, in order to eliminate red-lining (the practice of not providing mortgage financing in certain - usually poor, ethnic – neighborhoods), the Community Reinvestment Act required banks to provide mortgages to people in those communities. However, this well-intentioned law backfired. Trying to regulate people to do the right thing is harder than regulating them to not do bad things. The CRA wasn't the only cause of the Great Recession, but it was certainly a contributing factor. It opened the door and gave sanction to lower credit terms that motivated banks and other mortgage originators to take on much more risk than was prudent. The lenders charged higher rates for the riskier loans that generated more profits to compensate for the higher risk. The lure of extra profits drew the market away from the original intention of the law (to help out poor folks, remember?) and toward the rapid expansion of the sub-prime market ensnaring the government sponsored entities Fannie Mae and Freddie Mac in addition to many of the banks in the country. The cost of covering the losses for Fannie and Freddie alone were more than $317 billion. Many of those hurt worst by the crisis were those the CRA was intended to benefit.

Encouraging financial institutions to make risky loans is not an appropriate way to regulate the industry. Not giving loans to people with poor credit histories is not racism or discrimination (red-lining entire districts, however, is pure sloth and helping people improve their credit is poor business practice). There were better ways to help those people but the CRA fit the preconceived notions of those pushing the legislation (as well as the personal agendas of a host of community activists).

An appropriate type of financial legislation would be to limit private profit at public risk. The risk/return relationship must be assigned to the right people or entities. The use of government-guaranteed depositor money to make speculative investments is inappropriate because gains are allocated to bank managers while losses are covered by taxpayers.

Excessive Regulation

Regulation that does not support the smooth functioning of the American Social Contract and the free market economy is, by definition, excessive. Of course, good honest folks can disagree as to what constitutes the smooth functioning of the social contract, but at least that should be where the discussion begins and ends. All other factors are extraneous.

<u>Too Big to Fail</u>

Bailouts of banks because they were deemed too big to fail caused widespread outrage in the depths of the crisis. Not because of the bailout saved depositors, other financial institutions and numerous businesses with transactions going through these banks. It was the perceptions that bankers and owners got off scot-free. Of course, the owners didn't get off scot-free; many lost everything they had invested and others saw their holdings diluted. But the bank managers? They pretty much got off scot-free. And that pissed everybody off. (Including me!)

It is probably not a good thing to write regulations when you are pissed off. You focus on the wrong things and end up with regulations that cause more problems than they solve. Unfortunately, some of our politicians appear to be permanently pissed off – and a lot of our regulations reflect that.

A lot of people want to break up the big banks that are too big to fail into smaller banks that aren't too big to fail. But their motivation isn't to make a safer more secure financial system; it is to punish the bankers by failing their banks.

But the largest US bank, JPMorgan Chase, is only the sixth largest bank in the world, and only three US banks are in the top twenty. Other countries have more centralized banking systems than we do. We have over 5,600 banks in the United States, far more than any other developed country. Our banks need to be able to compete on a global scale (at least some of them) in order to be able to provide the global financial needs of American multi-national corporations. In order to do this, our banks need to be of a size and offer a range of services demanded by their domestic and international clients or they will lose business to their competitors. And that does not serve the interests of our country.

Being big isn't the problem. The problem is the risk/reward relationship between bank managers and the public. We can address this issue through appropriate regulation – and that is a lot better than regulating because we are pissed off.

An excessive regulatory burden impairs the smooth functioning of the free market system rather than facilitating it. But so does insufficient regulation. The level of regulation must be sufficient to provide the assurance of trust in our interactions (economic or otherwise) with our fellow citizens.

Shared Sacrifice

Shared sacrifice is like camping. When you go camping you are too hot or you're freezing. You can't get the campfire lit and when you finally do the smoke goes in the tent. The tent leaks, too. The mosquitos drive you insane. Your kids drive you even more insane with their mood swings and constant complaining. You are miserable. Everybody is miserable. Yes shared sacrifice is a lot like camping: it's not just that you survived it, it's that you survived it together. It's the stories that you tell about how miserable you were – together. It's the photos that you share showing your damp bedraggled clothes, your sunburn – your goofy smiles. Camping brings families and friends together (our son Charlie loved to go camping with his friends). Shared sacrifice brings citizens together: it's the glue that binds the social contract.

Shared sacrifice is serious business. The American Social Contract is just that – a contract (actually it is more like an amalgam of many different contracts, some written, some verbal and some based on mutual but unspoken understanding). The sense of shared sacrifice is an emotional response to some crisis or other problem that afflicts many citizens (a world war, a great depression, a civil war). The sense of shared sacrifice is the emotional bond that holds us together as a nation. The nations that lack this shared sacrifice require autocratic or dictatorial powers to hold the nation together (think Iraq under Saddam Hussein). This is why those dictators so often turn to conjured nationalism or fake enemies and plots to try to bind the people together: conjuring up a sense of unity.

As a democracy there is no force to hold us together (remember the Declaration of Independence) except our mutual commitments to each other. Break those bonds and the nation will fall under the spell of the next strong man.

Those bonds of commitment are being sorely tested. To reorder our nation and put it on the right track will require a great deal of commitment and hardship. How do we nurture a sense of shared sacrifice that will be supported by a large portion of the populace, from the poor to the wealthy, in order to deal with the very serious issues confronting us? There are several key elements that must exist in order to develop the consensus necessary to initiate positive change: There must be transparency in government operations, income inequality should not be "too unfair", and there should be no impunity for corrupting the social contract.

Transparency

Transparency isn't itself shared sacrifice but it is a condition precedent to the sense of shared sacrifice. A lack of transparency breeds mistrust among citizens that burdens are not equally shared. The government needs to keep some secrets, like when dealing with defense issues or diplomacy. Some things are just too sensitive (like what the State Department really thinks about some world leaders). But most things that government does must be open to public scrutiny. Bad things and evil deeds hide behind closed doors. Corruption and influence peddling are not things most people make public. In this book we will not try to address these criminal types of corruption but the more subtle debilitations of the social contract that hide in plain sight such as complex laws and regulations, inadequate accounting standards and self-serving financial analysis.

Government accounting (or the lack thereof) hides the true cost of government and especially obscures the true cost of entitlement programs. No one knows what the unfunded liability is for Social Security and Medicare. Governments of both parties have blurred and hidden these costs. One must conclude that this has been done with the intent to perpetuate a fraud on the American people as every attempt to remedy the situation has been blocked.

One of the goals of eliminating these entitlement programs and simplifying the tax code is to provide transparency to citizens. Complexity is the enemy of transparency. A lot can be hidden in a 77,000-page tax code. Much can also be hidden in a health care bill that the legislators haven't read, stating that they have to pass the bill in order to find out what's in it. What hogwash!

Have you ever noticed that when a politician talks about the cost of a program or the impact of a tax cut, they do it over a period of 10 years? Why is that? Well obviously, a tax cut will look bigger over ten years than in one year; but that's not the real reason. The real reason is that when forecasting costs and cash flows in the future, one needs to make assumptions. If the assumptions turn out to be true then the forecast might be reasonably accurate, but if the assumptions were erroneous the forecast could be wildly wrong.

Our politicians are political experts, not financial experts, and as a result their financial estimates are often proven ludicrously off base. Boston's Big Dig tunnel project was estimated to cost $2.8 billion and ended up costing a mind boggling $28 billion. If the citizens of Boston had known the project would cost even a fraction of the final amount, the project would never have been approved. So the political experts come up with calculations that get projects approved. And once started, these projects almost always have to be completed. You couldn't leave the Big Dig half dug. The first phase of the $68 billion California High Speed Rail project is already about two years behind schedule. Imagine the final cost if they run into Big Dig types of cost overruns.

For all their bean counting, the government doesn't really want you to know what is going on. The future costs of these government entitlement programs dwarf the losses incurred during the Great Recession. What we need is true accountability.

International Accounting Standards

The United States should adopt the accounting standards developed by the International Accounting Standards Board. The US, directly through its foreign assistance programs and indirectly through the Bretton Woods institutions, has long been urging developing countries to adopt these standards (Sauce for the goose?). It's about time the US also adopt these standards. First of all it is supreme arrogance on the part of the US to ignore these standards while pushing them on hapless third world countries. But that is not the reason I am urging the adoption of these standards. It is that the American people deserve this type of accountability from their own government.

Third Party Audit

"The U.S. Government Accountability Office (GAO) cannot render an opinion on the 2010 consolidated financial statements of the federal government, because of widespread material internal control weaknesses, significant uncertainties, and other limitations."

This quote from a GAO press release (December 21, 2010) says it all. Despite all the efforts of the over three thousand professionals working at GAO, it cannot only not render an opinion, it cannot even give some semblance of a report that makes sense. This is because the government does not take this obligation to the people seriously. Reporting as it does to Congress makes it subject to the political machinations of the members of Congress and clear reporting is always subordinate to politics.

The GAO should be spun off from Congress (or a new entity created) and made an independent agency of the government. Furthermore, I would recommend that the administrator of this newly independent auditor not be appointed by the President or named by Congress but elected directly by the people from candidates that meet a set of professional qualification standards (i.e.: not a politician). Further, this auditor must be given the teeth to do the job, the ability to demand compliance and the ability to apply sanctions.

Variance Analysis

We can never really get rid of forecasts. Without them we could never do any long-term projects. But forecasts are not the future. In my work I use forecasts as tools. If there is a variation in the outcomes from my forecast, I look for the reason for the variation; this is called variance analysis. Once I have determined the reason for the variance, I can look for ways to eliminate or reduce the cause of the variance or I must alter my forecast. More importantly, I must report the variance; recommend actions to be taken or why the forecast must be amended. Too many unexplained variances and I would be out of a job.

Our government doesn't want to provide you with this kind of variance analysis. Mostly likely because the reason for the variance would likely be "use of wildly over-optimistic assumptions in order to dupe the American people into doing something they would never sanction if they knew the truth".

The government and our politicians use many artifices to manipulate the information we receive about their programs: the benefits of new programs are front loaded will the costs are back loaded, the projections of costs are minimized while those of benefits are exaggerated. Better accounting won't change all that, but it will give us the opportunity to be better informed about government programs and who is benefiting and who is paying.

Income Inequality

Excessive income inequality corrodes the sense of shared sacrifice that binds us together. But income inequality is the essential driving force of the free market economic system. While all people are created equal, not all work is rewarded equally. People who work harder, longer or more productively usually receive higher compensation than those who don't. Those who take more risks by investing in business reap greater rewards. More importantly, people who invent and innovate can achieve great wealth. Hard work, taking risks, inventing things: that is what drives the modern economy.

So how do we discriminate between healthy compensation for hard work and innovation and excessive compensation that undermines the sense of shared sacrifice and corrodes the social contract? This is a fairness issue that offers no easy solution.

Progressives and socialists would flatten compensation through the use of state coercion. For them, the reason for income inequality matters little. There is a presumption on the left that great wealth cannot be accumulated ethically and morally: that some corner had to have been cut, some worker had to have been exploited; some government connection had to have been leveraged, some law had to have been flouted. This presumption is necessary in order to justify any tax or other means needed to extract this wealth from the rich: if the funds are ill-gotten the government has the right (no - the responsibility) to seize those funds and redistribute them to more worthy or needy people.

But their solutions do not address the causes of too much income inequality, which arises more from our human nature than economic theory. As I have pointed out elsewhere in this book, their theories don't work. Income redistribution doesn't solve income inequality: it depends on it. Redistribution needs the coercive power of the state to extract the money from productive sectors of society to give to less productive sectors. This coercive power is dedicated to sacrificing personal liberty on the altar of group material well-being.

Indignation at income inequality hits at the gut level: people get very worked up about income inequality (especially if their income is the lesser one). This is why it makes such a good issue for political campaigns. But setting up the wealthy as straw men for political campaigns does little to solve the underlying problem.

Income inequality is a good example of the fairness problem; it is impossible to build a consensus regarding what is a fair level of income inequality so we will have to find a solution that is not "too unfair".

Excessive Compensation
What is excessive compensation: how do you define it? To some, it is defined solely by amount: make x and it is okay, make 2x and it is not okay. But was Steve Jobs excessively compensated for bringing us all those innovative Apple products? Was Bill Gates excessively compensated for making Windows the ubiquitous computer operating system? High compensation is the reward for being highly productive. On the other hand, some of the most highly compensated CEOs in the US are heads of poorly performing companies. Their compensation could be deemed excessive (of course, so too could being paid $15 an hour for mindlessly flipping burgers — it just depends on your point of view).

Private Profit/Public Loss
Taking risks is an essential part of the free market economic system. Investors take risks by buying shares of companies. Businessmen and women take risks by investing in new manufacturing plants or retail outlets. Investors take risks by trying to look at problems in new or different ways. Sometimes they win/sometimes they lose. When they lose they take the hit or share in the losses.

Perverse Incentives and Moral hazard
People who make big bets expect to reap big rewards. The problem on Wall Street is that the people making the big bets and reaping the rewards are not the people taking the risks. This is because depositor and investor money is often mixed with proprietary funds (the bank's own money). When the trader's bet wins, he or she shares in the gains. But when there are losses they belong to others. Hopefully the investors knew the risks they were taking. But when the

losses can potentially affect the depositors of the bank, the government must step in to honor the FDIC guarantees backing the deposits. This situation creates both perverse incentives and moral hazard. The perverse incentive is that the trader is motivated to take larger and larger risks in order to maximize the bonus, but is not exposed to the risk of the loss.

There is an asymmetrical risk/reward relationship in much of the executive compensation on Wall Street and elsewhere in the business community. This means that when times are good for the company, they are very good for the executives while when the times aren't so good for the company they are still pretty good for the executives. Of course during hard times you want the best executives running the company so you would be foolish to scrimp on pay for top notch talent. The problem is that a lot of that talent that was paid so much during the good times wasn't really so hot. It's easy to make money in a rising market. And maybe some of those hotshots got fired and had nothing left to do but count all their money from their mansion in the Hamptons.

Income Inequality in the 21st Century

Income inequality in the United States (as measured by the Gini index) has been getting worse but before going too far down this road we need to keep in mind that the Gini Index measures relative income inequality and not absolute inequality. Norway (26.8 by World Bank measures) has more or less the same dispersal of income as Pakistan (29.6) however only the richest Pakistani has more income than a poor person in Norway.

Many people will cite Census Bureau studies that show median household income has been stagnant or fallen in recent years. However, the Congressional Budget Office issued a report in 2013, which noted that median household income is a pre-tax calculation and does not include in-kind payments by employers or the government. These in-kind payments have risen from 6% of household income in 1980 to 17% in 2010. Taking these factors into account, the Brookings Institution (a left-leaning think tank) stated in a January 6, 2014 opinion piece by Gary Burtless, "As the CBO statistics demonstrate, incomes in the middle and at the bottom of the distribution have fared better since 2000 than incomes at the very top."

But it is not in the interest of politicians of the left for people to be complacent about their levels of income. There is a widespread perception that income distribution is very unequal and that it is getting worse. It is the perception (rather than the fact) that undermines the social contract. But the left's solutions will only further divide the nation and do economic harm to the people they say they are trying to benefit.

Impunity

Impunity is a root cause of the deterioration we see in the American Social Contract. If equality before the law is a prime tenet of the American Social Contract then why were so few people punished for the damage caused by the Great Recession? Although many traders took outsized risks with other people's money, they were careful to not violate the letter of the law. The real crime was not the financial shenanigans but the corruption of the rule of law by Wall Streeters, K Streeters and Congress to allow such activity. How can anyone be asked to sacrifice if they know that others are protected from sharing the full burden of sacrifice through influence or clever dealing?

The Role of Regulation

Regulation is the legal framework the government uses to ensure the integrity of the American Social Contract. Regulation guides how the government can use its coercive powers to maintain the social contract and allows citizens and their commercial enterprises to know the limits of actions within the social contract. When regulation is used to support a particular interest or to enforce a political agenda, it works against the social contract and must be voided.

Clearly, linking compensation to risk taking is furtherance of the public good. Placing limits on the compensation of traders and bankers would be an unacceptable use of the coercive power of the state. However, limiting the damage to third parties arising from risky trading practices calls for the segregation of proprietary trading from other banking practices (especially those backed by the government such as deposit protection). I was originally in favor of the elimination of Glass-Steagall because the act impaired the ability of the US banks to compete internationally. However, I now think that some, probably more nuanced, version of this law should be reinstituted.

Bailouts

Bailouts are seen as another form of impunity. However, bailouts are generally used to prevent further economic damage rather than to save the asses of investors and management of the bailed-out institution (although saving their asses may be a side effect). In banking, bailouts usually occur during a liquidity crisis when there is little time for preparation and little information of the potential impact of a failure. The FDIC routinely resolves bank failures and makes sure that depositors get their guaranteed money back (the process is so smooth that bank customers barely notice that the name of their bank has changed over the weekend). The potential failures in the Great Recession were too large or involved non-banking institutions (like AIG) that required special treatment. But the TARP (as pointed out elsewhere in this book) actually worked, saving institutions from bankruptcies and eventually getting repaid. One of the critical functions of the Federal Reserve System is to act as the "lender of last resort" (a situation commonly called a bailout) providing confidence to the banking system as a whole.

The gut reaction (at least among many progressives) to banks deemed "too big to fail" has recently been to break up the banks. And it is true that the US banking system has become more concentrated over time, going from 12,343 banks in 1990 to 5,643 in 2014. But the US banking system is much more fragmented than many other countries. Breaking up banks could have unintended consequences so we must be careful to base financial policy decisions on rational thinking and not based on gut reaction.

Whether the government bailout comes in the form of taking equity in the company, or buying up toxic loans or other forms of bailout, the government is taking on equity type risks. Owners have rights regarding how the company is run including setting compensation levels. Would this imply that the government has an inherent equity stake in banks or other financial institutions that are considered too big to fail (because of the risk of systemic collapse)? By the time the government takes an actual equity interest the systemic damage has already been done.

Shareholders should demand clawback clauses for all senior executives and board members in their companies and these companies should be required to report that their executives are subject to such clauses. Mutual funds should make a policy to only invest in companies that have such policies.

Shareholder Responsibility

Ultimately, it is the shareholders of financial institutions that bear the risk of irresponsible behavior. When financial institutions are bailed out, shareholders still lose money. But my investments are too small to be noticed at these large institutions. And what's more, most of my investments are in 401(k)s and mutual funds that invest in a wide range of investments. These are the sophisticated investors permitted to invest in hedge funds and other risky ventures. The managers of these funds have a fiduciary responsibility to their investors (us) and need to be willing to speak out and take action at financial institutions that are taking unnecessary risks and paying exorbitant salaries and bonuses. They, and other large shareholders, should demand that managers indemnify the company for large paychecks, allow clawbacks of cash and stock granted in the boom times and require companies obtain insurance that guarantee that these measures will reimburse the companies for excessive compensation paid out by lax boards of directors.

What is not Shared Sacrifice

In a Bloomberg News National Survey done by Selzer and Company in December 2010, the people polled said they wanted radical change in the country's finances except do not touch their Social Security and Medicare. Oh, and they wanted somebody else to pay for it. Sixty-six percent said the country was on the wrong track while forty-eight percent said the budget deficit was dangerously out of control, while an additional forty-three percent said that the deficit was a burden that would require some sacrifice down the road (only five percent felt it was not a problem). At the same time 82% opposed cuts to Medicare, 72% opposed cuts to Medicaid and 65% opposed cuts in the cost of living increases for Social Security (although they were in favor of means testing – presumably unless their means tested positive).

One reason so few people are willing to make the necessary sacrifices is that many feel that the sacrifices will not be shared equally – that some will take advantage of the sacrifices of others. The financial crisis of 2008-2009 is a case in point. Many people looked to the outsized compensation packages of Wall

Street fat cats as a large part of the problem and, to a great extent, they were on target.

Well I've got news for all of you. Redistribution is not the kind of sacrifice needed to solve our problems. This survey only proves the insidious nature of these entitlement programs. People (you and me) have put the thinking part of our brains in neutral if we think that it is possible to receive more benefits than what we pay in and that the wealthy will willingly pay for the shortfall. More likely it will be higher taxes and lost economic opportunity for our children and grandchildren.

Common Goals

If the reforms impose a shared sacrifice, then they must be based on shared goals and aspirations. That may sound a bit odd coming in a book that is proposing radical reforms that will, at least initially, be opposed by many of the readers of the book as well as other citizens (opposition from people who haven't read the book and have no intention of reading the book must be expected: they wouldn't want to accidently learn something and then have to change their minds.). But I think that, on reflection, people will see that the goals are not so much radical but instead based on common sense and founded on our commonly shared principles. It is the contention of this book that those goals cannot be achieved by continuing on our current course of ever larger and larger government. Among these common goals are political freedom, a strong defense, peace in our land, economic opportunity, affordable healthcare and perhaps others. But always – freedom first!

Shared Sacrifice and the American Social Contract

The American Social Contract is founded on the principles of equality of opportunity and the level playing field so that all citizens can participate in the economic success of the country. Likewise, when times are tough all citizens are expected to bear some of the burden. It is safe to say that the economic burdens resulting from the Great Recession were not borne equally or (dare I say?) fairly. At the very least, we can state that the economic rewards reaped before (and since) the recession were negatively correlated to the economic hardships endured. This highly asymmetric relation of the costs borne and rewards reaped undermines the very fabric of the American Social Contract.

The question we face is: can we alter this perverse relationship within the context of the democratic (small d) American Social Contract and the free market economic system or do we need to adopt some new standard (such as socialism) to prevent this type of abuse. The position of many on the left is that the perverse sharing of cost and reward is inherent in the American system and that the entire system must be scrapped in the interest of fairness. The outrage on Main Street and the apparent impunity of business and banking leaders have caused many people to seek vengeance on their abusers through anti-business legislation and regulation and through massive expansion of the welfare state.

We must prove the polls wrong. We need to show that we are not a people that want to live beyond our means and stick the other guy (or our kids) with the bill. But we also need to show that we are the land of opportunity for those on Main Street as well as Wall Street. One way to do that is for government to make sure that the American Social Contract is operating effectively based on our founding principles.

American Exceptionalism

Many people believe that America is exceptional because it is the best country in the world. While I do believe that the US is the best country in the world, I do not believe that is why it is exceptional (if we investigate causality, America is the best country because it is exceptional, not the reverse). We also must include many caveats in a discussion of American exceptionalism because we have often not lived up to the ideals and standards that make us exceptional. It is the principles that undergird the American Social Contract that makes America exceptional in contrast to the social contracts of other nations that are enshrouded in ethnicity, religion or tribalism.

Revolutions around the World

Prior to the American Revolution most political violence and regime change was intended to determine who governed society not how the society was governed. The British may take exception to this claim citing the Glorious Revolution of 1688 however the revolutionary aspect of the Glorious Revolution was more the result (increased powers of Parliament and limitations on the divine right of Kings) than the intent (to prevent the establishment of a Catholic dynasty in England).

Although the American Revolution had many causes, some crass and some noble, the stated intentions in the Declaration of Independence were truly revolutionary. The concepts that all men are created equal (sorry ladies your time would come later) and that "governments are instituted among men deriving their just powers from the consent of the governed" were nothing but the wild theories of Enlightenment philosophers prior to the American Revolution.

Granted that America has not always lived up to its revolutionary ideal. But we must keep things in perspective. Keep in mind that the French Revolution led to the Reign of Terror and first modern dictatorship under Napoleon. The Russian Revolution led to the Dictatorship of the Proletariat by the Soviets after the Bolsheviks overthrew the provisional government in the October Revolution. The fact that the United States has not always lived up to revolutionary ideals is not the point. The point is that it always strives to live up to those ideals.

Melting Pot

The concept that all races and religions can come to America and be absorbed into a giant cultural melting pot may be a bit of a fantasy (it may be more of a stew where you can still identify the original ingredients) but it is more real than in any other country in the world. Europe is having many problems with migrant populations that are not being absorbed into the general population. Speaking French and even being a French citizen doesn't make you "French". Speaking Mandarin and living in Beijing won't make you Chinese. The Balkans are a prime example of how even the iron hand of Tito could not mold disparate ethnicities and cultures into a single country.

All around the world you see countries striving for homogenization. There are breakaway countries like South Sudan and East Timor. There are civil wars between ethnic groups and tribes lumped together by the borders imposed on them by their former colonial masters. In many countries, a person's primary affiliation is to his tribe or clan rather than his nation.

This concept is not limited to primitive or backwards countries. The 2014 vote on Scottish independence and the Catalan efforts to break away from Spain show that the concept of national identity in advanced countries in Europe is closely linked to ethnicity, language and local culture. People migrating from Madrid to Barcelona will still be Castilians generations later and not Catalans. Britons living in Scotland are still Britons, not Scots.

Anyone can be an American

However, Britons, Scots, Castilians and Catalans moving to America can be Americans. it is my firm belief (much of our culture is based on this belief) that anyone can be an American. Being an American means adopting our culture and believing in our goals and ideals. I have lived overseas for many years and have met many people who, while still loving their own country, love the ideals and opportunities represented by America. They want to make their own country more like America; these people are Americans in spirit even if not legal citizens.

Some will say that there are those who will never be accepted as Americans even if they are born here. It must be admitted that there is still discrimination in America. For some radical groups, whoever doesn't look like what they see in the mirror is not an American. They are wrong! It may be true in many other countries in the world, but it is not true here.

Because America is a concept. A grand concept. An aspiration. Yes, we fall short of the ideal. But that is the nature of an ideal. What we achieve on earth can never reach perfection. Nevertheless, in America we have set our sights high and strive to achieve them. It is this striving that makes us Americans.

The Shame of Slavery

Nothing illustrates how much we have fallen short of living up to our ideals as the enslavement of black people in America. The same man who wrote the words "all men are created equal" not only owned slaves but fathered children with by one of his slaves.

Slavery has existed since pre-historic times and still exists today in certain parts of the world. Slavery has afflicted virtually all the populations of the earth. The Roman Empire was built by slaves. Some 25% to 35% of the population of the empire was enslaved (perhaps as many as 60 million people). Muslims in medieval Spain regularly raided Christian regions of the Iberian Peninsula for slaves. The Aztecs ritualized warfare in order to obtain slaves for labor and sacrifice.

By the time of the discovery of America, the use of slaves was beginning to wane in much of the old world. This was not because of a major increase in the moral fiber of slave owners but due to agricultural economics, which made slaves less profitable. Slavery is only economically feasible for certain types of agriculture. Unfortunately for the Americas, cotton and sugar (two of the largest crops of the western hemisphere in the 16th to 18th century) are very suitable for large plantations manned by slaves.

At the time of the American Revolution, the economic strength of the South rested on the shoulders of slaves. From our modern perspective it is difficult to understand how men who held the high ideals of the Founders could countenance the existence of slavery let alone be slave owners themselves. It would be easy to state that they were evil men but that would be clearly wrong. They were good men that did things we now see as evil.

How could they not see the evil they were perpetrating? It was a different time, but the Founders understood that the United States that they envisioned would be something completely new and revolutionary. How could they not take the next logical step and free the slaves? Obviously their power to effect change was limited. The livelihood and wealth of many people was entwined in slavery and they struggled to find a way out. George Washington, on his death, freed his own slaves but declined to free the slaves of his wife, Martha, where he felt that he did not have the right to dispose of her property.

It would take seventy years and a bloody conflict to end slavery in the United States. Unfortunately for the black people living in the United States, the end of slavery was not the end of their problems.

The Condition of Black People in America

America has come a long way toward providing black people in America access to the level playing field available to others. However, if you ask most black people, they would say that we haven't gone far enough and that there is more work to be done.

Prejudice is innate in all people (recall our discussion on the instinctual brain as described by Dr. Kahneman). I have seen it in many forms, in many countries and against many different ethnicities. Government can try to solve the outward signs of prejudice (housing discrimination, segregated schools, etc.) but has limited ability to affect hearts and minds. Thought control is repugnant to a free people. But government must do its best to reduce and eliminate the remaining obstacles to full participation in American life, not only for blacks but also for all people that are discriminated against.

Prejudice, personal and institutional, has kept the playing field very tilted against blacks. Leveling the playing field will help everyone including blacks although tilting a little in their favor (through reverse discrimination such as affirmative action) may be necessary as a temporary measure. There is, however, one thing of which I am certain. Full participation in the American

Social Contract offers more potential for black people than can be found in any other country.

A Nation of Immigrants

You may be wondering why I am choosing to discuss immigration in the chapter on American exceptionalism. If you think about, however, it makes perfect sense.

America is a nation of immigrants. We all know that. Our ancestors arrived on these shore sometime between four hundred years ago and now (except for Native Americans who arrived here much earlier from Asia). We have immigrants from every country on earth, representing all the varied racial and ethnic identities, all denominations and sects of all world religions, speaking every language one can imagine. How is it possible to meld all these varied people into a unified nation?

Our founding documents state that "all men are created equal" and that the government shall not "prohibit the free exercise [of religion]". In a country of immigrants this is the only possible way of organizing society.

The principles of a diverse society

Most countries around the world find national unity based on ethnic or religious homogeneity. This has been especially true since the rise of the nation state. German language and the supposed "Aryan" racial stereotype were the basis of the rise of Nazi Germany. Jews were not considered "German' even though they had lived there for centuries. A person whose parents emigrated from Algeria is considered Algerian even though he might be a French citizen and speak perfect French.

Although China has been a nation state for millennia and has a millennia-old social philosophy (Confucianism), Chineseness is tied up in the Han ethnic identity and language. Although the Uighurs have been part of China for around 250 years (longer than the existence of the United States), they are not considered Chinese. The rise of China offers nothing to the non-Han billions that populate the globe.

Although as a British colony, what became the United States was considered largely made up of people from England. In fact the colonists came from a wide variety of European countries. Subsequently, people came from all over. These diverse people needed a unifying factor and that factor was the American Social Contract, which is based on principles – not ethnic or religious identity. Had we tried to forge a nation based on a specific ethnic type or a single sect of a single religion, we would be a nation of strangers. It would have been impossible to overcome the ethnic differences, the religious disagreements, etc. Instead of a great nation we would have ended up with a bunch of squabbling local and regional entities constantly at war or in competition with each other like the Balkans. We would not have been able to resist the Great Powers of the Nineteenth Century, the Axis Powers or the Soviet Union. We wouldn't exist – and the world would be worse off for it.

Being American and being an immigrant are inextricably linked. We are Americans not because of ethnic identity or religion but because we believe in American principles, the American Social contract and the Free Market Economic System.

A Flood of Immigrants

Most immigrants didn't come here to change us; they came here to be us. It is true that most of them probably only had a vague idea what it was to be an American. But they knew it was better than what they were leaving. They probably also had a hopelessly idealistic view of what life would be like in America. But it was better than the intolerable circumstances they were leaving.

I don't believe in the American melting pot: the concept that we are an amalgam of all the different cultures that have arrived on our shore. To a lesser or greater extent they came here to take part in the American social contract and the principles on which it is based: personal liberty, equal opportunity, democracy and the free market economic system.

It is true that many new arrivals live in communities that match their cultural and ethnic identities. Many find employment among their countrymen such as Korean grocers or Vietnamese nail salons. But over time they become integrated into the fabric of America: branching out into new employment opportunities, intermarrying with native Americans and other immigrant groups (some of which would have been prohibited in their home countries).

But the integration process is slow. It can take several generations before the American identity dominates the old world culture. The current volume of immigration is transforming and, in some cases, overwhelming local American culture. This comes at a time when American culture is in flux (when is it not?) and when American principles are under attack. Some say that the current administration is cynically encouraging immigration (legal and illegal) in order to promote the social welfare state and to undermine the basic principles of the American Social contract. Attacking the motivations of people that you disagree with (a tactic used extensively by progressives and others from left) does not address the underlying issues at stake and diverts attention from the search for solutions.

The real question is: what is the absorptive capacity of the American Social Contract and how much immigration can there be without undermining our basic principles?

I am not talking about the fact that most new immigrants are not from European countries but are people of color; from Central and South America, Africa and Asia (although it is probably true that earlier waves of immigration from Europe could more easily adapt to the enlightenment philosophy of the American Social Contract than current immigrants that come from very different cultures). The color of America is changing and people of European descent will soon be in the minority. This is demographically inevitable. But white people don't make America. It is our principles that make America what it is and it is those principles that we cannot let be disregarded or diluted.

This is why immigration is covered in the chapter on American Exceptionalism. Immigrants come here as the downtrodden, as refugees (remember Emma Lazarus' sonnet) and are transformed.

Immigration Policy
Unlike Millken's investment banking strategy, we don't want the influx of immigrants to change the successful formula of the American Social Contract.

The question is: how are we going to preserve the American Social Contract during an unprecedented influx of immigrants.

Staunch the uncontrolled influx

We can never completely stop in the inflow of undocumented immigration: our borders are too long, the seas are too wide and commerce too voluminous. Our free market economy demands high mobility of the populace including immigrants. But current administration policy actually encourages unrestricted illegal immigration. No other country that I know of allows unrestricted immigration (and a lot restrict emigration). Large influxes of refugees (such as is currently afflicting Jordan) occur because of war or strife in neighboring countries.

One time overseas, the taxi driver told me that what he admired most about America was the rule of law, not men. What does it say when the first act of illegal immigrants is to violate the rule of law. So the first step to an updated immigration policy is to enhance border security (also a benefit against increasing likelihood of terrorists sneaking in). We need to reinitiate deportations and make sure their home countries do more to stop their citizens from fleeing. One complaint I have heard is that illegals feel uncomfortable and marginalized because of worrying about immigration officials catching and deporting them. I say good! That is exactly how they should feel.

Increase the legal flow

We can increase the inflow of legal immigrants. One reason Central Americans hop onto death trains and Asians hide in shipping containers is because of the hopelessness of getting a legal visa. The reason they come here is hope, and if there is no hope of achieving a legal visa then they will try any other available alternative. We need to open up the legal immigration policy so that they have hope.

Change the family policy

Currently, there is a preference for family members of legal immigrants. This policy was created for humanitarian reason. It is a good thing to unite families. But this benevolent policy is being abused and converted into an immigration pipeline. We need to tighten the spigot to reduce this inflow. But how do we separate the family members of honest citizens from the abusers?

Sticking to our principles, we need to do this in a compassionate way. But we are not suckers either.

Birthright citizenship

People born in the United States and those whose parents are Americans automatically become American citizens. The right of citizenship based on solely location within US territories has been controversial as this practice has been subject to abuse. There have been increasing number of cases of "birth tourism" (women coming to the US to have babies and then leaving) and the problematic birth of children to illegal aliens. Other nations have a stricter conceptualization of citizenship, using a combination of location (including a period of legal residency) and parentage to determine the citizenship of the child.

It is not unusual for the United States to have a policy different from other nations of the world, and a fairly open policy towards immigration has been beneficial to our country. The language of the 14th amendment (ratified 1868) was designed to assure the citizenship to former slaves. However, in this case our liberal policies have led people to abuse our generosity and openness. To limit these abuses we need to tighten up the policies to require parentage or legal residency in order to qualify for birthright citizenship.

Temporary Work Visas (the Bracero Program)

Many people come to the US for work and not because they want to become Americans. A good American job can support many relatives back in the home country. Remittances from relatives working in the US account for a fifth or a quarter of the gross domestic product of some countries. Those who come illegally to work often stay because they fear if they returned home they could not get back in. If there were a temporary work visa program (like the Bracero Program but without its abuses) it would allow these workers to do seasonal or contract work and then return to their home countries and then come back to the US for the next season or contract.

English Language

I have lived in countries with more than one major language. It doesn't work. The two languages are emblematic of two cultures and countries do not work well with more than one dominant culture. I am not trying to stomp out all other cultures. Having many non-dominant subcultures provides variety and cultural opportunities but must be secondary to the dominant culture. In some countries beset by many languages, English is the official (Nigeria) or unofficial (India) language and is commonly spoken.

I have no problems with people speaking another language, or foreign language TV such as Univision, or signs that say "Se habla español aqui". But I draw the line at "Vota aqui". Citizens should be able to speak English and elections should be considered free and fair even if there are no voting materials in foreign language.

This isn't mere English language chauvinism on my part. Cong Wang and Bodo Steiner in their well-researched paper, *Can Ethno-Linguistic Diversity Explain Cross-Country Differences in Social Capital?: A Global Perspective* (Economic Record, 2015), found that countries that have high linguistic diversity (i.e.; many languages) tend to have lower social capital (as measured by confidence in institutions, rule of law, etc.). The study reviewed the correlations between these variables making tests (such as eliminating African countries) to make sure other factors weren't influencing their results. The United States was an outlier because we do have many languages and also have fairly high social capital. In light of this study (and hopefully others to follow) and in light of the many languages already spoken in the US, it would behoove us to restrain the slide toward multilingual society as a precautionary measure, at the very least.

So might say that this type of immigration policy is racially motivated. But it is not. The American Social contract is not intended to favor any particular race, ethnicity or religion although some people of certain races, ethnicities and religions may have difficulty conforming to the principles of the American Social Contract (keeping in mind our previous discussion on genetic determination). The people that risk death trains and travel in shipping containers are among the most daring and bravest people that their countries have to offer. They have the potential to be great citizens on the United States.

They deserve the benefits of the American Social Contract. That requires several things from us: first and foremost it requires us to preserve the American Social Contract that they are trying to achieve (sometimes called the American Dream): it requires that immigration policy is not used as a political tool but to benefit both citizens and aspiring citizens and residents; and finally it requires hope – a means for these immigrants to achieve their dreams.

Strategic Vision

The principal political struggle of the 2012 Presidential election was one of strategic vision. This likely will continue to be the principal issue of the 2016 election even though many groups will try to distract attention away from this issue. As I see it, it boils down to two views of America's role in the world: one vision sees America as one nation among a continuum of nations, some bigger, some richer, but all more or less equal on the world stage; the other vision is of American exceptionalism and leadership on the world stage.

Under the vision of America as just one nation among many (I'll let you guess which party espouses which vision), American exceptionalism is nothing more than mere jingoism (militant nationalistic fervor not backed up by reason or facts). According to this point of view, given the irrational basis for American exceptionalism, it is not rational to expend large amounts of money to assert America's primacy on the world stage. These monies would be more wisely spent at home, providing healthcare and retirement benefits to American citizens. This is the European vision; the "why can't we all get along" vision. Under this vision, cutting funding for the NASA Mars program to pay entitlements is completely reasonable. Cutting the US nuclear arsenal would be the right thing to do because (gosh darn it) it's just not fair that America has so many more nukes than the other guys.

However, we have been given a glimpse of what the world might look like lacking American leadership. President Obama has chosen a course to reduce the role of the United States on the world stage (and its attendant costs in terms of dollars and lives). The result has not been subsidence of conflict but rather an increase in violence and chaos around the globe.

The decision to completely withdraw troops from Iraq (and the pending, at the time of this writing, decision to withdraw from Afghanistan) has not reduced sectarian conflict but has resulted in the rise of one of the most dangerous terrorist groups yet, ISIS. In the aftermath of the Second World War, America did not quickly withdraw troops from Germany and Japan. In fact US troops are still there after more than seventy years. Germany and Japan are examples where bitter enemies have become stable democracies that are friends and allies. If the saying that those who ignore history are doomed to repeat is true, then a corollary must be that those who ignore history's successes are doomed to get a different result.

There are many (in America and elsewhere) who believe that America should not be the policeman of the world. But recent events have shown that the world needs a policeman. If that policeman is not the United Sates, whom would you recommend? Russia? China? Perhaps the United Nations? Don't make me laugh.

The post-WWII world created and funded by the United Sates has served the world very well. The Soviet Union was defeated without resorting to a nuclear holocaust. Europe has been prosperous and peaceful. Poverty has been greatly reduced worldwide. Perhaps not a golden age. But better than some of the alternatives I could imagine.

And this well-policed world has been good for the United States. We have benefitted from increased world trade and the expansion of free markets. Yes, Pax Americana has its costs, in blood and money. The recent wars in the Mideast (Gulf War I, Iraq War and the War in Afghanistan) have cost the U.S. over three trillion dollars, and around 7,000 American lives. A truly tragic cost of life that I believe has resulted in the national war-weariness indicated in polls.

But we need to put these deaths into perspective. The post-World War II wars of Korea and Vietnam cost around 40,000 and 58,000 lives, respectively. These costs pale in comparison with the 407,000 deaths America suffered in World War II (which were much less than the losses of other nations). Numerous battles in World War II suffered more losses than the three Mideast wars combined (Iwo Jima, 36 days, 6,800 deaths; Okinawa, 82 days, 12,000 deaths; Battle of the Bulge, 40 days, 19,000 deaths).

Were all these deaths in vain? No! They have saved us from oppression and terror. From the Nazis. From the Soviets. And now from al Qaeda and ISIS. It is sad that we have to sacrifice our young men and women to protect our freedom and the freedom of others. But the sacrifices in the Mideast are not so onerous as to make us shirk our global responsibilities.

The Duty of Exceptionalism

The fact of American exceptionalism demands a different policy, the policy of engagement and world leadership. The Declaration of Independence doesn't just apply to Americans. Jefferson wrote, "We hold these truths to be self-evident, that all men are created equal". These are truths that apply to all men (and women for that matter). He defines some rights but not all because the list is not exhaustive. He then states that governments are instituted to secure those rights. In just a few lines he has succinctly laid out the principles that guide America.

But these rights aren't exclusive to Americans. They apply to everybody. Don't we have a positive obligation to assist other peoples in obtaining these rights? Isn't that what we did in the aftermath of World War II? Didn't we help set Germany and Japan on the path to democracy? Didn't we provide assistance to Europe through the Marshall plan at great cost to a nation that had just endured a terrible world war? Didn't we protect the fragile democracies of Western Europe from the Red Army?

Don't we continue to have an obligation to proclaim these self-evident truths? To help others realize the inalienable rights that we enjoy?

I assert that we do. We haven't always been steadfast to this mission. The road is rough and difficult. We make mistakes. Many people will try and stop us from fulfilling our obligations to mankind. Many people may be philosophically opposed to our concepts of inalienable rights or be genetically predisposed to baser forms of social organization. But that does not relieve us of our obligation; it only requires that we act intelligently, compassionately and patiently in the fulfilling this obligation.

American exceptionalism is implicit in the concepts enshrined in the Declaration of Independence, the Constitution and other founding documents. The founders knew they were creating a new world vision and that this gave the United States not only a unique form of government but also a unique responsibility in the world. Many in America believe that we have lost this vision, that it has been corrupted and debased by America's past actions and therefore we must abandon our global responsibilities. It is true that we have not always lived up to our enshrined ideals, but that does not imply that we have lost forever our place among nations or that we can't regain the stature we had for most of the twentieth century. This vision, that the US can rebuild and reclaim our leadership role, stands in stark contrast to the people that believe in a diminished America.

It's a Matter of National Security

We have a choice. We can choose to honor the obligations placed on us by American exceptionalism or turn away from idealism and chart an alternative course. A course that denies that the concept of America is exceptional. A course that says we should emulate other nations rather than lead other nations.

There are many that will assert that this alternative course is superior to the ideals of the founders. That it is arrogant for us to think that we should lead the world. That it is chauvinistic to think our ideals are superior to those of other peoples. That this attitude leads other people to hate us (despite the fact that we were better liked when we did lead). They believe that the alternative course will make people like us better. That the alternative course will allow us to focus our energies on our own people rather than spending enormous sums of money fighting on the other side of the world for people that resent our presence and hate us.

What happens to a country that owes its creditors more than it can pay in a lifetime? Look at present day Europe where once proud empires are falling to their knees in the face of foreign creditors.

The European Example

In an article in the New York Times (*Can Europe be Saved?*, January 12, 2011) Paul Krugman made it clear that the European style nanny-state is, for him, the ideal style form of government. It is so civilized, the citizens are so well taken care of, they are so advanced that America pales in comparison. He neglects to mention that the European economies are on an even more unsustainable course than is the US; that the day of judgment (as it were) in Europe is not in the future, but, in many cases, now. He believes that the structural adjustments necessary to realign income and spending are unduly harsh. (We won't go into the supposed benefits of devaluation as a means of structural adjustment, noting only that currency adjustment is a zero sum game that changes the flows of wealth within a country and between countries. Nor will I note, having lived in Latin America during the Lost Decade, that the cost of devaluation is borne mostly by the poor.)

It is clear that Europe's welfare state is unsustainable. Even Germany is facing cuts or modifications in some of its programs. But even more importantly, it is clear that Europe has turned its focus inward, turning its back on the world stage and concentrating on the comfort of its citizens, their health and pensions and reduced work hours. But this model state of Europe has been accomplished within a protective envelope of security and access to markets provided by the United States. The US defeated the totalitarianism that afflicted Europe, paid for much of the recovery from the damage they inflicted on themselves, kept them from being run over by the Red Army and provided an international economic environment where they could flourish. The US even gave Europe an outsized seat at the table of the major post-World War II international financial and political institutions.

But Europe has focused inward. It has taken a step back from the world stage. Even in conflicts on their own continent European nations have taken a back seat – nor have they borne their fair share in Afghanistan and Iraq.

The United States cannot follow Europe into insignificance. Europe is not a shining example to follow but a pitfall to avoid. Sure, it's a nice place to visit on vacation and they do make some nice wine and cars. But Europe does not play a leadership role in the world even though some there still think they do. Only Britain, as a staunch US ally, plays a significant role on the world stage.

I agree with Krugman that the Euro is a non-starter. Many countries joined the Euro-zone thinking that it liberated them from credit restraints on their fiscal policy. They commenced a spending spree that included lavish pensions and retirement at 55. They took to the streets in Paris when the government, showing the beginnings of some fiscal sense, tried to raise the retirement age from 60 to 62. But there is more wrong with Europe than just the currency. They feel comfortable allowing the United States to take center stage (so long as they can criticize the US for its brashness, its lack of culture). The US has always been pretty friendly with European states. Many Americans are descendants of Europeans and the US has a friendly foreign policy for peaceable democratic states. Who will take center stage if the US bows out? Will they still be as friendly to a peaceable, democratic, Europeanized US? I don't want to find out.

American exceptionalism cannot be allowed to fall into irrelevance.

The mounting debt is the symptom of the malaise that America is currently facing. Even if by some magic the current debt disappeared, new debts would soon reach astronomical proportions because the basic structure of the economy is on an unsustainable path. If this were a benign world, perhaps we could choose the European path: a comfortable retirement from the world stage. The passing of the torch to a new generation: the end of the Age of America. But to whom would we pass the torch?

There is a reason for American exceptionalism. It is because America is a unique country, a new type of nation. It is a nation based on ideas and philosophies, a nation beyond territorial or ethnic considerations. True, colonial America was relatively homogenous and black and indigenous peoples were routinely excluded from the American dream. But the American dream transcended the petty prejudices of our ancestors. We remain committed to achieving those lofty goals and living up to our principles no matter how imperfect our attempts may be, no matter that the lofty goals are sullied from time to time by greed or expediency. Because of these principles and goals, America has developed into a truly unique nation, prosperous and ethnically diverse. Some ethnicities have not yet achieved all that this vision offers them but most are well on their way. Furthermore, we have tried to export not only our products, but also our visions of democracy and economic prosperity (even if some consider this imperialism). But the American Era is still young. Other dominant cultures lasted for centuries. Ours seems to have rapidly reached senescence before its time, like those poor children suffering from progeria. We seem to be suffering from a chronic disease when we should be robust and healthy.

If the American Era is to end soon, what will replace it? The Chinese may aspire to regional, if not global, dominance. But would a world dominated by China be a good place to live in? Well, maybe if you are Chinese but for others I'm not so sure. The current Chinese regime does not appear to have a dominant philosophy except nationalism founded on an incongruous amalgam of communism, mercantilism and Confucianism. It is a pragmatic and opportunistic philosophy designed to advance China's power and prestige throughout the world. China's foreign trade is designed to increase the wealth of the nation even if it comes at the expense of others (this is of course a fairly common theme). Of course, America was brash and rough-edged when it first came onto the world stage. Will the Chinese government mellow over time? Will the Chinese people stand up and demand civil rights and choose freedom? We do not yet know and I, for one, do not wish to stand by passively and see what kind of world the Chinese wish to create.

The World's Policeman

There are many people who say, *why should America be the world's policeman? Why spend money chasing terrorists in Afghanistan or bombing Libyan tanks that are shelling civilian neighborhoods? We are spending money that could be better spent on domestic programs.*

Sometimes I think there are people that would like the government to cease all functions except to take money from the rich and give it to themselves in the form of entitlements. But the money we spend in policing the world does provide real benefit to US citizens and fulfills the constitutional mandate to provide for the common defense.

The Founders warned against foreign entanglements. However, back then it took six weeks to cross the Atlantic Ocean. The world is a much smaller place now. We can be almost any place on earth in less than a day, often in a few hours (the US is working on a prototype plane that can travel at 13,000 miles an hour). What's more our commerce is worldwide and the world economy is becoming more integrated every day. We have citizens spread all over the globe and have millions of aliens (legal and illegal) residing in the US at any one time. It would be impossible (and foolish to even attempt) to disentangle ourselves from the rest of the world.

Our enemies do not need tanks and aircraft carriers and jet bombers to attack us. A few men with box cutters were able to kill almost 3,000 of us. In this chaotic and often dangerous world, a policeman on the beat can provide the security needed for commerce and general wellbeing. Our national interests cannot be narrowly defined. A peaceful world is in the interest of all our citizens.

Some might say that it is our involvement in everybody's business that makes us a target. That it is not policing but imperialism. But if we withdrew back within our borders others would seek to replace the US as the world's policeman. Alas, not our friends in Europe, but others whose motives are less well known and could easily be not in our interests. You need not look far to get an inkling of what the world would look like if we were not involved.

You might wonder why it couldn't be a joint effort. That would at least lower our profile and maybe save some money. Well, we've tried that. NATO has shown some promise on paper. The 28 member states are all democracies and we share many values. However, when NATO has been called to act the burden has usually fallen to the US, with many members providing only nominal support and others abstaining completely. The United Nations is not a world government, more like a world debating society (which serves a purpose but only a limited purpose). But since it includes all the countries of the world it includes many who do not share our values: dictatorships like Zimbabwe and Syria (I had included Libya but world events run apace), antagonists like Venezuela and others like Russia and China that simply have a different agenda.

There may come a time when the United States does not have to take an outsized role on the world stage. However that time has not yet arrived.

Foreign Assistance
Foreign aid and assistance would appear to be one of the easier budget items to target for cuts, but I would state that it is not only the ultimate expression of American ideals in tangible form but also helps to keep America safer. *What?* I hear you scream, *you want to give our money to foreigners while cutting or eliminating programs vital to Americans like Social Security and Medicare?* Indeed I do. Foreign assistance takes up around one percent of the budget and isn't programmed to increase uncontrollably for decades to come. Eliminating all foreign assistance wouldn't slow the entitlement program freight train more than a fly hitting the windshield.

Although a chunk of foreign assistance goes to strategic allies such as Pakistan, Israel and Egypt rather than the truly poor, even this assistance can be said to be helping to keep the world a more peaceful place. But much of American assistance goes to help very poor people in very great need. Many may think that a lot of foreign assistance is just pouring money into a black hole and it is true that many countries receiving assistance show few tangible results in the long term. But the US is constantly looking for ways to make foreign assistance more efficient and effective.

But that's not even the point. Helping others in need is who we are; it's one of our core values. *But what about Americans*, you shout. *This aid should be spent at home not eliminated.* The problem with entitlement programs (as noted above) is that they are not designed for people in true need but for all people. By cutting entitlements there would be more money for helping Americans that really need help. We should not try and solve our budget problems on the backs of our core values.

Leading from Strength

We can only fulfill this role if we are strong, truly strong. Given the growing chaos around the world we cannot reduce the size of our armed forces in order to save money. This is exactly what we are doing under the policy of sequestration where the military and other essential programs are starved so that transfer payments can be maintained. How can essential, constitutionally mandated programs be considered discretionary spending while transfer payments are non-discretionary?

How can we be the world leader while we are dependent on our rivals to fund our budget by buying our bonds? How can we lead the world when our unfunded future obligations dwarf our current debt? We need to get our financial house in order in order so that we can play the role we are obliged to play because of American exceptionalism. There are costs to world leadership but we and the rest of the world have benefitted from our fulfilling our duty.

The High Ground/The Final Frontier

In the effort to reduce the deficit somewhat (to call current efforts as trying to "balance the budget" is laughable) one vulnerable program is the civilian space agency, NASA. To some, the expenditure of billions to send space missions to probe the odd comet or bounce a little robot around Mars must be sacrificed so as not to have to force Americans to pay for their own healthcare. However those people are woefully shortsighted, the future of America depends on outer space.

C'mon, you say. *You're joking. I like Tang as much as anybody else*, you might say, *but what has NASA done for me lately?* Well, let me tell you.

The High Ground
The exploration of outer space has been a competitive, but peaceful race for knowledge. Except for the odd spy satellite, space has been generally unarmed and demilitarized by the Outer Space Treaty of 1967 which reserves all of outer space for the good of mankind (the Space Treaty is part of the world order envisioned by American exceptionalism). The Space Treaty has been signed and ratified by all countries with even a remote chance of getting into outer space, but realistically it is the idealism of the United States that has preserved the peace in outer space. The Soviet Union signed the treaty because they knew that if they didn't they would have been staring down the barrels of an array of space weapons they couldn't match. The US has dominated space since Kennedy began the race for the moon.

But now space missions are being pushed back by decades, the shuttle program has been phased out and, because there is no replacement program for the shuttle, our astronauts have to hitch rides from other countries. If the US cannot maintain its dominance of outer space, the Outer Space Treaty might not be worth the paper it's written on.

Other countries, especially China, are expanding their space programs while we are cutting back. China recently shot down one of its own satellites just to prove that they can do it (of course we went and shot down one of ours to show that we can do it too). If the US abandons space, other countries may not be as altruistic as we are in maintaining outer space as a peaceful preserve for all of mankind.

Outer space is the high ground. Anyone who controls it will have a military advantage over all the other countries in the world. The US has dominated but not sought to control space for many decades. But if the US gives up space dominance for the sake of Obamacare, we will be making a fateful, and possibly deadly, decision. The US cannot allow any other nation to take the high ground.

The Final Frontier

An equally important, but somewhat more subtle, point is that outer space is truly the final frontier. America as we know it (or more correctly, as we remember it) is a frontier country: always restless, always growing, always expanding. There are many who think this not a virtue, but it is who we are. We are always marching to that distant horizon; mapping out new terrain; trailing settlers in our wake. Not all of us, of course. There were many shopkeepers back in the frontier towns that supplied their wares to the frontiersmen. There were many farmers in the settled lands, tradesmen in the bigger cities, mariners and fishermen and all the great variety of people needed to make a country run. But the national imagination was on the explorers on the frontier. The dime novels were about the cowboys, frontiersmen and explorers who tamed the western frontier.

Of course, other countries had their explorers. America wouldn't exist without them. Many came here from the old country to explore the wide-open reaches of the American continent. Those left behind had a different vision than those restless roamers filling up North America. Are we fated to become those placid homebodies watching others leaving for the new territories? Outer space, the final frontier, is essential to the American psyche.

Physicist Stephen Hawking agrees that space travel is essential for human survival. He is quoted as saying that humanity would not survive another 1,000 years "without escaping beyond our fragile planet." We need to make sure that America not only participates in this effort but leads it.

The Private Sector

During the frontier days of American history, it was often the government that followed the explorers and frontiersmen into the west. In the beginning of the space age, it was government that led us to the final frontier (primarily to compete with the Soviet Union). At the dawn of the 21st century entrepreneurs and adventurers are pushing the envelope of space with more and more projects to take man into space without government involvement. This represents the true frontier spirit and the US government should seek to develop its space capacity by offering opportunities to these bold entrepreneurs.

Entrepreneur Elon Musk, in addition to creating electric car company Tesla, also formed the space exploration company SpaceX. SpaceX is already delivering cargo to the international Space Station with its free-flying spacecraft Dragon and hopes to soon transport astronauts. Musk, born in South Africa, gives proof to my contention that there are potential Americans all over the world. These people are drawn to America for its opportunities and often become American citizens, as Musk did in 2002.

This is a typical progression in America. The government does the initial basic research and early implementation. The government is usually not interested in the science for science's sake and certainly not in the commercial potential of the research. While the government doesn't compete for market share or profits, as do companies in the private sector, it does compete on the world stage with other countries. It is not profit but survival that drives governments. That was what drove the creation of the Internet. The Internet was one of the creations of the Defense Advanced Research Projects Agency (DARPA).

In most countries, the science uncovered by this research remains within the state intelligence apparatus, buried deep within the vaults of some bland government edifice. I am sure that DARPA has some projects that we know nothing about but many are known and are being developed in cooperation with the private sector. Civilian applications to military technology have changed our lives (remember the Tang).

DARPA and NASA need to be supported and enhanced. They must not become the underfunded stepchildren to "non-discretionary" spending. We must set our goals high and then go out and achieve them.

Energy Policy! What's That?

When I first started writing this book, oil was over $100 per barrel. As I revise this chapter, oil is $45 per barrel and headed south (note to author: be careful about using market quotes in book – oil now $55/bbl). What is going on? In order to understand what is happening and its implications we need to look at how energy has affected the United States, economically, strategically and politically. More important, I had to completely rewrite this chapter. What a drag!

Why do we need an energy policy? The free market economic system gives us access to copious amounts of energy from a wide variety of sources. This is true. But these sources of energy all have their limitations.

All our energy comes from basically four sources, each of which has its own unique problems. The sources of energy are: hydrocarbons (which includes oil, gas, coal and wood), nuclear power, hydropower, and a wide variety of alternative energy sources. Hydrocarbons create carbon dioxide pollution along with a number of other pollutants (although some hydrocarbons produce more pollution than others). Nuclear energy has a problem with the disposal of waste products, which can remain radioactive for many centuries. Also, the fear of meltdowns and accidents is real, both Fukushima and Chernobyl spread radiation thousands of miles from the site of the reactor. Hydroelectricity generated from dams is limited by topography and some say also disrupts the migratory habits of fish, which are a necessary element in their reproductive cycle. The widespread use of alternative energy sources (solar, wind, geothermal) requires new technological advances to be economically viable.

The critical factor about energy is that energy is fundamental to all other industry and economic activity in the world; the sources of energy are often not located in places where it is needed (it requires transportation on a massive scale); delivering it requires massive investment in capital; some energies are not very transportable (geothermal) while others are not very storable (wind, electricity); much of the energy business is trans-national in nature,; and it carries drastic implications for the environment in which we and other creatures must live. So it is no easy thing to meet our energy needs.

More importantly, for the last fifty years we have been dependent on foreign countries for much of our energy needs (primarily oil and its derivatives). This dependence on foreign oil gave monopoly power to a small handful of countries that could control the price of oil. This pricing power was an political and economic weapon in the hands of countries not in line (and often opposed) to US foreign policy. Our foreign policy was constrained by our dependence on oil and forced in directions we would otherwise not have taken. Would we be up to our eyeballs in the Mideast quagmire if we were not dependent on that oil? What policy choices did we forego in order to keep the oil flowing?

And what has our government in Washington done about this situation? Well, like most other difficult problems facing our government, Washington has done - nothing.

Rather it has been our private sector entrepreneurs that have made the most progress in solving our problems (hint: why don't we let them take a crack at some of our other vexing dilemmas?).

Since the Arab Oil Embargo in 1973, the Organization of Petroleum Exporting Countries (OPEC) has been able to control the international price of oil by adjusting the levels of oil production of its members. The price of oil declined in absolute and real terms in the eighties and nineties due to new non-OPEC producers coming on line but remained significantly above previous levels. Throughout this period, the US was always a price-taker because, although we are a large producer of oil, we consumed far more than we produced.

Because oil-consuming nations can purchase oil from anywhere in the world on the international oil market, disruptions in supplies of oil in a single country can impact the international price of oil. Being a price-taker meant that we were dependent on the oil production of others and that the necessity of keeping oil flowing was a huge constraint on our foreign policy. Our addiction to foreign oil meant that we had to put aside our democratic principles in order to maintain that flow, much like a drug addict abandons all his ethical instincts in order to get the next fix. The US struck a kind of "grand bargain" under which the US would buy oil from the middle east and guarantee the security of certain countries (Saudi Arabia), and in exchange OPEC oil would flow and prices would be denominated in US Dollars, giving the US and its dollar enormous clout in the world as the reserve currency.

Since the 911 attack the United States has been deeply involved in the Middle East, partly to avenge the attack but also to protect the precious supply lines that guarantee the flow of oil. The Mideast turmoil drove oil prices to over $100 a barrel and we were advised to become accustomed to the new normal.

But the free market works in funny ways, at least in the minds of politicians and economic planners. High oil prices have generated a wave of innovation in oil production. Wildcat oil producers came up with a technique called hydraulic fracturing (fracking) as well as horizontal drilling to get at previously hard to get at oil and gas. US production of oil and gas has risen rapidly and the US is approaching energy independence, a goal always promised, but never delivered by the politicians in Washington. (Note: we still import oil but can export other forms of energy as well as petroleum derivatives like gas).

US oil production has completely changed the equation of the oil market that has existed since the seventies. It is clear that US energy production is now the driving force in the world oil market. Oil prices have gone down dramatically and there is no end in sight. The Organization of Petroleum Exporting Countries (OPEC) under the leadership of Saudi Arabia has adopted a strategy of continuing high levels of production in order to drive down prices in an attempt to bankrupt the new sources of supply from America. As a low cost producer, this strategy makes a lot of sense for Saudi Arabia but it has a very different impact on other producers. Higher cost producers like Venezuela and Ecuador are facing significant losses that will impact their economic strategies and financing capabilities. Other producers facing sanctions, such as Russia and Iran, will find those sanctions biting much harder.

The falling oil prices also are pinching oil companies from Texas to North Dakota. New production has ground to halt and many of these companies face bankruptcy (fracking is a high cost production method, needing a market price of $50 per barrel or more). Saudi Arabia and other low cost producers are hoping that they can drive these new interlopers out from what they consider their proprietary market.

The lower oil price provides a strategic benefit to the United States. Previous oil price declines were temporary because the United States consumed far more energy than it produced, contributing to a very large trade deficit. But more than deficits, the lack of US production made us dependent on foreign oil and this affected (or rather infected) our formulation of foreign policy. Dependency on foreign oil has kept us kowtowing to oppressive regimes, medieval monarchies and tin-pot dictators for far too long. It is time for the United States to take hold of its energy future and resist the attempt to bankrupt our energy independence.

The US Strategic Petroleum Reserve (SPR) was designed to protect us from temporary supply disruptions, usually caused by political events such as the Arab Oil Embargo of the seventies. But with a reserve of only around 40 days' supply, the SPR is hardly strategic. It is more a tactical reserve that was designed to assuage the concerns of US consumers than as a strategic ability to control our own energy future. As noted above, OPEC is trying to drive US shale oil producers bankrupt and with it our energy independence. As such, OPEC under Saudi leadership is acting in direct contravention to US strategic interests. We cannot allow this to happen.

But the US does not need to produce energy in order to be energy independent. We need only the ability to produce the energy. Even if all the shale oil producers go bankrupt, the oil and gas is still locked up within those shale formations. The US should acquire the shares of these failing companies in order to protect our production capabilities. The price should offer a reasonable return to the owners as they have provided the United States a vital strategic capability and deserve reasonable compensation for their service.

This would appear to go against our free market principles; however, oil is being used as a weapon against US strategic interests by other countries while we have floundered for years without an energy policy to protect ourselves. The government should not allow OPEC (which is run by other governments) to attack the interests of our private sector, especially when that private sector is providing so much strategic value. War is no longer a matter of planes, ships and tanks; it is also cyber-attacks, non-state militants and economics.

The ability to turn the shale oil spigot on or off would make the United State the price leader for the international oil market. We would replace the Organization of Petroleum Exporting Countries (OPEC) with the Controlling Petroleum Exporting Country (CPEC). This would liberate us from the shackles of the Middle East. We would be free from having to ingratiate ourselves to kings and sheiks that use the money from oil exports to fund the export of fundamentalist Wahhabi Islam and the financing of terrorism. Without oil money these petty princes might have to join the twenty-first century, offering their citizens productive employment instead of oil entitlements. It would also limit the ability of countries opposed to our foreign policy that use oil windfall profits to threaten our allies and undermine the spread of democratic institutions around the world. We would be able to base our foreign policy on American democratic principles rather than economic necessity.

It will take bold action to seize this opportunity that has fallen into the lap of the current administration, an administration not known for taking decisive action on the foreign stage. If the current administration does not move to take advantage of this opportunity, Republicans should pass the enabling legislation to move forward on this matter. I would like to see how President Obama could justify vetoing such legislation.

The "Inevitability" of Socialism

"Karl Marx got it right, at some point capitalism can destroy itself."
Nouriel Roubini, Economist, NYU

"We will bury you", Nikita Khrushchev, Premier, USSR

Each year it seems the US government grows a little bit bigger. Every January the President includes in his State of the Union address a laundry lists of new things the government can do for you: a list of benefits or giveaways to tie you more closely to government. With each step the welfare society grows, enveloping more and more of our daily lives. Will this encroaching tide of government morph from the welfare state to the socialist state?

Friedrich Hayek felt so. He felt that big government inevitably grew bigger; that when a government program proved ineffective that the response was not to get rid of the program but to increase its scope and coverage (the US education system comes to mind). He also believed that with each increase, we the people gave up a bit of freedom, our precious sovereignty.

What is the cause of this ever-encroaching tide of government? How can we stop or should we even attempt to?

There are a number of reasons why government tends to grow ever larger. The reasons are rooted in our basic human nature, which is why it takes discipline and resolve to resist this tendency.

<u>Government Growth as a Result of Recession</u>
As noted previously, the free market economic system is subject to booms and busts. But booms and busts inevitably cause harm to many people in the short run. Jobs are lost. Savings are wiped out. The people demand that something be done. They turn to Washington: Do something! Politicians who counsel patience will soon be looking for jobs themselves. (Ask Herbert Hoover.)

Keynesian economic theory offers a convenient way out. Deficit spending and government handouts are, according to theory, supposed to maintain aggregate demand that supports the economy and provides jobs. New programs are added to channel the deficit money to the needy and the additional bureaucrats required to process the payments only add to aggregate demand.

The deficit spending is usually also accompanied by increased regulations to assure that this will "never happen again" as well as to punish the perpetrators of this economic crime (because somebody must be at fault).

If these measures were temporary, such actions might seem reasonable. Once the economy returned to growth the debt that financed the deficit spending could be repaid and the extra government workers could be let go to return to work in the private sector. (Keynes, as we have noted previously, himself had this in mind.)

Wait a minute! Time out! Our Keynesian friends will say. *We need the additional bureaucracy to control the excesses of the private sector and to make sure that a recession doesn't happen again.* And the new government workers? No way they want to go back into the cutthroat world of the private sector, especially if they are unionized.

So the government doesn't downsize after the recession is over. Government is a little bigger. It takes a little bigger bite of the national economy. There are a few more government workers. But, so what? If it prevents recessions, it's worth it. Except it doesn't. Booms and busts are part of the free market economy. Recessions occur every 7 or 8 years, so when the next recession hits (even little ones are likely to be labeled the worst since the Great Depression) the response of our Keynesian friends in government is to push deficit spending, grow the size of the government and take another little bite out of the national economy.

Even in an expanding economy there are people that want additional benefits from the government. Some of these people truly need help; the disabled, the discriminated. Targeted programs could be beneficial for these people. But targeted programs (or temporary programs) do not have the kind of electoral impact our politicians seek. So the programs are larger and more permanent than the need requires.

The Lack of Creative Destruction in Government

There is another reason why government slowly and inevitably grows in size. The concept of creative destruction does not exist in government (except in the military however there the destructive takes precedence over the creative). Inefficient programs continue on aimlessly for years or decades. The Rural Electrification Administration, created by Roosevelt as part of the new deal with a goal to bring power to rural areas, continued on until 1994 even though rural electrification was essentially completed by 1950. It continues on today although it has morphed into the Rural Utilities Service.

Even failed programs continue on seemingly forever. Even worse, the failure is almost never attributed to an ill-conceived or poorly executed program, but rather to the non-compliance or intransigence of the people affected by the program. As Hayek noted, this brings about the most evil aspect of this creeping socialism, forced compliance. The government uses the coercive power of the state to force compliance to these cockeyed programs dreamed up in some ivory tower or smoky backroom (of course, it's not tobacco any more). The employer mandate of the Affordable Care Act, that requires companies to provide health insurance to employees, is a good example. Likewise, uninsured individuals not taking advantage of this "benefit" are fined.

Government Programs can Exacerbate Problems

Another element is that government programs often exacerbate the problem they are intended to resolve. During the great recession unemployment benefits were extended from 26 weeks to 99 weeks, Legislators trying to cap this benefit and staunch the outflow of funds were portrayed as heartless and mean. Now come reports that it is more profitable to remain on welfare than to go back to work. This is a contributing cause to the fall of participation in the workforce from 66.1% in 2004 to 63.7% in 2012. That's millions of people! Worse than that, in 2014, six years after the Great Recession and during a modest expansion, workforce participation is still declining, reaching 62.7% in 2014.

Crowding Out Civil Society

Big government not only expropriates the economy from the private sector, it also crowds out civil society as well. In the early days of our social contract, many of the functions needed to hold our society together were performed by civil society, groups of citizens banding together to achieve a common goal. In the early days of our Republic, the central government was very small and far away – many days travel to the capital. In rural communities, towns and cities, citizens formed organizations or groups to provide services that the central and local governments were not capable of delivering. In 1731 Benjamin Franklin and others founded the Library Company of Philadelphia to create a library of books (rare and precious commodities back then) that would provide intellectual backing to the discussions of Franklin and his friends. The Library Company still exists today, but in most towns the city government provides library services. This is a rather benign example of government taking over the functions of civil society. But as government has grown, more and more of the functions of our civil institutions have been taken over by the state.

This progression to convert civil society into government institutions is inevitable as the size of government grows. As the government takes over more of the economy, these supplemental services must also be controlled. As big government morphs into socialist government, this conversion becomes essential, as independent voices would be seen as a critique of the government plans. In socialist and communist countries, the state not only takes over the means of productions but also the means of social networking and all that involves. The state is the answer to everything.

The Morph to Socialism

So how does a country go through a transition from big government, to the welfare state, to a socialist state (and eventually a communist state)? The changes are political and economic but also cultural.

We have seen the retreat of democracy and the Washington Consensus in several countries in Latin America. The transition began as people became disaffected by the slow pace of change under democratic governments, and became enamored with populist demagogues such as Hugo Chavez who promised more rapid change. These countries espousing socialism of the twenty-first century are now floundering under years of economic mismanagement. Change for the better may not be in the offing as free and fair elections are now hard to come by in these countries.

Europe has a much more advanced welfare state than the United States. But Europe has reached a point of inflexion and it is hard to determine which course it will take going forward or even if it will be able to hold together. The large welfare states of Europe, sometimes comprising 40 to 50 percent of the economy, are now having problems fulfilling their social benefit obligations in spite of heavy tax loads.

The heavy state participation in the economy has slowed growth. Government enterprises operate on a different set of principles than the private sector. They are not profit oriented and are usually not great innovators, which slows economic growth. Progressives assert that by eliminating profit and unnecessary middlemen, the state can provide service to the people more efficiently and cheaply. That may be true in theory, but it is rarely case in actuality. Free market societies have always been able to supply more goods at better quality and at lower prices, than any other system. The slow growth inherent in large welfare states makes it difficult to generate the revenue needed to fulfill their benefit obligations.

It is difficult to tell how things will work out. As this is written, Greece is trending socialist while other countries turn to the right. The Euro is tanking and most of the countries in the EU haven't come back from the 2007/2008 financial crisis.

The slow growth endemic to large welfare states generates discontent among the citizens and the urge for the government to do more. Populists will point out anecdotal evidence of the government's poor response to the people's suffering. High taxes needed to support the giant welfare state cause capital flight, further reducing surplus needed to spur growth.

The transition to a socialist state is rarely smooth. Civil strife often precedes the conversion as occurred in Venezuela and Bolivia. The democratic institutions that allow socialist demagogues to accede to power are usually then abandoned or corrupted because the state cannot allow any recidivism from the socialist goals.

The Seduction of Socialism

Under socialism economic values are subordinated to other, supposedly higher, values for the benefit of all mankind. This appeals to our better nature, but it's a setup. There are a number of problems with this benign view of socialism.

A monastery is a Christian commune where economic values are subordinated to Christian values. Many of these communes are relatively self-sufficient and have existed for centuries if not millennia. The monks join voluntarily and live an ascetic lifestyle of privation and prayer. Their values are established by the church and their lives are dedicated to those values. What are socialist values? While the monks can point to religious or philosophical values as their guide, socialist values appear inherently materialistic but are actually aspirational. Marx envisioned a world where people subordinated their individualism for the benefit of the community. Marxism is not just a change of economic systems; it requires a change of people. Gulags and worker re-education centers are not prisons so much as a mechanism to destroy the individual and replace him with Socialist Man. This Socialist Man has no loyalty to himself, his family or his god. His only loyalty is to the state.

Socialism for the 21st Century

There is an eerie parallel between the recent rise of a movement promoting socialism for the 21st century and that of the rise (and ultimate fall) of a similar political movement in the 20th century. Both leaders of these movements led abortive attempts to overthrow existing democratic governments; both were thrown in jail for their efforts. Both leaders were eventually released from jail, returned to leadership of their political movements and eventually were democratically elected to lead their countries. Both leaders were given to bombastic oration and suffered from megalomaniacal narcissism. Both leaders used nationalism as the justification and state control of the means of production as the basis of the economy. Adolph Hitler and Hugo Chavez indeed had much in common. Once in power, the democracy that they used to achieve power was choked off.

After Chavez' cancer-shortened life, Venezuela has now embarked on a downward spiral under the leadership of Chavez' chosen successor, Nicolas

Maduro. Maduro has an even shakier grasp of socialist ideology than Chavez. The marginal improvements in the lives of poor Venezuelans in the early days of the Chavez regime could not be sustained. This was due, in part, by incompetence but also to the inherent slow growth nature of the socialist economy. It is dangerous to think that Venezuela's problems are only due to incompetence. Economic stagnation is the ultimate fate of socialist economies. The coming collapse of Venezuela will be a spectacle to behold.

The Inevitability of Socialism

There are many people who think their lives would be infinitely better if they could use the vast wealth of the one-percenters. The welfare state is the first step in gaining access to that wealth. When the heavily taxed wealth of the one-percenters proves insufficient to meet the demands of the masses, socialism is the next logical step. But the people who willingly, even eagerly, embrace socialism will find that dragging down the elite still doesn't solve their problems.

The only inevitability of socialism is eventual collapse and decay. Remember Adam Smith's pin and all the economic DNA required to create a simple straight pin? Even if computers could be programmed to manage the millions of variables that would be needed to make centralized planning effective, the human operators would lack the capacity (or will) to continuously input all that data. Instead of diversification and constant product improvements and innovations as exemplified in the free market system, socialist production will tend to reduce variety and will push toward a few approved products that ease the centralize planning process and increase economies of scale (at your expense). Socialized medicine will have only approved procedures – experimentation and innovation will cease.

At best, the future under socialism would be a dull drab world with worker drones trudging to the factory to produce the same old stuff. All personal services (to the extent they exist) will be proportioned out by bureaucrats, with your future determined by your socialist masters and an omnipresent secret police to stifle dissent.

That's why the Soviet Union collapsed. Under their Soviet masters, the USSR's population was declining and alcohol abuse became a widespread way to cope with the ennui of Soviet life. That's why China abandoned communism (except for the dictatorship part) and embraced a semblance of the free market system. That's inevitability for you!

The New Dark Age

The success of socialism as a world economic order would be the beginning of a new dark age for the human population of the world. Economic growth would slow to a crawl and then stagnate. The cornucopia of products and services that we are accustomed to would dwindle as economic planners opted for efficiency over choice — long production runs of the identical product.

If combined with radical environmentalism, socialism would require a drastic reduction in the population of the earth. Food lines and ration cards would be the order of the day.

Socialism and radical environmentalism go well together because both movements require a brutal dictatorship to enforce their programs. Freedom would be wiped from the face of the earth for decades or even centuries. What modern technology remained would be dedicated to the preservation of the state. Innovation, to the extent it existed, would be dedicated to advancing the power of the state. The arts and literature would be dedicated to extolling the glories of the state. North Korea is not an outlier of the socialist universe; it is the epitome of the socialist state. People who tell you otherwise are lying to you or deluding themselves.

Socialism cannot achieve its goals while there remains one bastion of the free market in the world. At the height of Soviet power, many people in the world were searching for a model to emulate. Many were attracted to the Soviet communist model. But the United States and its European allies were a beacon of freedom and prosperity to people all over the world. The Soviet puppets in East Germany had to build a wall to keep their people from fleeing their tyranny. The people of Cuba flocked to the port of Mariel to escape Fidel's Caribbean "paradise" (and still do).

The Soviets created the Comintern (Communist International) to foment communist revolution in all the countries around the world. The goal of Comintern was to fight "by all available means, including armed force, for the overthrow of the international bourgeoisie and for the creation of an international Soviet republic". The economic growth and technological advancement of free market economies are ever-present dangers to socialist regimes and must be destroyed.

Human progress has advanced because when one civilization collapsed or was overrun, another eventually took its place. The fall of Rome led to many centuries of chaos and war. Ancient knowledge was lost, books were burned. But some fragments of this knowledge survived to form the basis of the renaissance and later the enlightenment. Worldwide socialism would make this recovery much more difficult. It would extend the dark age for many centuries. The end would not be bloodless as was the case of the collapse of the Soviet Union. With a tragic cost of life, the survivors would emerge having lost centuries if not millennia of knowledge.

I do not want my children and grandchildren to live in this unholy lost age. I cannot leave them a legacy of despair and hopelessness. The purpose of this book is to a better path for the future and to convince people that socialism is no paradise but a dead end.

The True Cost of Going Green

Many environmentalists will tell you that the cost of going green is minuscule, making you feel guilty at not putting out even the small effort necessary to save the planet. And most articles discussing the costs of going green will tell you about the costs of buying a Prius, or of putting solar panels on your roof. But these types of discussions do not even touch on the true cost of going green.

Climate Change
The world's climate does appear to be changing although the change from calling it Global Warming to Climate Change is an indication of some of the uncertainty as to what is actually going on. Although some people may scoff at the impact that man has had on the environment, for the sake of argument let us accept as true Al Gore's contention that the increasing levels of carbon dioxide produced by our modern civilization are responsible for the rise in global temperatures. Will all of us driving Priuses save the planet?

I think not. There are greater implications involved in halting the increase in carbon dioxide in the atmosphere than driving Priuses or throwing solar panels on your roof.

First of all, any solution to the rise in carbon dioxide must be global. It will do little good if the United States cuts its carbon emissions if China, Indonesia, Brazil and India continue to spew out carbon dioxide. Keep in mind that carbon based energy is cheap. It's what powered our industrial revolution and developing countries have too little surplus to use anything else to power their industrialization.

But if developing countries cannot use carbon based energy to industrialize, how will they be able to meet the development needs of their people? They don't have the money to build nuclear power plants and others sources of energy are even more expensive. The answer is they can't do it without carbon-based power. They will not be able to develop and grow and provide their peoples with a decent way of life. The only solution would be a massive redistribution of wealth from the US and Europe toward developing countries to the south.

This redistribution of wealth will come about while the economies of the US and Europe are stagnating due to restrictions on the use of carbon. Would the free peoples of the developed world be willing to make such an enormous sacrifice to save the planet?

Global Dictatorship

It will require a global dictatorship of enormous power to redirect resources around the globe in the face of massive resentment of the people involved. The distribution of wealth and resources would have to be centrally planned making the dictatorship a communist or socialist dictatorship of enormous scope and power. Stalin and Mao had no hesitation in moving vast numbers of people and reassigning land and wealth as they saw fit. Of course, millions died in the process. In order to assure a stop to global warming (assuming that carbon dioxide is the cause) the global dictatorship will move millions more. And millions will die.

Demodernization

Without modern farming based on machines consuming carbon based fuels and fertilizers from petroleum products, agricultural productivity will decline drastically. Of course the global dictatorship will proclaim worldwide vegetarianism as belching cows with methane-producing poop will be banned (except for members of the Politburo). How many humans can agriculture support without tractors and fertilizers? A billion? A couple of billion? Whatever the total, billions must die to save the earth.

And after the worst genocide the world has ever known, how will we live? In some sort of pre-industrial 17th century agriculture based economy subject to the rule of a global dictator that subjects our freedoms to ecological rules, keeps most of us as agricultural workers practicing primitive farming supporting a small elite of green party apparatchiks and quasi-scientific ecologists?

What happens if the world keeps getting warmer?

A Principled Environmental Policy

Don't get me wrong. I enjoy a clean environment as much as anybody. But we need to look at things differently if we want to get anywhere.

The Right to Pollute
We have an affirmative right to pollute the environment. All human bodies create waste products: feces, urine, carbon dioxide. We have a right to life but if we can't rid our bodies of these waste products we would die. Therefore we have a right to pollute the world with our waste products.

Our body's wastes are by-products of the biological processes to give us the energy needed to live. Producing energy results in a lot of waste products, whether it is our normal biological functions or coal burning energy plants. Our modern society needs energy to function and that energy creates a lot of waste products (i.e.; pollution). There are no easy answers to the problem of pollution from all kinds of energy. Even green and renewable energy sources are fraught with problems.

Bjorn Lomborg wrote in the Wall Street Journal that the production of an all-electric vehicle such as the Nissan Leaf requires 16,000 more pounds of carbon than a regular car, much of that coming from the production of the lithium batteries needed to run the car. This carbon footprint hole can be eliminated over time through the usage of the electric car. Keep in mind however that the car still needs energy and right now most of that energy comes from fossil fuel burning power plants. As a result it takes a long time for the electric vehicle to erase the carbon footprint hole that began with its production. Also keep in mind that lithium batteries don't last forever. That electric car's carbon footprint goes back in the hole whenever it needs to replace its batteries. Eventually the electric car will begin to provide a benefit to the environment but that gain is fairly negligible in the overall scheme of things.

Other forms of green and renewable energy have their problems as well. Hydroelectric dams disrupt the spawning activities of the fish in the river. Large wind turbines disrupt the migratory patterns of birds and could cause other problems. A study published by the Wildlife Society Bulletin stated that wind turbines kill 573,000 birds and 880,000 bats each year. A lot of energy is required to produce solar panels and the process creates toxic by-products if they don't reprocess these materials.

This doesn't mean we shouldn't use these products or try other new ideas of how to produce energy more cleanly and efficiently. It just means there is no silver bullet. Modern society requires energy and energy production causes pollution in one form or another.

Mitigation

That leaves us with the challenge of mitigating the problems created by the waste and pollution produced by energy production and the other products necessary for our modern lifestyle. Waste and pollution are challenges for the free market economy because in most cases these by-products have little or no value while their mitigation is very costly. In the early days of industrialization there was virtually no attempt to mitigate the production of waste products. The result of this inattention was cities choked by smoke and soot, acid rain and rivers that caught fire (the Cuyahoga River in Ohio caught fire numerous times). When I lived in New York City, newscasters regularly warned against jogging because of poor air quality (of course it was worse in Mexico City where the birds fell out of the sky, dead from heavy metal poisoning).

In reaction to this poisoning of our environment, Richard Nixon created the Environmental Protection Agency in 1970. The EPA has been a lightning rod for controversy ever since. Rules to limit toxic emissions into the sky and the discharge of pollutants into our rivers can be very expensive. Industrial corporations and their army of lobbyists fight against almost all regulation with mindless fanaticism. It is an ideological dictate of many politicians on the right that regulation is bad and that environmental regulation is particularly bad.

But as was noted earlier, regulation is one of the key functions of government and is necessary to maintain the social contract. The right to pollute is offset by the right to breathe unpolluted air and drink uncontaminated water. The right to pollute ends when it affects other people's rights.

It is obviously impossible to reconcile the right to an unpolluted environment with the right to pollute. As a practical matter, modern civilization would be impossible without some by-products and pollution. And we must keep in mind that the incremental costs to mitigate pollutants and other by-products are not linear but increase exponentially. At some point it just doesn't make sense to invest more money into mitigation of pollutants (it is my personal belief, not backed up by research, that the slow growth of the 1970's – stagflation - was due in large part to environmental regulation that channeled new investment into pollutant mitigation instead of increased production, thereby stifling GDP growth).

Conclusion

Pollution is an unavoidable side effect of civilization and economic growth. The production of energy upon which our civilization is based is an especially dirty process. The developed countries have made substantial gains in reducing pollution as a percentage of GDP but still are very large producers of pollutants. The less developed countries say, "Don't force us to remain impoverished in the name of stopping global warming. We are entitled to development as well".

It would be easy to blame the free market economic system for this sad state of affairs. It was the industrial revolution that created the need for more and more energy to power economic growth. But keep in mind that some of the worst polluters were command and control economies of the eastern bloc.

So the United States cannot solve the global pollution problem by itself. But that doesn't mean it must do nothing. Innovation and technological advancement (the hallmarks of the free market economy) are the pathways to resolve this difficult issue. It is the role of the social contract to create sustainable policies and regulations to manage pollution.

An Educated Citizenry

I think we have lost sight of why taxpayers fund public schools. It is not so Dick and Jane can feel good about themselves and have high esteem. It is also not so that teachers and school administrators can have job security no matter the outcomes of their teaching efforts.

The purpose of public education is to prepare young people to be productive citizens. The public schools are failing miserably at this task. The study prepared by Mary Meeker of Kleiner Perkins tells the story. While the performance of US students is below mediocre our kids rank at the top in self-confidence and self-esteem. High confidence without underlying skills is just a way to get hurt. If all we wanted was to have our kids feel good about themselves they could just stay home and play video games all day and stop wasting the taxpayers' money.

A good education is an essential element of the social contract and the level playing field. If certain segments of our population are allowed to flounder in school it will be impossible for them to achieve the equality of opportunity that is the foundation of the American dream. We cannot afford to allow American schools to fail to develop educated citizens with the discipline needed for a productive life. School systems and their administrators and teachers must be held to this standard. Common Core testing is not sufficient.

It is time to make some changes. The time of teaching sinecures without regards to results is over. It is time to instill some discipline on our teaching corps as well as our students.

I think most teachers will welcome this change. The teachers I have known have been good decent people. It is the system that has let them down. They often feel helpless to control order in the classroom, hamstrung by labyrinthine regulations (often required by their own unions) that restrict their ability to maintain discipline over little Dick and Jane (or Antwaan and Maria).

A school trying to enforce a dress code required one little darling to ditch all her body piercings before attending classes. Not only did the little darling squeal in protest, her loving parent sued the school saying that she and the little darling belonged to the Church of Body Modification and that the piercings were her expression of freedom of religion (and the good old ACLU backed her up and won in court). How will children ever have respect for their elders with this kind of nonsense? It's no wonder that discipline has fallen apart in US schools (I wouldn't advise the little darling to try that nonsense in a Chinese school).

It's not that I am against freedom. This book is all about freedom. But citizenship involves more than rights and freedoms, it also include duties and responsibilities. If an adult wants to have nose piercings and tats, I have no problem with that; but children need discipline and need to show respect to their school and teachers. Schools need the ability to maintain discipline in the classroom and protection from crackpots like the little darling's mother.

The Rights of Children

Like all human beings in America, children have rights. However the rights of children differ from those of adults. When we talk about personal liberty and individual rights, we are discussing the rights of adults. Adults can make rational decisions about exercising their rights (although don't always employ this ability) and are considered to be in agreement with the social contract. Children are considered to be too immature to enter into contracts and therefore are not members of community governed by the social contract but, rather, wards of the community. They deserve the protection, not only of their parents, but also of all adults in the community.

Children are too young to understand the nature of the social contracts and the freedoms and responsibilities it provides to citizens. Scientific research has shown that the frontal lobes of young men are not fully developed until their mid-twenties (although the age of majority is 21 or 18 depending on the circumstances). Not only can children not enter into contracts, children are not held to adult standards of criminal responsibility unless this assumption is waived by the court. Because children cannot bear the full responsibilities of adult citizens, their rights are likewise limited.

So if children do not enjoy the full rights of adults, what rights do they have? It would be nice if we could say that children have the right of love and affection but that is impossible to grant. Children do have the right to be protected. They have the right to be protected from adults who would take advantage of them or do them harm. They have the right to be protected from other children as well. Most importantly, they have the right to be protected from themselves because they cannot always understand the consequences of their actions.

Agent or Delegate?

As children grow, they spend more and more time away from parents and family. Much of this time is spent at school. Schools, whether public or private, are institutions of the social contract charged with preparing young people for adulthood as full participants of that contract.

A question arises however. Is the school an agent of the child's parent or does the school have delegated parental authority? As a practical matter, it would be impossible for the school to acting as an agent of the parents as they would be directly responsible for all the elements of the child's education (as they are when home schooled). Group learning would be impossible as each child would have a different curricula, different texts, etc. The parents would be overburdened with all the work and study necessary to prepare the teacher for each child.

So the school is clearly acting under delegated authority and prepares lessons, text and classes within certain parameters (usually determined by a school board or other governmental authority). Under this delegated authority, the school would also have the ability to create and enforce dress codes and other forms of discipline as necessary and properly approved.

Boundaries and Security

Children are always testing limits. This is what they do. This is how they grow. It is the responsibility of their parents and other adults to identify clear boundaries of acceptable behavior. Within those boundaries they are safe to play and learn.

There are some parents who make poor choices about the boundaries of acceptable behavior such as the woman who allowed her child to get tattoos and body piercings. In these cases it is up to the community through the schools and courts to protect children against irresponsible adults.

Within the acceptable boundaries children need to feel safe. In the madhouse of today's public schools it is as if it was being run by the patients. Teachers and administrators appear helpless in the face aggressive students who know no boundaries (my kids were totally traumatized by junior high school but could not communicate this to me until they were adults). I believe that many of the school shooters we see these days feel that they were unprotected and betrayed by the system, leaving violence and/or suicide their only resort.

Discipline and Love

Some parents are afraid to discipline their children for going beyond the acceptable boundaries of behavior. They want to be liked by their children. They want to be friends with their children. They fear losing the love of their children. But without clear boundaries, children fail to understand what is acceptable behavior. They become self-centered and demanding. Their sense of right and wrong becomes warped (this relates to the fairness problem we discussed previously). Their ability to become good citizens of the social contract is impaired.

It takes love to be able to properly discipline your children. Although children need disciple, they resist it. They will fight you all the way. They will say they hate you (and will meant it at the time). Many parents fear these words and hot emotions. But love does not encompass just the child's current situation. You have to think: what will this child be like as an adult. Will he or she be happy? Will he or she be a productive member of society?

Excessive discipline and excessive leniency both fail the child. We have societal mechanisms such as Child Protective Services that attempt to protect children (not always successfully) from abuse of which excessive discipline is an example. Excessive leniency is harder to define. It is less likely to cause physical harm to the child and so there are less societal protections in place. In the past schools demanded that students be respectful and maintained strict (sometimes harsh) discipline. These days schools can't even enforce a dress code. Children see this impotence and act accordingly.

The Duty of Adults

It is the duty of adults generally, as members of the community that comprises the social contract, to provide and support this boundary of security and protection. Of course parents don't like others disciplining their children even when they are running around a restaurant like a horde of barbarians.

Adults are citizens bound by the social contract. They enjoy the freedoms but are also bound by the rule of law. If they disagree with the law they are not free to violate it without suffering consequences, although they are free to try and get the law changed if they can convince enough of their fellow citizens.

Public schools are institutions of the social contract and their duty is to prepare children to enter into society. Private schools may have additional goals but they would lose their validity (and accreditation) if they did not fulfill their principal duties. In order for children to grow as their frontal lobes develop, these institutions must provide the secure circle of protection by providing clear boundaries. Parents (and teachers unions, the courts and various child advocates) need to allow these institutions to do their job.

Public Schools and the Social Welfare State

I am not much into conspiracy theories and it is a stretch to believe that it was all planned this way, but it is clear that the progressive thought process behind the social welfare state is the same thought process leading to the mediocratization of American public schools. The emphasis on self-esteem over performance and ability is paralleled by reconceptualization of charity as entitlements.

Well-educated, ambitious people do not make good citizens of the social welfare state. What better way to insure a placid malleable population than by educating them to believe that self-esteem is independent of performance r success. That the only outlet for ambition is in sports or entertainment. It is ancient Rome all over again: nothing but bread (welfare) and circuses (distraction).

Principled Policy

Part 3

Tacking to Our

New Course

So we have set a very ambitious agenda: fix the fiscal structure of government, restore the free market economy, change the entitlement mentality (including revamping the retirement and health systems), strengthen our military and foreign policies, and fix public education (oh, and don't forget, we have to get our asses back in space). Whew! That is a long list of very difficult, very complex problems to resolve. In order to do this we have to fix the broken political process in the US.

For decades (many decades) politics as usual has made government more complex, more opaque, more unresponsive and larger (much larger). But size alone is not the main problem. Our modern civilization requires a government capable of dealing with our modern complexities. Wal-Mart has sales of almost a half a trillion dollars and over two million employees worldwide. That is the equivalent of a small country. Other large companies have complex business processes that impact the economy, the environment and everyday citizens. It takes a large, sophisticated government to appropriately regulate these businesses in order to secure the level playing field required by the social contract.

Around the world we are faced with many rivals, enemies and potential enemies. We have to protect ourselves from enemies ranging from large countries to rogue terrorists. We must defend against weapons ranging from thermonuclear ICBMs to box cutters. We need a large and sophisticated military along with a robust foreign policy to provide for the common defense.

So size is a problem but it is not the problem. We need a government that can deal with these issues and that means that we have to deal with politics. The Founders felt that factions (i.e.; political parties) would lead to alternating factional domination and ultimately despotism. Nevertheless, our country fell into the morass of factionalism almost immediately. Today we are faced with a factional divide just as sharp as that between Adams and Jefferson.

This factional divide between progressives and conservatives, left and right, Democrats and Republicans has been papered over for decades. There has been no collegiality or compromise in government. Rather than building consensus, each faction has gone its separate ways, funding their divergent visions with debt. The cause of the current gridlock in Congress is not a sudden peckishness arising in our politicians: rather it is the realization that we can no longer continue down the divergent paths of these visions because our ability to finance both schemes with debt is running out.

The Revolutionary Spirit

In order to effectuate the monumental changes proposed in this book, we not only need to rethink how we structure the American Social Contract but also how to organize politically to be able to effectuate change.

The Founders of America were not conservatives they were revolutionaries. If the Founders were alive today I do not think they would be conservatives. I am pretty damn sure they wouldn't be progressives either. We need to take the principles on which America was founded and transform them for the 21st Century.

The societies, cultures and demographics of a country are dynamic entities. America has evolved into a very different country economically and politically from the small, rural backwater it was at the end of the eighteenth century. In the course of two hundred years we have become an industrial and military giant. Instead of living in fear of the great powers of Europe we are the sole super power of the world. A power that we have tried to use for the benefit and well being of the entire world, creating global institutions to promote peace, stability and economic growth.

We have lived through the Industrial Revolution, the Age of the Railroad, the Age of the Automobile, the Computer Age and the World Wide Web to reach a post-industrial society that we struggle to understand. The challenges we face are enormous and to a large extent unknown. Advances in medicine and computerized artificial intelligence will greatly alter the world we live in. Modern medicine is on the cusp of overcoming the frailties of old age and greatly extending our useful lives. At the same time, artificial intelligence will greatly reduce the demand for unskilled (and probably some skilled) labor. A reduced demand for labor combined with longer life spans could create a heaven or hell on earth. We have little idea and virtually no control of how this will impact our children and grandchildren.

The purpose of this book has been to review our founding principles and determine if they are still relevant in this strange new world we confront. I have striven (you may judge how effectually) to show that our founding principles are still relevant and perhaps even more essential in this evolving modern world. I have shown that the underpinnings of socialism are softheaded good intentions that have horrible results in the real world. Finally, we have come to learn that our human frailties undermine the working of the free market economic system as some try to circumvent the framework of trust created by the social contract. The goal of government must be to strengthen the framework of enforcement of the social contract in order to build trust among citizens so that society can function smoothly.

How do we rebuild that trust (and yes, even the pride) necessary for the proper functioning of the social contract?

The Demise of Traditional Political Parties

Around the world traditional political parties are breaking up and new parties are being formed. I first noticed this in Latin America where traditional parties, often controlled by the elite families, were abandoned by voters in favor of radical new parties. There was disenchantment with democracy in general throughout the continent. The Washington Consensus was supposed to have brought prosperity and greater freedoms for the people but results were limited as traditional elites gobbled up most of the new wealth. New political parties won left wing victories in Venezuela and Bolivia. A split in the left-of-center Liberal party in Honduras led to a coup-d'état and the eventual formation of a new far left party (although the party was not able to win the following election).

The same is happening across southern Europe with new political parties forming in Greece, Italy and Spain. In Greece, widespread disgust with corrupt traditional parties led to a Syriza victory in recent elections. Left-wing Syriza, however, has found that governing is more difficult than protesting and is now faced with a revolt among its adherents that could lead to a splitting up of this newly formed party.

We are seeing something similar in the United States during the 2016 election cycle. Non-politicians dominate the Republican field of presidential candidates as voters reject politics as usual from Washington insiders. A very wide spread in policy positions (combined with very nasty campaign tactics) could lead to a breakup of the GOP. Likewise the Democrats face a revolt within their ranks as an avowed socialist gave the traditional candidate a run for her money. While no breakup of the party seems eminent, hard-core socialists and left-wingers dominate the political agenda of the party leaving no alternative for more mainstream adherents. In the 21st century each presidential election cycle appears to have drawn each party more toward the radical elements within their ranks, which has led to a ideologically based political impasse in Washington.

It is reasonable that voters are becoming alienated from traditional political parties. The traditional parties have become divorced from the founding principles of America and locked in to policy positions that are designed to attract voters but that don't work in the real world.

Winnowing Traditional Values
Conservatism for conservatism's sake is a barren exercise. Things that worked in the past won't necessarily work in the future. Many traditional concepts are simply wrongheaded such as the Republicans' obsession with taxes. It is true that for much of our history the United States had a very small government and super low taxes on a national level (the government also had a budget surplus most of the time). But those times are gone and we can never go back.

Likewise, many people entwine Judeo-Christian values with traditional values. But the Founders studiously avoided religious references in the founding documents of our country. To them, the social contract was the product of reason, not faith. While the values based on Judeo-Christian principles and traditions are laudable, they are not shared by all citizens of our country, many of whom come from other religious traditions or who may be atheists. Jefferson stated that there should be "a wall of separation" between church and state as much to protect religion from the evil influences of politics as to keep religion from infecting the government.

The Valid Complaints of Progressives
Progressives in America make some valid points; the deck is stacked against many of the people in our society. This book has reviewed many of the ways that the social contract fails to live up to its obligations to the people. The trouble with progressives is not their complaints but in their solutions. They

seek to increase state power so that the state can confiscate the property of certain citizens in order to give it to other citizens. This not only destroys the liberty of the propertied citizens but that of the recipients of the confiscated goods who become little more than wards of the state. And when the property has all been confiscated and redistributed there is nothing left but the state.

But the problem is not the distribution of property but in the capture of the social contract by special interests. The progressive solution does little to change this problem and in fact is dependent on its continuation.

A New Dedication

We need to rededicate ourselves to fully implementing the social contract among United States citizens based on the principles established by the Founders. This book has tried to establish the case for many of these basic principles; personal liberty, equality before the law, equality of opportunity, respect for the rights of others, free market economics, sound fiscal policy, future generations free of the burden of excessive debt and American exceptionalism.

History has shown that we have often fallen short of the full implementation of these ideals. If we want to remedy this situation we have to examine why we have fallen short and failed to live up to these, admittedly, high standards.

We have seen that the fault usually lies with us, the people. Many citizens try to capture the system for their personal benefit. Others try to ignore standards of conducts for their convenience or profit. But people make up all societies so other economic and political systems suffer many of the same problems or worse.

It is through the institutions and procedures that we establish to protect and nourish the integrity of the social contract that we can flourish. Government is one of these institutions: ordained by the people to guard the integrity of the social contract. But government was intended to be only one of these institutions. When government grows too large, it overwhelms the other institutions of society. The founders placed limits on the role of government (and therefore its size) and included checks and balances to prevent the domination of one branch of government over the others.

In the following part of this book we look at some of the actions we can take to restore the social contract and preserve our democracy.

The Future of Democracy and the (Base) Nature of Politics

Everyone thought the 2012 presidential elections would be a Republican romp: the economy was in the tank and everyone blamed the incumbent president, Barack Obama. Despite the conventional wisdom, the President Obama won and Democrats gained in the House and Senate. How did Obama and the Democrats do this? They were able to turn the political discourse away the economy (and their poor handling thereof) and introduced a series of supposedly less important social issues such homosexual marriage, birth control for female college students, the "war on women" and etc. How could these side issues displace the overwhelming importance of the economic morass we were in?

On reflection, however, these supposedly side issues were emblematic of the larger issues I am trying to analyze in this book: the size and role of the government, the proper use of the coercive power of the state, the level playing field guaranteed by the American Social Contract. I thought at first that raising these social issues trivialized the political discourse. However, I ultimately realized that these social issues were anecdotal in nature: diverting the discourse away from the deeper issues by featuring, for example, a coed whining about have to pay for birth control pills. The fact that she wants to use the coercive power of the state to force others (taxpayers) to pay for her pills is totally obscured. The use of anecdotal events to sway our vote (both parties do it) is an appeal to our instinctual brain over our rational brain.

Anecdotes are insufficient material for the development of policies. We must resist the appeal of anecdotal stories and focus on the underlying principles that formulate policy. By basing policy on our American principles, we will set the best course for the future. There will be anecdotal exceptions: there always are. But these can be managed on a case-by-case basis rather than a reformulation of policy.

Whatever changes we need to implement in order to fix our economy and set a new course for our country must be done through the democratic political process. Putting a Mussolini in power in order to get our trains to run on time or a Pinochet to get the Chicago Boys to fix our economy is not a price we are willing to pay.

I know that some of you are throwing your hands up in despair at the thought of trying to get true reform accomplished in the broken down system that is Washington inside politics that seems to have hijacked our democracy.

A Little Historical Perspective
The Founding Fathers of the American Democracy were unique men at a unique time that created a unique nation – a nation that has profoundly shaped the course of world history. But the Founding Fathers were not all of one mind and there were many bitter struggles among them, especially the struggles between the Federalists led by Washington, Hamilton and Adams and the Republicans (not the current one – these Republicans morphed into the current Democrats) led by Jefferson and Madison. These struggles led to some very serious political maneuvering and campaign skullduggery.

The Founders tried to create an enlightened nation and were appalled to see it become a political nation (not just within their lifetime - but almost immediately). The polarization of the first decade of our republic (and how our country not only survived but thrived) should give us hope that all is not lost and that the American people will find a way to overcome the great obstacles we currently face.

The Not So Sacrosanct Constitution
Nowadays there are a lot of folk who are saying that we have to stick to the Constitution and that if something is not in the Constitution it should not be done. That we must abide by the Constitution in all things. But remember, the Founders almost immediately amended the newly approved Constitution in the form of 10 new amendments (the Bill of Rights). In fact the original thirteen States, in the process ratifying the Constitution, submitted 210 proposed amendments to the document.

The Founders, in their wisdom, provided for a process to amend the Constitution but did not make it an easy task. Amendments have a high hurdle to surpass before becoming the law of the land, requiring approval of three-fourths of the state legislatures. The implication is that the Founders did not want the Constitution to be eminently flexible nor did they want it subject to modification through interpretation. The Supreme Court's proclivity to make new law based on re-interpretations of the Constitution is clearly not what the Founders intended.

It is up to the people, whose will is expressed through the State legislatures (in this case), to change the Constitution. This requires consensus, not divergent visions.

Can Democracy Survive?

Aside from all my ranting and wisecracks about the flaws of American politics, there is a serious question at the base of all these discussions. Is democracy a viable form of government? More specifically, can American democracy survive? Extrapolating from the current trajectory of our country, the answer would seem to be NO.

The latter half of the twentieth century appeared to demonstrate the triumph of American style democracy as the Washington Consensus (democracy and free markets) was widely adopted around the world. But the dawn of the twenty-first century has seen an ebbing of the high tide of democracy across the globe. Country after country has fallen under the spell of populist strongman leaders who, for now at least, still maintain the official trappings of democracy. But leaders such as Chavez (now Maduro) and Putin don't believe in democracy, they only use its forms to maintain their grip on power. If and when these democratic trappings become an impediment to their thirst for power, they will be discarded without a second thought.

In America, there is no focal point we can blame as the cause of our diminishing democracy. We have to look in the mirror. The problem is us, ourselves. We are letting democracy seep through our outstretched hands like so much sand. Democracy says that the majority rules. But if the majority only wants entitlements that no one can afford, what is to become of democracy? Some might say that we can afford the entitlements that have been established, we just need to tax the rich. But the greed for entitlements is insatiable and we have just scratched the entitlement surface. There are so many more that could be claimed. Based on the work of Hayek, we have discussed the inexorable creep toward socialism that requires the increased coercive power of the state to enforce.

A new threat to democracy has risen from within. The government is now committed to the promise that terror attacks such as 9-11 will "never happen again". Such absolute promises require strong measures. In order to keep us safe, we are allowing the government to tap our phones, inspect our e-mails and invade almost all aspects of our privacy. Police SWAT teams now look (and act) like Seal Team Six. It is a paradox that in order to remain free, we must give up so much of our freedom. Isn't there a better way?

There are many external threats to our democracy and in the past we have been able to defeat all comers. The main threat we face now is internal even as our attention is turned outward to the many problems in the world. This is the essential question that we face today – and we have to come up with an answer soon.

I've Fallen and I Can't Get Up

Everyone knows that Washington (along with many state capitals) is broken. The only controversy is about how badly it is broken and what needs to be done to fix it. My feeling is that it is very badly broken and that major reforms are necessary to get things back on track.

I once worked on the Congressional campaign for a fellow I knew to be a pretty good guy. I liked his politics and his family and he treated me as a genuine person. We worked very hard to get him elected and he ended up with an upset victory over an incumbent with powerful inside connections. I also worked on a second campaign to get him re-elected. By the third campaign he didn't know me from Adam. I wasn't a big money man and didn't bring in the big donors. He not only lost me as a supporter he eventually lost his family and his seat in Congress. He had changed and it was Washington that had changed him.

Many of the people we send to Washington are decent folk. They are well intentioned and trying to do their best. But Washington changes them. They are feted, wined and dined, treated like American royalty until they become to believe that they ARE something special – a cut above - that they deserve the royal treatment – the members-only elevators, special subways beneath the streets of Washington, VIP parking at Washington National Airport, et cetera, et cetera, et cetera. They become like little megalomaniacal dictators that believe narcissistically that their business is the people's business (more about that later). They believe that they must be re-elected in order to continue doing the people's business, not realizing that they are betraying the people's interests in their striving for re-election. This is because they must sell out to the special interests in order to get the money and support needed for reelection. They lose faith in the integrity of the people believing that only manipulation and slick television ads (with a preference for attack ads) can garner the votes necessary for reelection. This eventually leads to elitism and a disdain of the common folk.

We have all seen the Congressional committees skewering bankers and CEOs for their greed and other misdeeds with what they think are especially pointed or witty probes; seen the pontificating Senators and Congressmen crucifying these (not so hapless) giants of the business world; and we wonder that they are so obtuse that they don't realize we can see right through their phoniness (such as castigating CEOs for flying to DC in private jets while the then House Speaker routinely took government owned private jets to go to and from her home district). We know that their speechifying to an empty gallery for home consumption or a sound bite for the next campaign does not show leadership- only shallowness.

It is what they do to perpetuate their term in office that is a principle cause of the problems that are destroying our country. They may try and convince us that it is all very complex but it really boils down to two things; promising more than they can deliver, and doing special favors for friends (in order to be a friend you have to donate very large sums of money).

Promises, Promises

Campaign promises have been around since the Ancient Greeks and you would think that over two thousand years of history littered with broken promises would render such banalities futile. Our modern politicians, however, have come up with several new variations of the game that they hope will delude us: future promises, promises on borrowed time and un-provable promises.

Politicians often promise something very big in the future but deliver very little in the present. It doesn't matter that the country cannot afford the future benefit. It will be up to future generations to find the funding for such promises. And the good thing about these promises is that they are bipartisan. Whether it is some future health benefit or a tax cut we cannot afford (and that will not generate an offsetting growth in the economy), politicians will keep trying to offer us something we neither can afford nor deserve.

If politicians do not have the resources needed to deliver on a campaign promise, then the government can always borrow the money necessary to deliver the promised goods or services. It doesn't matter to them that our children and grandchildren (and presumably theirs as well) will have to repay this largesse. That will be somebody else's problem and is clearly subordinate to the truly important goal of their reelection.

Politicians always like to fall back on impossible and unprovable promises. The greatest of these is jobs. Politicians are always promising to provide employment but except for a few juicy appointments for their kids and brothers-in-law they are always falling short. But it matters little that the government is a feeble generator of jobs – politicians can always take credit for generating jobs. If the economy generates 700,000 new jobs in a month the politicians will be out front preening and crowing about the fine work they are doing on behalf of their constituents. It's as if the private sector had nothing to do with it. Even if there are job losses, they will crow that lacking their efforts, the job losses would be even greater. How can you determine how much impact government policies have had on generating employment? The simple answer is that you can't. My even simpler answer is (based on the previous discussions about the economy) that government really can't do much about jobs except get out of the way so don't believe anything they promise you in this regard. Nevertheless, whenever people are interviewed on the street (at least by the mainstream media) people are always saying, "I want the government to do more to generate more jobs." As long as some of our benighted fellow citizens keep repeating this mantra, politicians will be rushing to fill this void (at least with their rhetoric).

Special Favors for Special Interests

Have you ever thought why the IRS tax code is almost 77,000 pages long? I can tell you one thing. It isn't 77,000 pages long for your benefit. It's for the benefit of special interests. What is a special interest? It could be almost anyone or anything that has some sway with Congress. Take any random tax provision such as the one at right which was taken from the Government Printing Office website when I did a search for Title 26 Internal Revenue Code (http://www.ecfr.gov/cgi-bin/text-idx?SID=6d2d69d21f2163ee931c8e91b0d825ad&mc=true&node=se26.15.1_19 004&rgn=div8). What do brick and tile clay, fire clay and shale have to do with your taxes – probably nothing unless you are one of the few special interests that qualify for such benefits (unless you are a mine owner or operator for such products). But if you are one of the lucky few, this provision would provide a benefit, a benefit that would likely motivate you to make campaign contributions to Congressmen or Senators willing to support such a provision.

When you have a fiduciary relationship you try to make sure that there is an alignment of interests between the service provider and the beneficiary. There is an alignment of interests between our elected officials and the special interests. Unfortunately citizens and especially taxpayers are not included in this alignment.

There have been many efforts to break up this unholy alliance in the form of campaign finance laws, limitations on lobbyists and ethics provisions limiting ex-federal employees representing special interests before their former employer. None of these provisions seem to have worked very well.

The way Congress currently operates, a single member or a small group of members can introduce specific clauses into legislation and get it approved by a majority of other members by agreeing to their specific clauses. This is a very cost effective way of cramming all sorts of special interest clauses into our laws. Reducing the members' ability to introduce these special interest clauses into legislation and to get them approved would increase costs and reduce the effectiveness of the special interest lobbyist. This would at least be a start in resolving some of the complexity that overshadows the level playing field.

Discovering Our Democratic Selves

Many of the scientific advances discussed in this book about how we think and act both politically and economically are fairly recent. We have discovered that we don't always act rationally and that we can sometimes be easily manipulated. The work of Professor Kahneman and other economic behaviorists has given us greater insight into ourselves; however, more work needs to be done.

Politics and economics are closely linked. Philosophers of the 17th and 18th century such as Adam Smith studied the political economy. More modern economic theories have tried to separate politics and economics; however, recent studies have shown that they are inextricably linked.

The thought processes we use to make economic decisions are very similar to those we use for political decision-making. Greater understanding into the psychology of decision-making is essential to the process of improving the functioning of our democracy. Like all knowledge, this understanding can be used for good or evil. We know that advertisers use many tricks to get us to buy their products. We are aware of the concept but are often unaware when these tricks are being used to manipulate our decision-making. Everyone hates attack ads that proliferate at every election cycle, but they keep on coming. They keep on coming because they work.

The research on human behavior will continue. We just need to make sure that this information is public. We have a better chance to protect ourselves from misuse of this knowledge if it is widely known. The concept of democracy has come into question recently and democracy in many countries is threatened. Dictators like the Castro brothers or Kim Jung Un are relatively easy to identify and isolate. Manipulators of democracy like Putin, Chavez, Maduro and Correa use the forms of democracy to stay in power. They actually win elections by using the powers of the state to manipulate people to vote for them. They control the media. Independent voices are isolated and often imprisoned on phony charges. The Internet is censored.

While these international despots are relatively easy to spot we have manipulators in the United States as well (many of which are not so apparent to us). Richard Thaler and Cass Sunstein wrote a very scary book called Nudge. Nudge has a subtitle of "Improving Decisions about Health, Wealth, and Happiness". They think it is not only acceptable but also laudable to manipulate people into making better decisions. But who defines which decision is better? The manipulators, of course. Thaler and Sunstein think it is not just a good thing but a great thing that could be applied throughout our society.

The thought of a bunch of do-gooders working behind the scene to make me do the "right" things is a truly scary thought. We see these nudgers all around us. The abortion of a fetus is converted into a woman's right to choose to take away the sting of death. Homosexuals are converted into gays to make them appear friendly and approachable. Charity and the dole are converted into entitlements to ease the shame of having to take handouts. All these are done to make things more palatable. Entitlements have even gone through a second conversion. Regular government expenditures (mandated by the Constitution) are discretionary parts of the budget, while entitlements (transfers of wealth) are non-discretionary.

You can agree or disagree with particular policy decisions. But let's describe them accurately so that we can make a reasoned decision. We need to shine a bright light on manipulation wherever we find it. We also must structure our democracy in order to resist manipulation. Manipulation is tinkering with the level playing field and, as noted previously, the level playing field (the equality of opportunity) is essential to the democratic social contract that is the United States.

Taking Back Our Democracy

The fundamental change necessary to restore our democracy must start with the Congress because the Congress is the heart of US sovereignty. Although the Executive has ample powers, the President cannot pass laws (despite what President Obama is attempting to do) that govern the implementation of the social contract we call the United States of America. Much of the dysfunction of Washington arises from the Congress because of its pivotal role as defined by the Constitution. The Founders created a system of checks and balances between the branches of government in the hope that these different branches would act to limit the abuse of power by other branches of government.

In 2008, citizens voting in large numbers for "change" gave the Democratic Party an overwhelming victory, electing a Democratic President and giving Democrats large majorities in both houses of Congress. In 2010, these same citizens gave an overwhelming victory to Republicans, giving them back the House and strengthening their position in the Senate (the only thing preserving the Democrats was the limited number of Senate seats up for election and the off-year for Presidential elections). Were the voters just being fickle? Were they being bratty little kids that take away their ball if they don't get their way? Well, yeah they were! They were saying, we don't want to play by your rules in Washington. We want you to play by our rules – or we will vote you out of office. And you know what – they were right!

The rise of the Tea Party movement is a reflection of this. The left branded the movement as a bunch of right wing (and probably racist) extremists. The Republican Party welcomed them with the same trepidation as a male black widow spider about to mate. The Tea Party followers voted for Republicans but probably because that was the best way to kick out the incumbents who were mostly Democrats. They immediately put the Republicans on notice that they were on "probation" and that the Tea Party groups would be watching to make sure the Republicans don't return to "politics as usual" as they did after winning both houses of Congress in 1994.

Taking back our democracy isn't a Republican or Democrat thing. Both parties have failed to act in the interests of the people and the country. It may not be a Tea Party thing either. Time will tell. The Tea Party is basically a rejection of the status quo and a call for change. But much of that change is yet undefined. Other than kicking the bums out (over and over again if necessary) what can the people do? How can they be a force for positive change and not just a rejection of the status quo?

There needs to be a new philosophy of government and an action plan to bring about positive change. This book hopes to point out the fundamental principles that can be the basis for such change as well as recommend some tangible actions that can be de implemented in the short to medium term future.

Let's start with revamping how Congress works (because it surely isn't working for us right now). Most reform efforts in the past have focused on making changes to the forces that can influence Congress, primarily the lobbyists that roam those venerable halls. But it takes two to tango and the men and women of Congress are subject to the same human failings as everyone else. Efforts to try control the money available to influence Congress is bound to fail if the incentives of the members of Congress do not change.

For over two hundred years, Congress itself has defined the rules under which the Congress operates. The Constitution gives the legislature wide latitude. Congress can pass legislation to reform itself but can also pass legislation to undo the reforms when things get uncomfortable or inconvenient later on. In order to make reforms more permanent we need to change the Constitution. So let's amend the Constitution!

The 28th Amendment - Term Limits

Our Congressional leaders have their own sense of entitlement. They feel entitled to their offices and its privileges. They aren't! They are elected to office to do our business and it appears that we need to remind them of this from time to time.

Term limits have been approved in a number of states and municipalities. This has not ended democracy in these communities but rather enhanced it. The Constitution does not address the concept of term limits for Congress, probably because in the days of the Founders, the concept of a career as a lawmaker was totally alien to them. Serving in government was a duty and obligation (as well as an honor). It was not a career that you could make a living from.

This was partially based on the elitist attitudes of the Founders. The Founders felt that men of public service had to be "disinterested' by which they meant that they had no interests that would come before or have a higher priority than their obligations to faithfully serve the interests of the government. This disinterest would give them independence and the ability to act impartially. A disinterested person was probably wealthy or retired or both. Benjamin Franklin sold off his business interests and retired in his fifties in order to devote the rest of his life to public service and science. George Washington was one of the wealthiest people in the Colonies (at least before his government service). They were all gentlemen (no matter what their origins).

Unfortunately, the concept of an American democracy led by disinterested gentlemen was more an Enlightenment ideal than a practical political solution. It wasn't long before people with interests before government became the norm rather than the exception. During his life, Aaron Burr was vilified for his conflicted interests even though such conflicts of interest are now common (his actions did endanger the fragile republic but no more than the actions of his successors that are currently imperiling America).

If we must be resigned to the fact that our lawmakers will have conflicts of interest then we are obligated as good citizens to limit the damage that these conflicts can create. This can be done in two ways: one, limiting the amount of time anyone can serve in a particular office; and two, limiting how and in what way such individuals can represent "interests" before the government.

It took an amendment to the Constitution to impose term limits on the President of the United States. I had thought growing up that this was done out of kindness because the job of being President of the United States was too crushing to be borne for too long by anyone (I have since changed my opinion). I believe that we need a new amendment (or possibly an amendment to Amendment #22) placing limits to the number of terms that can be served in the House of Representatives and in the Senate. I think 4 terms as a Representative (8 years) and 2 terms as Senator (12 years) would be appropriate. Ex-representatives could run for the Senate but not the reverse. Ex-Representatives and ex-Senators could rerun for offices after spending a time out of office equal to the amount of time served. Ex-Representatives and ex-Senators would not be allowed to represent private or foreign interests before either House of Congress or work in associations with others that do (lobbyists).

This should stir the pot enough to keep icky burnt stuff from sticking to the bottom.

The 29th Amendment - Line Item Veto

There was a push in the 112th Congress to place a voluntary ban on earmarks (the neutralized term Washington has come up with to replace the more earthy term of pork barrel projects). However, at around $30 billion a year earmarks represent only about one percent of the Federal budget. They are not a budget problem, but they are a symptom of the feeling of elitist entitlement rampant on Capitol Hill: a prerogative of elected representatives to spend our money as they see fit (and usually to benefit some particular interest that could provide future campaign help). The El Salvadoran Constitution has an interesting provision we may want to consider including in ours. Their Congress can only approve or reduce the budget items submitted for approval by the Executive Branch – they cannot add items or increase existing ones.

While the President has the power to eliminate such earmarks by vetoing bills containing earmarks, our wily politicians usually tack earmarks onto larger and more important legislation totally unrelated to the earmarks but which are deemed essential for one reason or another (such as funding for our troops in Afghanistan). But the reluctance to throwing the baby out with the bathwater is the basic strategy employed by our representatives to prevent anyone with common sense from getting rid of this wasteful spending. A line item veto would not only prevent earmarks (potentially) but would also give the President the power to eliminate riders and other provisions or amendments to bills where they don't belong (such as some sort of social legislation attached to a bill funding benefits to military veterans). This would require the earmarks to get a straight-up vote in order to override the line item veto. Something that is unlikely to happen once their cover has been blown.

The line item veto would change the economic dynamic that drives the special interest lobbyist machine. Rather than putting limits on special interest campaign donations, it makes them less profitable. A single member or a small group of members could no longer guarantee the legislation needed by the special interest. They would need the cooperation of two-thirds of the legislators to override the veto of the President. It would take a lot more campaign contributions and other favors to push these bills through after a line item veto.

Lobbyists and other special interests invest money in campaign contributions and other favors (like speaking fees or book deals) because they get a good return on their investment. Lobbying pays off. The line item veto changes this equation by increasing the uncertainty and lowering the return on the investment. The lobbyists will have to dole out a lot more money without the certainty that it will ever be made into law. That doesn't mean the special interests will never be able to get their way from time to time, but it will make it much harder, much more expensive and less profitable.

The 30th Amendment - Unfunded Mandates

A recent trend in the Federal government has been to write a law entitling people to certain services or benefits and then require the State governments to provide the service or benefit. I, for one, do not understand how this has passed the scrutiny of the Supreme Court as it clearly is an imposition on the rights of the various States by Federal authority. The federal government clearly has a great deal of power and can require the States to do a large range of things (often to require equal treatment of citizens among the States).

An amendment requiring the Federal government to provide the funds necessary to implement new legislation would prevent the Federal government from hiding the true cost of such programs. It is disingenuous for the Federal government to claim that some new Federally mandated program has little or no budget impact when what they truly mean is that it will have only limited impact of the Federal budget. The true impact to you as a taxpayer in Federal, State and municipal jurisdictions may be very different. Citizens deserve to know the true cost of such programs.

The 31st Amendment - Government Accounting Standards

A related amendment would be to impose clear accounting standards on the Federal government (most state governments are already subject to these requirements). The Federal government has resisted this reform for decades and for good reason: a less transparent (and more obscure) budget process gives Congress the freedom to act based on politics rather than sound financial principles. Congress and the government need to be held responsible and a positive step would be to impose strict accounting standards on our government. I recommend that the US adopt the use of the International Public Sector Accounting Standards as developed by the International Public Sector Accounting Standards Board (IPSASB) based on the International Financial Reporting Standards. Many people will immediately respond that such action endangers our national sovereignty but many of the loudest complainers will be those with the most to hide. The days when the US could chart its own course and be oblivious to the international standards while we try to hold the rest of the world accountable (do what I say, not what I do) are almost gone. Such a move would be welcomed by the rest of the world, including those nations that are our largest creditors as well as the credit rating agencies that are warning us of future downgrades (oops) if action is not taken soon.

These standards must also be made to apply to contingent liabilities. The US has enormous contingent liabilities arising from the unfunded benefits promised under Social Security, Medicare/Medicaid, veterans' benefits etc. Valuing contingent liabilities is always tricky because you have to make a lot of assumptions about the future such as future inflation and interest rates. But this uncertainty is compounded when no estimate is made at all or is made by someone who has an interest in skewing the result (whether higher or lower). Implementing the International Public Sector Accounting Standards would be an enormous task, but one well worth the effort.

The 32nd Amendment - Sinking Fund

At first I thought the idea of a sinking fund was a dumb idea. A sinking fund is sort of an old-fashioned concept where a debtor must set aside a certain amount of money each year that will be used to retire debt in the future. Modern financial markets have largely eliminated the need for sinking funds as most borrowers can refinance debt as it comes due with relative ease. I would create a sinking fund, not so much for credit reasons, but as a constant reminder to the people of the amount of debt the government has incurred. I would require that 5% of debt outstanding be repaid each year and, in addition, I would require that all citizens be sent a bill for their share of the sinking fund plus interest due. This would be separate from their regular tax filing. Assuming a total debt of $18 14 trillion and a population of 319 million the total debt burden of each citizen would be around $56,426 and the sinking fund payment for each person would be $2,821. How happy would you be with your Congressman if every year you had to write a check for $11,285 for a typical family of four? The chances of getting such an amendment passed are probably pretty low, but one can only imagine the changes that would be made in government if people had to write checks to pay directly for those excesses.

The 33rd Amendment- Popular Amendments

One final thing. Under the Constitution, only Congress can propose an Amendment (or the state legislatures can call for a constitutional convention). Citizens should be allowed to propose Amendments as well. The hurdles to start the amendment process should be appropriately high as are the hurdles currently imposed on Congress. I would also propose that the State votes be by popular vote rather than by the State legislatures. This would be an appropriate reflection of modern popular democracy in America.

The Reluctant Amendment – The Balanced Budget Amendment

I have always been against a balanced budget amendment despite all the calls for its passage by fiscal conservatives. There are four reasons why I thought such an amendment was a bad idea; 1) while it's been stated that countercyclical measures in a downturn are ineffective, a balanced budget amendment would be pro-cyclical (i.e.; it would make a bad situation worse) limiting the government's ability to respond to a down economy, 2) debt isn't bad or evil in itself but the problem is in how it is used (borrowing to build infrastructure projects can pay off in the long run but to pay for current entitlements is a bottomless pit) , 3) the world economic system is based on the availability of dollars (and dollar investments in the form of Treasury bonds), and 4) domestic capital markets are founded on the reference points established by US government debt.

Pro-cyclicality

We have noted that countercyclical measures such as increased deficit spending have been proven to be ineffective; however, much of that is due to the fact for much of the past fifty years the government has been operating in a continuous deficit which debilitates the impact of additional deficit spending. Deficit spending to offset temporary shortfalls in tax revenues due to recessions or other economic downturns could prevent massive layoffs of government workers and a continuation of benefits for citizens most hard hit by the recession. These actions would have to be countered by surpluses as the economy improved.

Productive Debt

I am not one of the people that think all debt is bad. Like any tool, debt can have its toxic effects like other modern tools we have such as nuclear energy and even fire. Used wisely, debt can greatly enhance the productive efforts of both the private and public sectors. In the early republic the role of government in the development of infrastructure projects was a hotly debated topic. Many people feared the government's participation in such projects thinking it would curb private initiative, increase the size of government and reduce the freedom of all citizens. While these concerns are valid and real, large projects like hydroelectric dams and the interstate highway system are often not feasible without government participation. A consensus has developed that government participation in certain infrastructure projects is a valid use of national government power. However, large infrastructure projects require large amounts of cash and, while it may be very prudent to use only available cash for such project, the judicious use of public debt can accelerate the development of such projects and thus accelerate economic growth generally. The projects should generate additional income for the citizens benefiting from the projects, which will provide the tax revenue necessary to repay the debt incurred by the project. This is how modern business operates on a daily basis and it is not inappropriate for government to do the same. This is very different from borrowing to pay current expenses, subsidize favored groups or dole out entitlements.

Governments, however, are often not very good at estimating the costs of these projects (remember the Big Dig we discussed earlier). Care must be taken to assure that the costs of any project of the government do not outweigh the benefits.

The International Money Supply

Because the US dollar is (essentially) the international reserve currency, there is a continuous demand for US dollars by foreign governments, companies and individuals. Traditionally, Europeans, Brazilians, Mexicans and others around the world have wanted to receive dollars compared to the domestic currencies of their trading partners. International companies borrow dollars for plant expansion or to buy inventory. Foreign individuals need dollars for tourism and often for savings because they lack faith in their domestic currencies. This demand for dollars has grown as the world economy has grown and become more globalized. This international demand for dollars has allowed the US to operate a continual trade deficit over a long period of time and, because foreign countries, companies and individuals need a place to store their dollars they want to invest in America, especially in US government bonds which are very liquid and easily converted into cash. This constant demand for US dollars and government bonds allows America to operate differently than other countries in international markets. A moderate trade deficit combined with a moderate fiscal deficit financed by government bonds has been one of the driving forces of international trade and development for more than half a century. Of course, the key word here is moderate. Excessive trade and fiscal deficits will debase the US currency, increase domestic inflation and motivate our trading partners to find a more secure store of value.

Domestic Capital Markets

People on Main Street may think they are far removed from the fast paced trading of government securities on Wall Street, but the hectic trading and the liquidity derived therefrom create a risk free reference yield curve which is the basis for most domestic (and international) borrowing; whether by large multinational companies, small businesses or individuals. The car loan or mortgage you get on your major purchases is linked (directly or indirectly) to the yield curve of US government securities. If the government paid off all of its debt, this important reference rate would disappear making day to day business more difficult and less transparent which would be to the cost of everyone.

What we need is a government that has a mature and adult attitude toward debt that can be used for the long-term benefit of its citizens. Unfortunately, our politicians have shown themselves unable to resist the temptation of buy now, pay later. We need a flexible balanced budget amendment that addresses the issue of excessive borrowing without eliminating the positive benefits from having a reasonable level of debt.

While We Are at It

One piece of legislation that needs to be repealed is the Full Employment and Balanced Growth Act of 1978, better known as Humphrey-Hawkins. The bill outlines a number of goals for the government's economic policy, almost none of which have been accomplished (a balanced budget and no trade deficit as two prime examples). The bill also establishes full employment as a primary goal and mandates the Federal Reserve to conduct monetary policy to achieve this goal. In addition, the act requires the Fed to report to Congress how it is doing on achieving these goals twice yearly.

Humphrey-Hawkins is deeply rooted in Keynesian economic theory which explains the very limited results of the legislation. What the legislation has done is to force the Fed to conduct aggressive Keynesian measures to try and reduce unemployment. This has resulted in zero interests rates and asset price inflation but not much employment. Although the unemployment rate was down to under five percent in 2016, labor participation was at a 30-year low, which means that almost ten million people left the work force and were no longer counted as unemployed.

Asset price inflation has made the wealthy wealthier (because they own most of the assets) but has done little for the middle class. All of the Fed's mandated Keynesian activities (Quantitative Easing or QE 1, 2 and 3) and near zero interest rates have driven up the stock exchange. All the money went into equities while bonds paid almost nothing. All this activity has disoriented the economy and destabilized markets as because financial services grew faster than manufacturing or other services. Financial services are important as a facilitator of economic activity but do not generate much economic growth or employment.

We are asking the Fed to do more than it can which has resulted in the current market turmoil. When a central bank is functioning properly people are hardly aware of its existence, not guessing Fed policy by the thickness of Alan Greenspan's briefcase. Repealing Humphrey-Hawkins would let the Fed get back to doing what it is supposed to be doing, proving stable monetary conditions and backing up the financial system.

Getting It Done

How, you might ask, is it possible to get these amendments proposed and passed if the politicians whose power we are trying to limit through the proposed amendments control the entire amendment process? Well it won't be easy but it can be done. It can be done through the concerted actions of citizens such as you and me. We can make a list of the amendments that need to be approved and ask each person running for Congress to pledge to propose a bill to enact each amendment, telling the candidates that without such a pledge there will be no votes for them, no matter how good their record on other matters might be or how alluring their campaign promises appear. If they take the pledge but then renege, vote them out. Keep this up until there are enough votes to get the job done.

This will not be an easy task but amendments to the Constitution are not meant to be easy. If amendments were easy there is no telling what type of folderol would end up in that precious document (believe me, I have seen the constitutions of many other countries, and ours is by far the best, most succinct and understandable one of the bunch. A constitution that can be changed easily soon ends up a useless mess.)

You may say that you are not a one issue voter and I believe you. But believe me, there is nothing more basic and essential to saving our great country than getting these amendments passed and instituting the others changes recommended in this book. These are not issues of right or left, Republican or Democrat; these are issues of good governance that should be supported by all citizens.

Checks and Balances

The proposed reforms are not meant to weaken Congress but to make it more effective and relevant. Congress has fallen into a trap that makes its members captives of the election cycle, as they must be constantly raising funds for the next campaign. The money grubbing makes them beholden to those with money to donate and weakens Congress as an institution. The proposed reforms would lessen the power of money and reduce the power of incumbency. Although some members may suffer (by losing elections) the institution would be improved.

Likewise, reform to reduce the ability to paper over differences through debt will force members to work with each other in order to build a consensus. Again, some individual members will suffer and the road toward building a consensus will be long and arduous.

Congress's inability to pass effective legislation (the government has operated for five years without a budget) has created a power vacuum. President Obama has taken advantage of the crippled Congress by acting independently through executive orders and other administrative actions. This is precisely what the Founders feared and tried to forestall when they created the system of checks and balances in our government.

So the situation we are currently faced with is that of a sitting president using unconstitutional means to take advantage of an ineffective Congress in order to advance and entrench the un-American welfare state. And he has the chutzpah to call his opponents radical (please recall the quote by John Adams[3]).

---

[3] 1 Abuse of words has been the great instrument of sophistry and chicanery, of party, faction and the division of society. John Adams

Turning the Ship

The America of the future is going to look very different from the America of today: only we don't know if this will be a good thing or a bad thing. All we really know is that what we are currently doing is unsustainable. Will we find ourselves in a giant welfare state dominated by state services and income redistribution or in an economically and, more importantly, spiritually revitalized country.

I have stated my thinking several times in this book about why I think the welfare state is a dead-end. The end probably wouldn't happen in my lifetime (although the current descent has my stomach contents in my throat), but my children would live to see it and my grandchildren would be the ones living impoverished in a dark post-American world.

The ideas expressed in this book are not inclusive and I encourage all of you to try and think of additional ways we can bring the country back on course. I started charting a new course by thinking of ways to improve the functioning of Congress so that government can try and fulfill the obligations imposed on it by the American Social Contract. But the amendment process is a slow one and we cannot wait for those changes before implementing the reforms needed in the other areas we have looked at.

Tax Reform

There are a number of principles that must be included in any tax reform measure:
1. The only purpose of taxation is to fund the operation of the government of the United States.
2. All citizens must pay taxes
3. Taxes must be consistent for all citizens with no special treatment.
4. Taxes must not be confiscatory or used as punishment.
5. Taxes should not be used to motivate any action to be taken by citizens.

The potential to abuse the tax code or divert it from the goal of raising funds for the government is inherent in the nature of politics. But taxes should not be used as political tools because taxes come from the citizens and elected leaders have a fiduciary responsibility regarding the use of the money taken from citizens through the use of coercive state power.

It is the duty of all citizens to pay taxes. It is part of the shared sacrifice that all citizens must bear. Keeping in mind that all citizens do not feel the burden of taxes equally, progressive taxation is consistent with the concept of the level playing field, which is part of the American Social contract.

There should be no special treatment for any taxpayer. The application of this principle can be difficult because taxpayers, especially corporations, have very specific circumstances that can obscure what would be considered special treatment. A mining company is very different from a manufacturing company but certain basic principles should apply.

Taxes should not be used as punishment. The state has enormous coercive power at its disposal. It doesn't need additional powers with which to afflict citizens.

Taxes should not be used to motivate or urge any actions by citizens. If the government wants to promote the purchase of hybrid vehicles in order to preserve the environment it can right a check. This has the same impact on government finances as providing a tax subsidy but it will make the tax code simpler and easier to use while providing transparency to the government's environmental program. Similarly, special programs for poor people that can result in a negative income tax can be replaced by income supplement payments.

Very high taxes and very low taxes are counterproductive. Very low taxes deprive the government of the ability to perform its functions in support of the social contract. While changes in tax policy may cause a spurt of tax flows, undermining the rule of law through lack of funding will, ultimately, reduce economic output and a breakdown of the cohesiveness of society. Very high taxes are confiscatory and are used as a means to punish the wealthy for being wealthy. Confiscatory taxes will be seen as unjust and will prompt affected individuals to seek ways to avoid such taxes. Unjust laws break down the rule of law just as do very low taxes.

The last element we need to incorporate into tax policy is that of stability. Businesses and investors already face a lot of uncertainty in their economic activities. Bringing new untested products to market or investing in volatile equities incurs inherent uncertainty. They do not need additional uncertainty in a changeable and capricious tax policy. This added uncertainty can only dampen economic activity.

The National Commission on Fiscal Responsibility and Reform (known as Bowles-Simpson) tried to get control of the runaway budget deficits and mounting debts but did not alter any of the functions of government: being unimaginative and draconian at the same time. It made no attempt to unwind the welfare state or reform the tax code.

The recent proposal of Senator Marco Rubio has some promising elements but is, essentially, a campaign promise rather than a serious proposal.

So a tax reform that would work would embody the following elements: 1) a progressive system of personal taxation (the top marginal rate should not be confiscatory and there should be a sufficient number of tax brackets such that moving from one bracket to another is not onerous), 2) no deductions except for the standard deduction for the taxpayer and dependents (no mortgage deduction, no environmental subsidies, no welfare support or negative income tax), 3) no double taxation (dividends) and no double exemptions (healthcare – see below); 4) a capital gains adjustment for inflation during the holding period, 5) elimination of universal taxation and 6) a corporate tax equivalent to that of our main trading partners. .

Unwinding the Welfare State

It will take a generation to unwind the welfare state. The Baby Boomers and the elderly have been paying into the Social Security System and Medicare for many decades. A substantial portion of their retirement funds is locked up in these systems. Any plan to unwind these welfare Gargantuas will be complex and long term and would require a book of its own to be fully fleshed out. Nevertheless a couple of key elements are clear.

<u>Social Security</u>
There are two principle problems with Social Security as a pension system: 1) the contributors have few rights to the funds they pay into Social Security, and 2) the funds they pay into Social Security are used by the government for other purposes resulting in a largely unfunded pension system. Corporations would be in big trouble if they treated their employees and pensioners in this manner. Most Social Security contributors are totally at the mercy of the supposedly benevolent government for their retirement security. This is not the American way! These contributors worked hard for their money and have a right to determine its usage. After all, it's not the government's money, it's theirs.

Privatization of Social Security would have to have three basic options for contributors. For the retired and those about to retire the social Security System would be basically unchanged. They would continue to make payments and eventually receive payments as under the current system. For the middle-aged and those in their prime earning years, they would have the option of placing their current contributions into their new privatized accounts and freezing their social security accounts. At retirement they would receive checks from both sources. They would also have the option of converting the social security account into a privatized account (depending on how many chose this option, the government would probably have to come up with a payment plan to put funds into the privatized accounts). The third system would be young people who have not yet made large contributions into their Social Security accounts. All of these accounts would be converted and placed into privatized accounts (again with a payment plan for the government).

There would be an enormous cost to government for this conversion. I don't know what it would cost in the US but in other countries it has run around 3-5% of GDP a year. In the US, that would be more than $500 billion a year. This amount would gradually reduce as people under the old system die (although it might increase initially because of the baby boomers).

If you think this amount is not supportable, keep in mind it represents the net present value of the future pension payments that the government owes but does not report.

Fixing Healthcare

Fixing Social Security is easy compared to fixing healthcare. The healthcare system has been totally screwed up by previous government policies and it will take a long time and a lot of work to get things back on track.

But the first thing we need to do in order to get started on fixing the healthcare system is also the easiest. As noted previously, we need to eliminate the double tax deduction for healthcare expenses. The double deduction is one of the root causes for the current malaise of the healthcare system. The elimination of the distorting deduction should be an integral part of any tax reform.

I am no healthcare expert but reintroducing the free market system to healthcare should eventually provide better healthcare at lower cost as competition and innovation kick in. The government will still have an important role to assure that the rule of law and the level playing field prevail, especially during a lengthy transition period. Consumers will have an important role as well and will bear increased costs not the least from having healthcare benefits from employers considered taxable income. People who have private insurance don't get this benefit, which violates our principled tax policy of not providing special benefits.

We should also get rid of the employer mandate. Since when did it become the responsibility of employers to provide healthcare insurance? They provide salaries: that should be enough. The employee has the right to determine how his salary should be spent and insurance may not be a high priority.

All this government meddling means that the free market economic system does not work well in the provision of healthcare. When the free market system doesn't work well as a result of government rules and regulations, the government creates mandates enforced by the coercive power of the state. As these mandates further distort the market, additional government mandates backed by coercive power will be needed. Recall now what Hayek said about the path to Socialism. The free market economic system has been the mechanism for the United States to become the most powerful nation in the world and to have an economic system that provides enormous benefits to its citizens. It is irrational to not let the free market system provide these benefits in the area of healthcare.

Many additional reforms will be needed to make our healthcare system healthy. I am no expert is this field but believe the expertise is available to recommend the necessary reforms while still providing superior levels of service.

Restoring Our Defense

There are two things that we must do to restore our defense capabilities to their previous preeminent position: 1) implement fiscal integrity to assure that we have the financial and economic power to field a powerful military presence, and 2) make sure that defense is adequately funded by these resources.

Sequestration (defunding the military in order to make transfer payments for the social welfare system) and a hesitancy (if not antipathy) toward military action and the military itself have debilitated our defensive capabilities. Once we had the capability to wage a two-theatre war (the ability to fully wage two wars in two different theatres at the same time as we did in World War II). This capability was initially downgraded to a one-and-a-half theatre capability (the ability to block or forestall military action in one theatre while conducting military operations in another). Ultimately, the military has been downsized to a one-plus capability (where we have the ability over time to increase our capability to more than one theatre).

The capacity to maintain a two theatre capability means that an aggressive nation or non-state entity knows that it would have to take on the full capability of the United States if it engaged in aggression against us or its neighbors. This capability kept the forces of aggression and terror at bay for many decades (keeping the Soviet Union held in check while engaged in proxy wars such as Viet Nam). As our military power has been degraded, we have seen more aggressive activities from a wide range of actors who feel that they can attack their neighbors or initiate terroristic activities with impunity.

We cannot allow our national security to be put in jeopardy by this downsizing of our military. The world is a dangerous place and is full of lots of bad actors. We could try and negotiate a peaceable settlement of our differences, assuming the other side is negotiating in good faith (when in fact they often aren't). But negotiating from a weakened position only emboldens the other side.

We need to provide our armed forces with an adequate budget and also assure that our veterans are well cared for. This means realigning our budgetary priorities even if it pinches other discretionary or non-discretionary expenses (ultimately everything is discretionary unless expressly mandated by the Constitution).

At the same time we need to revitalize our economy in order to make sure we have the resources to meet all the needs of government. I have always ascribed to the saying, "the lack of money makes a strong man weak".

Transitions

Achieving this new and greater America will require a protracted struggle and a long, uneasy period of transition. Americans of our generation are unused to this type of sacrifice. We are accustomed to watching our wars on television from the comfort of our living rooms: only a tiny fraction face actual combat (God bless them!). The efforts to transform America will affect everybody and for an extended period of time. It took us a lot of time to get in the mess we're in, and it will take a long time to get us out.

Start Digging

Some of you may be surprised to find out that one of the first things we must do to get from under this mass of debt we have accumulated, is to take on more debt. *What?* You say. *How can that be? If you find yourself in a hole, the first thing you do is stop digging.* But the conversion of the entitlement systems to a more competitive, free-market basis cannot leave millions of people with no coverage at all. Generations have grown up piling money into entitlement systems with the expectations that their retirement or healthcare will be taken care of. (The assumption behind Social Security was that the contributions of young workers would cover the Social Security checks of the retired - ooops, they forgot to take demographic changes into account.) It does not matter that their contributions were squandered or that there is now little left in the Social Security Trust Fund or that there are too few young workers to pay for the benefits they deserve. These are commitments that must be honored.

Healthcare is even worse than Social Security. In the sixties when Medicare was created, the average life span for white males was around 68 years and for other males around 60 (75 and 69, respectively, for females). Now, the average lifespan for white males is 76 and 72 for other males. We are living longer, which is a good thing. But if we look at the Medicare coverage period it has gone from 3 years (68-65) to 11 years, a 267% increase (males of other ethnicities have gone from unlikely to receive benefits to 7 years of benefits). Add in the outside increases in medical costs and the cost of providing healthcare in Medicare has exploded. The Medicare tax rate has been unchanged for almost thirty years. You do the math. It doesn't add up.

We will have to borrow the funds to honor these commitments even as we redirect the taxes of younger citizens to more fiscally sound programs as outlined above. The unfunded benefits of these legacy programs run into the trillions. A study prepared by Mary Meeker of venture capital giant Kleiner Perkins (www.kpcb.com) estimates the net present value of the future benefits to be paid out at $64 trillion! There are many millions of people that are already retired or about to retire that must continue to be paid their benefits although they make little or no contributions. The outstanding obligation to these people runs into the trillions. The actual amount we pay out will be determined by the transition program adopted.

The debt required to meet those commitments isn't really new debt, it just monetizes the unfunded obligations that we have been too blind to recognize (and which politicians have been trying to cover up for decades). Taxes may be able to cover some of these obligations but it is quite likely that additional debt will be required for many years. Unwinding the entitlement programs will be the labor of a generation.

Social Security will be the easiest to work ourselves out of. Not that it will be easy. Ms. Meeker estimates that the net present value of unfunded Social Security benefits to be around $8 trillion (the smallest of the major entitlement programs). Actuarial studies can estimate with reasonable accuracy the cost to unwind the system and convert it into a defined contribution plan instead of a government defined benefit program. Social Security payments go up more or less in line with inflation and other variables can be controlled or subjected to limited changes (unless some wonderful new discovery changes the average longevity of Americans). Juggling with the numbers through lengthening the retirement age and including means testing can greatly reduce the final cost. In fact, if it wasn't for the inherently insidious nature of entitlements themselves, Social Security probably could be fixed (at least to the extent of kicking the can way down the road) without bankrupting the country.

The same cannot be said for Medicare and Medicaid. Medical costs are rising much faster than inflation. The solution to the health care problem is in using competition to reduce costs, but we don't know how quickly this will take effect. We don't yet know how this reform will be implemented. It may take place in stages, as some reforms may not be able to be implemented until some other reforms have taken place. There will be many people fighting against these reforms. To wring out costs in the health care system, a lot of people must lose their jobs. Hopefully the losses can be concentrated in bureaucratic paper shufflers (currently the fastest growing area of the medical field thanks to increased red tape) and not medical professionals like doctors, nurses and technicians.

The other big transition will be in our personal and group psychology. We have become accustomed to being dependent. Many people will say we cannot (I cannot) survive without Social Security or Medicare. Well, for most of our history we didn't have those programs and we not only survived but became the greatest country in the world in the process. *Well*, you might say, *why can't the greatest country in the world provide all these things to us?* The answer is: it could —secure retirement and affordable medical services would be available if you would let America do what it does best — COMPETE. You're asking why America can't provide retirement and health care services (plus a few other entitlements we haven't thought up yet but that the politician's will come up with by the time of the next election cycle) while unmaking America at the same time, dismantling America's strength through debt and deficits. People are trying to change America into Europe so that it can provide these services to Americans. It just won't work that way. You're killing the golden goose and all we're going to end up with is goose gizzards and no gold.

The Role of Compassion

The goal of the proposed reforms is not to deprive people who truly need help of the support they need. It is the insidious nature of the welfare state to provide benefits to those who are capable of providing for themselves, making them ever more increasingly dependent upon the state. They become creatures of the state: forgetting that the state is their creation. This is not the America the Founders envisioned.

But being independent and taking care of ourselves does not mean that we lack compassion or that we should throw the less fortunate to the wolves. The proposed reforms to level the playing field would help those disadvantaged by the system to succeed in life. But there will remain those who, for whatever reason, lack the ability to make it in modern society. There are also those, such as the recently unemployed, who need temporary help. Basic decency requires that these people be helped. This is what any civilized society would do.

The difference would be that only those that truly need assistance would get help and those that needed temporary assistance would get that too. A society where everyone needs help is just as dysfunctional as one where everyone is oppressed. America became great because of the strength of its people, not because of the strength of the government.

In a reformed America, those in need would receive assistance. But this is not an entitlement: it is compassion. Assistance doesn't come from government: it comes from taxpayers and taxpayers deserve to know their money is being well spent. The reforms would get rid of tax credit and other methods used to hide the true cost of these programs. Critics could argue that this is just a cover-up of ways to reduce costs on the backs of those in greatest need. But a program to provide assistance that is based on deception is morally wrong.

How can we possibly borrow more?
How can we possibly afford all this new debt if we already have more than we can handle? You might ask. Big creditors like China are already getting nervous and threatening to diversify into other securities while the rating agencies have already begun to downgrade our creditworthiness. But the problem isn't the level of debt, no matter what Bill O'Reilly says. Debt service only takes up about six percent of the Federal budget, a big chunka change but nothing we can't handle. The problem is the deficit and the trajectory of the debt.

Our debt is growing faster than our economy and that means that at some point in time in the future we will not be able to service our debt. Worse, the debt is pre-programmed to continue growing as far into the future as we can foresee because all the entitlement programs are locked in and running on autopilot. Our creditors see this. The rating agencies see this. That is why they are worried (China is not too worried. If they have to spend a couple of trillion dollars to become the world's greatest superpower they would consider it a bargain.)

But if we could break out of our pre-programmed vicious downward spiral then all that worry would dissipate. If the creditors and rating agencies knew that we would go further into indebtedness during the transition but that once the reforms were in place debt would go down, that we had a solid plan for sustainable government spending, that we had a tax regime supported by the people that paid for the necessary government services, then our credit rating would be golden again.

How Can This Be Done?

It's pretty easy to write a book about changing the course of history in America (actually it was a lot harder than I thought) but it is a lot harder to actually implement the reforms I am recommending. The reforms recommended in this book are really hard to do: amend the Constitution (not once but several times), eliminate entitlement programs that have been around for many decades (generations actually), fundamentally change the tax regime (and how Congress does business), save the free market capitalist system and take back our democracy. WHEW!

Presidential Leadership

We could always wait around for a leader to come and save us. There are, however, a couple of problems with this approach (in addition to the fact that we have been looking for this kind of leadership for years and keep coming up short). A leader espousing the goals in this book would be committing political suicide (remember the third rail of American politics), and a leader having the strength of character to implement these changes might also have the strength to take our freedoms from us.

We were lucky that our first leader was George Washington. He could have grabbed the reins of power and ruled as a king for the rest of his life if he had wanted to do so. Instead, he resigned his position, first as Commander in Chief after the Revolutionary War and later as President after two terms in office, establishing a precedent that has been followed by every President since (except for Franklin Delano Roosevelt).

Modern Politics

Even before Twitter and Facebook modern politics seemed to dwell eternally in the gutter. For those that aspire to high office, every aspect of that person's life is subject to intense scrutiny. Every foible and human weakness is subject to exposure and ridicule. It takes a special man (or woman) to be willing to endure these indignities to be President. Recently the public discourse has fallen to the point that it is not sufficient to merely disagree with an opponent's ideas, his or her motive must be made suspect, the opponent's intent evil. It is just not clear that the qualities a person must have to endure the requirements of modern campaigning are actually the qualities that we want to see in a President.

Congressional Leadership

It has been Congressional leadership that has largely gotten us into this mess. It is very hard to find the courage to take the hard positions. Taking an unpopular stand is just another way to lose an election.

Grass Roots

It will be up to you and me to work ourselves out of this mess. We have seen the first inklings of this grass roots movement in the various Tea Party organizations that have spontaneously sprung up across the country. Although some people and the news media have disparaged their motivations, they appear honest in their outrage at what's being done to our country. And the Tea Party caucus in the House of Representatives hung tough in the debate over raising the debt ceiling (although I felt their opposition unwise as limiting the debt ceiling without solving the structural imbalances would have only made things worse).

But opposition alone is insufficient. To rally the American people you have to be _for_ something. This book has attempted to put forth a plan to change the course of the American ship of state. As with any humongous supertanker changing the course of the American ship of state will be a slow process and patience will be required. We have spotted the iceberg up ahead. If we wait the turning of the ship will be too slow to avoid the oncoming disaster. We need to start changing course now.

How do we get our representatives in Washington to start making the needed changes? (Presidential support would be helpful but most of these recommended changes are aimed at Congress. The Congress enacts the law and the President implements the laws enacted by Congress.) We need to make sure that the political candidates support the affirmative program outlined in this book. Require them to sign a pledge similar to the one shown here. If they are elected make sure they honor their pledge. If they make excuses and dawdle, fire them. Elect representatives that will honor the pledge. It may take several election cycles to get enough elected representatives to support this program – so patience and determination will be required.

To win this war and save our country (save it from ourselves) we need to get started now!

<u>Good luck!</u>

Conclusion

You probably think me naive; a hopeless dreamer (I prefer - paraphrasing the 1984 movie, _Romancing the Stone_, - a hopeful dreamer). You may think it impossible to accomplish all the changes outlined in this book; that the changes are too big, too radical to be accepted by a population accustomed to living beyond its means, a population that thinks of personal comfort instead of individual liberty and responsibility.

I feel a bit like Captain James T. Kirk confronting the Kobayashi Maru test: I don't believe in the no-win scenario (Star Trek II: The Wrath of Khan). This is a job that must be done, no matter how hard, no matter how long it takes. It will only get harder the more we wait.

It is not just our personal liberty that's at stake (that might be of little consequence to others). It's the fate of our nation that is in the balance, the future of our children and grandchildren. It would not be an exaggeration to say the fate of the world is also at risk since I don't think a world without a strong United States would be a very nice place to live in.

But as great as is the task that confronts us, it is no more daunting than that faced by the founding fathers who had to conceive of a country without monarchy in a world of monarchs. It is no more daunting than that faced by Abraham Lincoln who had to hold the nation together at its time of greatest stress. It is no more daunting than that faced by our grandfathers and great-grandfathers to confront and defeat the fascist war machine while preserving their own democratic way of life. It is no more daunting and no less consequential. This is not a time to be found lacking.

Essential Reading

The Road to Serfdom, Freidrich Hayek

The Wealth of Nations, Adam Smith

Common Sense, Thomas Paine

Second Treatise of Government, John Locke

The Constitution of the United States

The Declaration of Independence

Democracy in America, Alexis de Tocqueville

This Time is Different, Carmen M. Reinhart and Kenneth Rogoff

The Black Swan, Nassim Taleb

Capitalism, Socialism and Democracy, Joseph Schumpeter

The Commanding Heights, Daniel Yergin and Joseph Stanislaw

Thinking Fast and Slow, Daniel Kahneman

The Great Degeneration, Niall Ferguson

Coming Apart: The State of White America 1960-2010, Charles Murray

A Troublesome Inheritance, Nicholas Wade

Misbehaving, The Making of Behavioral Economics, Richard H. Thaler

A Capitalism for the People, Luigi Zingales

Why Nations Fail, Daron Acemoglu and James Robinson

<u>Supplemental Reading</u>

The Communist Manifesto, Karl Marx

Animal Spirits, George A. Akerlof and Robert J. Shiller

The General Theory Of Employment, Interest And Money, John Maynard Keynes (if you suffer from insomnia)

Capitalism in the Twenty-first Century, Thomas Piketty

Nudge, Improving Decisions about Health, Wealth and Happiness, Richard H. Thaler and Cass R. Sunstein

Paul Krugman (Save your time)

Leviathan, Thomas Hobbes

Websites to Investigate

www.newyorkfed.org

www.kpcb.com

http://www.usconstitution.net

www.pbs.org/wgbh/commandingheights

www.economist.com

www.thefederalist.com

www.wsj.com

www.whynationsfail.com

About the Author

Victor Bolles

Victor has worked in the Office of Technical Assistance of the US Treasury Department for over twelve years specializing in the issuance and management of government debt. He has just wrapped up an assignment working with the Vice Minister of Public Credit in the Ministry of Hacienda of the Dominican Republic on several projects including modifying the legal framework for debt management, developing the debt management strategy, developing an office of Investor Relations, and improving communications between the Ministry and Central Bank. Victor has also finished and copyrighted a new book, Principled Policy, which at the relevance of the American social contract as envisioned by the Founders in today's modern world.

Previously he was a resident advisor in the Ministry of Hacienda of the Republic of El Salvador and was the Resident Advisor in Tegucigalpa, Honduras where he worked with the Minister of Finance and the President of the Central Bank. Victor was also an intermittent advisor working with the Consejo Centroamericano, an organization of the central banks of all the countries of Central America. Prior to joining Treasury, Victor was an independent investment banker working out of San Antonio, TX. Victor worked at Citibank for many years in New York, Mexico City, Quito, Ecuador and Lagos, Nigeria where he was head of the investment bank and regional treasurer. His first job after graduate school was with Swiss Bank Corporation (now a part of UBS). Victor has lived overseas for 16 years, speaks Spanish fluently and has traveled extensively. Victor has an MBA in Finance from the University of Michigan. He is married to Diane and has three children and three grandchildren.

February 2, 2016

(This book and its contents are the sole work of Victor Bolles in his capacity as a private citizen and should not be considered to be a statement of policies or opinions of the Department of the Treasury.)

Read Victor's blog at: http://www.bollesfinancial.com/#!principled-policy-blog/ig1ub

(Victor@bollesfinancial.com) (www.bollesfinancial.com)

Acknowledgements

I want to thank Geoffrey Finch for his patient and diligent review of my early drafts of this book. His rigorous review made me rethink many of my arguments and forced me to strengthen many of my analyses.

<<<<>>>>